Praise for Bill Bonner from Dear Readers of *The Daily Reckoning*

"As a follower of Bill Bonner's *Daily Reckoning* from its beta days more than 10 years ago, I find the *DR* over the years has been the best guide available on money and the national and international economic picture, bar none. Here pounding sand in the oil patch in the Middle East, I eagerly await availability of Bill's next book."

—Curtis T.

"You make more sense in one e-mail than a month of CNBC."

—Ken K.

"Eloquent and elegant musings on the apocalypse, leavened with humor and a profound appreciation of human folly."

—Chris H.

"I've been a *Daily Reckoner* since 2007, when I decided the mainstream financial media really didn't know what they were doing. I decided to figure out how world markets really worked. I remember the first *Reckoning* I read, about the history of gold as money. I read it twice, and I've been addicted ever since. I didn't lose a cent during the meltdown of '08 and have watched my net worth soar since, but what I am really thankful for is the knowledge of world markets I've gained these past few years. Bill's writings have really taught me to think like a contrarian, and think for myself."

—Matt W.

"Bill Bonner's clarity of thinking is astounding! I only wish our leaders and the population would study the point that Bill has mastered: *How do you learn to think!* And then apply it."

—Steven F.

"It is rare to find an honest voice in the world of finance. So reach around and pat yourself on the back; you just might touch my hand as you do."

—Jerry C.

"I enjoy reading Bonner a lot! One of the best financial reads … financial thoughts put across in a factual and most humorous way!"

—Lakshminarayanan K.

"Best well-rounded economic commentator of the new century."

—Peter L.

"Mr. Bonner is a man of rare intelligence and culture, and I enjoy reading his *Reckonings* every day."

—Henri V.

"Your style is so personal and down to earth; it is difficult to remember your audience is bigger than just me!"

—John B.

"The first thing I hear when I come up from my office downstairs every morning is "Did *The Daily Reckoning* arrive yet?" My wife thinks it's the best thing since the Internet; me, too!"

—Jack C.

"What a refreshingly witty, erudite, finger-wagging, sensible, and insightful piece."

—Elaine

"What I've enjoyed most from Bill Bonner's comments are his bemused and skeptical attitude toward the everyday market and his ability to evaluate the daily nonsense in the clear light of his own values. I find that not many can do that. He is willing to stand apart from the crowd and point out that the emperor is, well, ah, er, naked."

—John

"I thoroughly enjoy your *Daily Reckoning* and have quite unabashedly become addicted to your mental agility. You fall into the category of Mencken and Buckley and other essayists for whom I have the highest regard."

—Robert O.

DICE HAVE NO
MEMORY

DICE HAVE NO MEMORY

*Big Bets and Bad Economics
from Paris to the Pampas*

WILLIAM BONNER

WILEY

John Wiley & Sons, Inc.

Published by John Wiley & Sons, Inc., Hoboken, New Jersey.
Published simultaneously in Canada.

For general information on our other products and services or for technical support, please contact our Customer Care Department within the United States at (800) 762-2974, outside the United States at (317) 572-3993 or fax (317) 572-4002.

Wiley also publishes its books in a variety of electronic formats. Some content that appears in print may not be available in electronic books. For more information about Wiley products, visit our web site at www.wiley.com.

Library of Congress Cataloging-in-Publication Data:

Bonner, William, 1948–
    Dice have no memory : big bets and bad economics from Paris to the Pampas / William Bonner.
        p.   cm.
    Includes index.
    ISBN 978-0-470-64004-3 (cloth); ISBN 978-111-8-05796-4 (ebk);
    ISBN 978-111-8-05812-1 (ebk); ISBN 978-111-8-05813-8 (ebk)
        1. Money market—History—21st century.   2. Finance—History—21st century.   3. Investment analysis.   I. Title.
    HG226.B66 2011
    332'.042—dc22

                                                                                            2010051234

Printed in the United States of America
10 9 8 7 6 5 4 3 2 1

To my mother,
Anne Bonner,
with much appreciation

◼ *Contents* ◼

CHAPTER 6   THE ZOMBIE STATE: WHEN GOVERNMENT FAILS

181

DICE HAVE NO
MEMORY

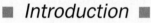

Introduction

I t was 10 years ago, or a bit more, that I began writing the Internet series called the *Daily Reckoning*. The collection of essays and short notes you have in your hands developed over the course of the years that followed.

When I began, I was ahead of the innovation curve. I was blogging before blogs had been invented. Day after day, I watched what happened in the world of finance, economics, and politics. And day after day, I found myself entertained. I merely described what I saw happening.

This was something fairly new in the press. Journalists believe their job is to report the facts, not to laugh at them. Even the commentariat and editorialists believe they need to take the news seriously; who will buy their papers and magazines if they make a joke of it? The lectorat, too, had become convinced that the world of finance, investments, and economics was serious business. Many believed that the latest developments—both in technology as well as in financial theory—would make them rich. They had heard that the Internet made wealth secrets available to everyone. You could now go onto the Internet to find out how to make a nuclear bomb, or a fortune. "Stocks for the long run" seemed like an almost risk-free road to riches. Readers weren't going to pay someone to mock their ambitions and undermine their hopes.

But the *Daily Reckoning* was free. Readers could not complain that they were not getting their money's worth.

The period began with a bubble in the dot.com stocks. Back then, investors believed they could make money by buying companies listed on the Nasdaq, even those that had no plausible way of making money. Often, these new-technology dot.com companies were managed by people with no business experience. Indeed, the lack of a track record was seen as a benefit. Ideally, what investors looked for was a callow CEO with his baseball cap on backward, who spoke the gibberish of the era. Incoherence and pimples were all the evidence they needed that the company was run by an Internet genius, untarnished by the rules and lessons of the old economy.

The Nasdaq bubble blew up in January 2000. The Internet impresarios moved on—often to the mortgage industry. What followed was the strangest recession in U.S. history. Consumers and businesses are supposed to correct their mistakes in a recession, cutting back on spending and debt; that's what recessions are for. But in the micro recession of 2001, consumers borrowed and spent more than ever. Something very odd was taking place.

On September 11, 2001, came the assault on the Twin Towers in New York. This too was freakish. At least you expect freaky people to do freaky things. But if the attack surpassed our expectations, so did the Bush administration's reaction to it. Rather than put the cops on the case, run the miscreants to ground, and punish them, the United States launched a vast and implausible "war on terror." As far as we know it was the first fighting war against nobody in particular ever proposed. "September 11 changed everything," said the neoconservatives. And so it seemed, as I recall in "The Dark Years" in Chapter 4.

The public should have been appalled; the war on terror looked from the get-go like an expensive military misadventure. Instead, the voters closed ranks. Americans imagined that they were under general attack. In Dubuque, they bought tape to seal their doors and windows against chemical attack. In Dallas, they stopped opening their mail, afraid that the towelheads were aiming to poison them. Even to this day, electronic billboards along I-95 north of Washington, D.C., tell travelers to "Report Suspicious Activity." Another says "Terror Tips. Call 1 800 4XX-XXXX." I was tempted to call to ask for a tip, but this would surely get us on a list of suspects.

The war on terror soon proved a letdown. As far as we know, not once in 10 years was a truck spotted headed south on I-95, with Arab fanatics at the wheel and drums of fertilizers and gasoline in the back. The terrorists went limp. The terror hotlines were silent.

Apparently, the terror pros were dead or under deep cover. But the amateurs soon took over. In the years following the original terrorist strike, the media reported only three additional incidents worthy of comment. In one, a man tried to get his shoes to explode. In another, a man actually did scorch his own genitals before an alert passenger overpowered him and put out the blaze. In another, terrorists allegedly drove a vanload of explosives into Manhattan, but then were unable to get it to blow up.

There were real wars too, even more expensive and even more absurd. The nation with the largest nuclear arsenal in the world accused poor, desolate Iraq of having "weapons of mass destruction (WMDs)." An invasion was launched. The *Daily Reckoning*, always on the side of the underdog, the lost cause, and the diehard, doubted that the war was a good idea. Not that we had any opinion on who would win the war, or whether the world would be a better place as a result; we just thought it was mildly indecent for such a big country to pick on such a small one. Readers were incensed. Many wrote to accuse us of a lack of patriotism (we pled nolo contendere); some wrote to suggest that the U.S. Air Force should drop bombs on us, too. We were in Paris at the time. Had the French not refused flyover rights to U.S. bombers, one of them might have done it.

Those were heady times. Imaginations ran wild. Besides Iraq there was Afghanistan. And more bombast, bickering, and bunkum. No WMDs were ever found. These wars made little sense in terms of U.S. strategic interests, said critics. But perhaps they missed the point. Men have desires. History has destinations. Maybe the point was not to win, but to lose. The United States faced no real enemies or probable threats. Nature abhors a vacuum and detests a monopoly. After the Berlin Wall fell, the United States had a near monopoly on military power. She could not find a worthy opponent. So, she had to create one. She sought to destroy herself by spending money she didn't have on wars she couldn't win. More on this in Chapter 4.

Most of our attention in the *Daily Reckoning* was focused on what was going on in the world of money. Both politics and money are often absurd and funny. But the world of money is not lethal; you can laugh without risking a firing squad. There too, in the 2000 to 2010 period, the United States was so far out in front of other economies, she had to be her own enemy. In economics as in warfare, Americans fought to lose.

So it was that the micro recession of 2001 was met with a dramatic and practically suicidal response. Alan Greenspan's Federal Reserve took its key interest rate down below the rate of inflation—essentially giving away money for free—and kept it there. The Bush administration also used fiscal stimulus to disastrous effect. It quickly replaced the surplus of the Clinton years with a large and growing deficit. All together, this was the strongest official intervention ever undertaken.

It had results. But not ones any sensible person would want. You can see for yourself in Chapter 5. The new stimulus spending went into speculative assets—stocks, commodities, and (most important) real estate. With mortgage money so readily available, the U.S. housing market took off, rising at roughly twice the rate of gross domestic product (GDP) over the five years to 2007. Soon, ordinary householders began to treat their bedrooms as a kind of automatic cash machine. They believed they could simply take out the equity they had "earned" in their houses and spend it. Why not? There would just be more next year. At the housing market's peak, house trailers sold for $1 million and more, house flippers bought and sold houses two or three times before they were built, and homeowners "earned" more from their house price increases than from full-time employment.

Of course, that couldn't go on for long. It came to an abrupt end when the bottom fell out of the subprime mortgage industry in 2007. Over the next few months, homeowner equity disappeared. The mortgage debt, however, remained. Even today, three years later, a quarter of U.S. homeowners have mortgages larger than their remaining equity. And house prices are still going down.

This was probably the funniest episode of the whole period. The authorities were lost at sea. U.S. Treasury secretaries, Fed chairmen, and leading economists told the world that everything was all right one day . . . and then the next day some new disaster happened. Illusions of competence collapsed along with Wall Street.

The talking heads should have shut up. Instead, they kept talking. And it became more and more obvious that they had no idea what they were talking about. You'll find that glorious period recalled in various memoirs such as "Said the Joker to the Thief" in Chapter 6.

The financial authorities were not the only ones whose reputations were bruised. Economists, finance professors, investors, and business leaders all were black and blue. Nobel Prizes had been won. CEOs had become celebrities. Hedge funds had made fortunes. All based on theories and formulas that were demonstrably flawed, if not preposterous.

But now, that era is years behind us. Since then, the world's focus has shifted to rescue and recovery efforts. These efforts were designed and controlled—like traffic at a busy airport—by the same people who had just proven that they were fogged in. That alone should have told us what to expect. But what the central planners lacked in sagacity they more than made up for in stupidity. Once again, they flew in the rescue teams and heavy equipment willy-nilly. And once again, the accidents multiplied.

It was breathtaking to watch. Trillions of dollars of the public's money was wagered on the basis of ideas that made little coherent sense in theory and had never been effective when put to the test. Yet, the brightest minds in the country asked few questions; everybody's bread was buttered on the same side—toward more spending, more stimulus, more cash and credit.

The scale of the previous major contracyclical relief effort—in 2001 and 2002—was monstrous; this time it beat everything ever before seen. This time the Fed took its key rate down as close to zero as it could get it. And as for fiscal stimulus, the U.S. government ran a deficit of nearly $3 trillion over the following two years. Including financial guarantees, backups, subsidies, and contingent financing plans, the total put behind the rescue and recovery effort surpassed $10 trillion.

What was amazing about this effort was that so little real thinking went into it. You'd expect the wisest men on the planet to think twice before putting in play an amount equal to almost the whole private sector output of the entire United States over a complete year. But they seemed not to think about it even once.

Instead, they bumbled and stumbled forward, with that same can-do activism they had just shown in the wars on terror, Iraq, and Afghanistan. Did any of them bother to ask how likely it was that the people who so poorly understood the problem would be able to find the remedy for it? Did they take the time to consider the matter practically: How would the economy be able to put $3 trillion of new spending to use sensibly and efficiently? Where exactly would the resources come from? How would anyone be better off if those resources were redirected into the government's "shovel-ready" projects—the very same projects they judged not worth doing a year earlier, when they still had the money to do them? You'll see some of these questions raised in the first and second chapters. I was always dumbfounded by how little serious reflection went into these trillion-dollar decisions.

Did the authorities trouble themselves with the philosophical implications? The government had no extra money. It could borrow, but that would only take money away from other projects. And what if it created new money—as, in fact, it did—out of nothing? How could you expect to get something out of nothing? How can wealth created at the stroke of a key turn into the kind of wealth you can spend, eat, live on, or use to floss your teeth? If you could do it so easily, why not do it more often? Why not do what Gideon Gono had done for Zimbabwe? If you could make a nation richer simply by adding more zeros to the national currency, surely Mr. Gono had proven out the trick. See page 30 for "Gonoism!"

Instead of thinking, the authorities pushed ahead. Then, in 2010, came the "recovery" sightings—like mirages in the desert. The economy was improving! And then the improvements receded into the distance. Unemployment wouldn't go down. Housing wouldn't go up. Alas, there was more desert to cross. And then there were disappointments, alarms . . . and more calls for more stimulus.

The simplest explanation for what was happening could be put into four sentences: People had spent too much. They had borrowed too much. Now, they had to spend less so they could pay down their debt. Until the debts were paid down, the economy would suck.

Making more cash and credit available was clearly the wrong course of action. It was like offering another piece of custard cake to a fat man on a diet. If the temptation works, it makes the man need to diet even more.

And yet the economy improvers chose not to notice. The neo-Keynesians believe the solution is for the government to spend more money it doesn't have. The realists think they can engineer a recovery by more central planning, forcing whole economies to run surpluses or deficits as their theories suggest. The idealists want a whole new, global monetary system over which they would have more control.

And only a marginalized kook would dare suggest that the lot of them—Nobel Prize winners et al.—are quacks and scalawags. You will find my own kooky thoughts on the subject in "Plumbers Crack" in Chapter 2, "100 Years of Mismanagement" in Chapter 1, and various other essays throughout the book.

Probably the most remarkable proposition of the whole decade came into sharp focus in the past six months. It was the idea that the Fed could spur a recovery by creating money out of thin air. In the desperate atmosphere following the Lehman bankruptcy of 2008, the Fed had already used its "quantitative easing (QE)" tool. But it had done so as a way of loosening rusty nuts in the banking system. In August 2010, it proposed to do more, no longer using the tool to provide emergency liquidity; this time it was using QE as a stimulus measure. And this time it was not just putting money into the banking system; now it was funding U.S. government spending. There was no substantive difference between the Fed's QE II program than Gideon Gono's money-printing in Zimbabwe or Rudolf Havenstein's money-printing in the Weimar Republic. Here was the world's leading central bank printing up paper money to pay for federal salaries, missiles, Social Security, Medicare, and other expenses. In broad daylight. And yet, professional economists looked on coolly. Many even approved. It was as if all the lessons of financial history had been unlearned. Forgotten. Ignored.

At the *Daily Reckoning* our mouths dropped open when we heard the news. And then we all started laughing.

"Buy gold," we said to each other, chuckling. Gold goes up when people lose faith in central bankers. Paul Volcker had restored investors' faith in the Fed in the early 1980s. The price of gold had gone down for 20 years as a result. Now, Ben Bernanke was giving goldbugs a huge gift.

"Ha-ha . . . when he's finished, the price of gold ought to be $3,000 an ounce," said one of the *Daily Reckoning*'s merry staff.

"Are you kidding? It will be $5,000, at least." See Chapter 7.

Ha. Ha. Ha.

WILLIAM BONNER
Baltimore, Maryland
February 2011

P.S. Man does not live on finance and economics alone. In Chapters 8, 9, and 10 you will find reflections on a variety of subjects. I traveled widely during the decade and lived most of the time outside of the United States. I wrote about what I saw—particularly in France and Argentina.

Over the course of the 10 years I also lost a few friends. You will find them recalled in the final chapter.

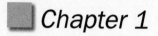 *Chapter 1*

The Incompetence
of Economists

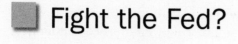

Fight the Fed?

May 17, 2001

"Almost half of the 1,300 employees of the Peruvian Central Bank of Reserve are related to one another," Bloomberg reports. Central banking is, after all, a government job. It is different from, say, the local Department of Human Resources, only in that its employees are better paid and get better press. Even the Federal Reserve—perhaps the world's most powerful and prestigious bureaucracy—is still, like every other government agency, a scam, a sinecure, and waste of money.

At least, that is the working hypothesis of today's letter.

Not much in life is certain. That is why it is such a comfort to have government. One of the few things you can depend on is that government officials will do the wrong thing. Even when they occasionally seem to do the right thing—it turns out later on that it was at best accidental, and at worst, the wrong thing after all.

"The last successful government program," observed New York mayoral candidate Jimmy Breslin, "was WWII." Since then, there have been a number of wars declared and undeclared by Washington hawks. But in almost every instance bureaucratic instincts and motives were hopelessly wrongheaded.

In the war on drugs, as we observed here just the other day, the government seeks to put drug dealers out of business by interdicting supplies. This is just the wrong thing to do, since it increases profit margins. The more taxpayer money spent trying to keep illegal drugs off the market, the more profitable the business becomes and the more entrepreneurs rush in to fill the unsatisfied demand.

Yesterday's *USA Today* brought news that the shooting war has moved to the suburbs as dealers battle it out for control of the Ecstasy market— made especially rich by government decree.

If government really wanted to put dealers out of business it would flood the market with illegal drugs—give it away on street corners for free. But what profit could there be in that? Not only would it put the drug dealers out of business—it would also put the DEA out of business, too.

Likewise, if the bureaucrats really wanted to win the War on Poverty—they would tax poor people at a higher rate . . . not reward them with subsidies and handouts. So, too, would health officials cease to coddle the sick and infirm. If they really wanted a nation of healthy people, they would revoke public health insurance benefits for people who eat too much or watch TV all day, and perhaps shoot a few smokers and fat people in the streets.

Thus do bureaucrats go about their business—making worse whatever problem they're supposed to be fighting, while actually increasing their own power. It is a rare person who will not give up his dignity and his common sense in a bid for riches, fame, or public office.

Even Alan Greenspan, once an Ayn Rand devotee, could not resist the lure of power. In order to get his picture on the cover of *Time,* something he could never do as an "Individualist," he has become a collectivist central planner.

Unlike other activities in life—from shopping for vegetables to running a Rotary club—government distinguishes itself in a singular way: by its ready use of force. Instead of coming to terms with people in a polite and dignified way, government orders them around like prisoners of war. The results are almost always pathetic and absurd.

Could it be any different with Alan Greenspan and the Federal Reserve? Could the interest rates proclaimed by the Greenspan Fed be superior to those set by buyers and sellers? Could this be one—and perhaps the only one—instance where government is superior to the market, and where the judgment of powerful government bureaucrats is superior to that of millions of investors and lenders?

Raising these questions, I realize that I put myself directly in the path of the rush of popular opinion. "Don't Fight the Fed" blows the common sentiment.

The odds favor the Fed, it is believed. Because easy money has to go somewhere . . . and because stocks rise more often than they fall, anyway. The Fed, clearly committed to cutting rates until the economy turns around, seems to be offering investors a no-lose wager. If at first the Fed's cuts fail to boost stock prices . . . Greenspan will try, try again—and keep trying until the market finally responds. And yet, anyone betting on government bureaucrats to win the War on Poverty, the War on Drugs, or any of its other wars since 1945 would have found himself on the losing end of the wager.

Even the Fed itself has a reliable record. Charged with protecting the currency, it has done the exact opposite. In the 100 years preceding the creation of the Federal Reserve System, the dollar went up and went down, but it ended the period about where it began, worth as much in 1913 as it was in 1813. Since then, thanks to the Fed's management, it has lost 95 percent of its value.

Having failed so miserably, the Fed has done just what every government agency seeks to do—expand its mandate. Now, the Fed has taken on the job of managing the economy as well as the currency.

Mr. Greenspan believes, at least publicly, that the Fed can manipulate key interest rates and keep the economy expanding almost eternally. And the public believes it, too.

Even people who have not yet begun to shave believe it. Teddy Chestnut, of Montclair (New Jersey) High School, said he was "almost positive" that the Fed would cut another 50 basis points this week. "People are losing confidence," he explained, "and right now spending is the only thing keeping us out of a recession."

If the Fed merely cuts rates, Teddy seems to think, consumers will be inspired to do more of what they do naturally . . . and the economy will continue its record expansion. It is, of course, possible that the economy functions in exactly the way Teddy imagines—with the complexity of a grandfather clock. Greenspan has merely to adjust the pendulum to make it run faster or slower as desired. This view helped Teddy's team win $40,000 from Citibank in a remarkable competition called the "Fed Challenge." The challenge for the kids is to think like central bankers. That is, to think like central bankers who believe that Alan Greenspan is a bureaucrat like no other . . . one whose decrees actually lead the nation where it wants to go.

How likely is that, dear reader? Should you "fight the Fed" or not?

The 17-Year Itch

August 30, 2001

Thus is the universe alive. All things are moral. That soul, which within us is sentiment, outside of us is the law. We feel its inspiration; out there in history we can see its fatal strength. "It is the world, and the world was made by it." Justice is not postponed. A perfect equity adjusts all parts of life.

Oi chusoi Dios aie enpiptuousi—the dice of God are always loaded.

—Ralph Waldo Emerson

Yesterday's news brought new evidence, not necessarily of a moral universe, but of a symmetrical one. Nature gives . . . but it takes away too.

Far from Wall Street, the law of regression to the mean . . . of "return to trend" . . . has been invoked. A sentence has been handed down and carried out. "Japanese Stocks Plunge to New Low," the BBC reported.

Ten years ago, the Dow in Tokyo and the one in New York were 35,000 points apart. Fewer than 1,000 points separate them today.

Yet, there is still a big difference between Tokyo and Manhattan. Wall Street is still on top of the world, the way most people view it. Tokyo is on the other end.

Daily Reckoning masochists will recall the Japan story. It has been recited often in this space, once as a cautionary tale, then as moral lesson, and most recently as a preview of things to come in America.

In 1989, it was hard to find something negative to say about the Japanese economy. Every word was flattery as the Nikkei Dow rose toward 40,000. The triumph of "Japan, Inc.," as it was called, was thought to be inevitable. Japanese labor was more disciplined and harder working than labor elsewhere. Japanese management was willing to look further ahead and take bigger risks than its competitors. The Japanese government was thought to be capable of guiding the economy more artfully than Western counterparts.

Japanese terms—such as *kaizen*—sprang from the mouths of investors in January of 1990, as they rolled the dice again, expecting to win as they had in every year since the "Japanese Miracle" began. Little did they know that the dice were loaded.

The head follows the heart, reasons dress up reality, and markets make opinions. In January of 1990, the Nikkei began its descent. Eleven years later, it is hard to find a good word to say about Japan.

Columnists—so recently busily trying to explain why the Japanese would dominate the world economy for a very long time—now explain why Japan will not recover anytime soon. With an alarming lack of imagination, they turn to the familiar reasons, merely giving them a spin in the opposite direction. Japanese government is out of date, managers are incompetent, and Japanese laborers will never learn the secret of a healthy economy—that is, borrowing and spending!

Rarely (perhaps not since the peak of the Nasdaq), has the financial press been so unanimous. Every headline about Japan makes the country sound hopeless. Yesterday, not only did we learn that stocks "Plunge to a New Low" in Japan, we also discovered that "Japan's Jobless Rate Surges" to its highest level since WWII (*USA Today*) and "Japan's Industrial Production Falls for 5th Month" (*Financial Times*).

The Nikkei dropped to 10,9779 . . . below 11,000 for the first time since 1984. It has taken more than a decade, but Japan has erased 17 years of stock market gains. Over a period of 11 years, investors have lost 75 percent of their money as the Nikkei Dow has come from a high of nearly 40,000 to within 900 points of Wall Street's most popular index.

Tokyo's unemployment rate—once almost a nonexistent number—has risen to 5 percent . . . almost exactly the same as America's current level.

Even Japan's GDP growth and that of the United States have converged—both presently at about 0.2 percent . . . an eight-year low for the United States . . . and very nearly an eight-year average for Japan.

My, my . . . might not other things converge, too? How long will it be before American reputations are flattened by a bear market just as those in Japan have been? Will people come to see that U.S. stocks, U.S. central bankers, U.S. corporate managers, and U.S. politicians are big losers . . . just like their Japanese counterparts?

"There is a crack in every thing God has made," explains Emerson. "It would seem there is always this vindictive circumstance stealing in at unawares, even into the wild poesy in which the human fancy attempted to make bold holiday, and to shake itself free of the old laws—this back-stroke, this kick of the gun, certifying that the law is fatal; that in nature nothing can be given, all things are sold."

"Great bear markets take their time," says Jeremy Grantham. "In 1929, we started a 17-year bear market, succeeded by a 20-year bull market, followed in 1965 by a 17-year bear market, then an 18-year bull. Now we are going to have a one-year bear market? It doesn't sound very symmetrical. It is going to take years."

"Every one [bubble market]," adds Grantham, "went back to trend, no exceptions, no new eras, not a single one that we can find in history."

Japanese stocks have returned to their 1984 trend line—17 years later. The U.S. bubble market began in 1995. If the United States repeats the Japanese experience, stocks may be expected to return to their 1995 trend line . . . with the Dow below 4,000 in the year 2012 . . . almost the very moment at which America's baby boomers will most need the money.

Nature in her wisdom . . . and God in his grace . . . always make sure people get what they've got coming, not what they expect.

From Funeral to Funeral

November 21, 2003

I n a world where science and reason do not suffice—and where the future can be anticipated, but not predicted—lives and dies a funny little creature called man. . . .

> Come now, you who say, "Today or tomorrow we will go to such and such a city, and spend a year there and engage in business and make a profit." Yet you do not know what your life will be like tomorrow. You are just a vapor that appears for a little while and then vanishes away.
>
> —James, Chapter 4

The *New York Times,* as reported in France's *Le Monde,* marks the 25th year of its science coverage with a worry. It notes that while 90 percent of Americans say they are interested in science, barely 50 out of 100 are aware that it takes a year for the earth to make a full circle around the sun.

In an election year, of course, people will believe anything. A politician might go all the way to the White House, in our opinion, by proposing to add a month to the calendar in order to give everyone an extra four weeks vacation. He might also suggest rounding off the number Pi in order to make it easier to remember . . . or reducing the boiling temperature of water, in Fahrenheit, to a round number, say, 200 degrees.

But how the chattering classes would screech! They have come to adore science the way jackals adore road kill; they would be nothing without it. "Better living through chemistry" was their motto back in the 1960s, when mood-altering drugs were popular. We mustn't lose "the primacy of reason," says French president Jacques Chirac, 40 years later.

The burden of the following little reflection is that Jacques Chirac is a dreamer and much of what pretends to be scientific is a fraud.

Reason never was primal. Not even secondary. Whoever made an important decision based on reason alone? What fool ever decided what he would eat . . . what he would drink . . . with whom he would sleep and work . . . and what he would do with his life . . . on the basis of unadulterated reason? No one we have ever met.

Instead, reason is so heavily diluted with greed, fear, envy, love, hope, and other emotions, you can barely taste it. It is rarely more than a rationalization for what people want to do anyway. "The head is merely the heart's dupe," noted La Rochefoucauld famously. Reason is really only used for things that don't really matter, such as choosing stocks and cooking eggs.

Still, when the Federal Reserve tells us that the economy is likely to improve in the coming quarters, most people believe that there is something more in this pronunciamento than just wishful thinking. They imagine there is some science backing it up. A man reads such a forecast like a favorable report from his latest physical examination. "All clear," he thinks the doctor wrote. He cannot hear the quacking noises in the background. Nor does he realize that there is no real science behind the Fed forecast at all. Just statistics . . . and many of them phony.

Science is marvelous; who are we to argue with it? But *Daily Reckoning* readers are cautioned: Don't take it too seriously. We recall that Harry Markowitz won a Nobel Memorial Prize in Economics for proposing a model to predict future risk in markets. Two of his disciples and fellow Nobel winners, Myron Scholes and Robert Merton, used his work to help them run a hedge fund, Long-Term Capital Management. Within four years, Long-Term had come and gone—blown up by a science that any decent trader would have laughed at.

Science evolves from funeral to funeral, it is said. Each corpse is another lesson . . . another scientist gone mad and another theory gone bad. Each exquisite cadaver is another reminder that there are only two kinds of scientific theories—those that have been disproved, and those that have not been disproved yet.

Science is all very well for predicting when a soft-boiled egg will be done. But it is little help in predicting when people will get spooked by the market. At sea level, water will begin to boil at 212 degrees Fahrenheit. Investors could boil over any time.

Scientific market forecasts . . . and detailed economic models . . . pretend that man is something he definitely is not—reasonable and rational. He is neither. If he were, the whole jig would be over. Since he could be expected to act in a rational way, scientists could model his behavior and figure out what he would do next. Would he buy stocks . . . or sell them? Having the answer, the rational investor would position himself immediately to benefit from whatever future the model showed. But in a matter of minutes, the model would blow up . . . for our rational investor's positioning would have changed the model's inputs.

People believe that things improve. They think Darwin's Theory of Evolution describes a world constantly mutating toward perfection. Every day, we add more and more information . . . and every day, our formulas become more accurate and more reliable.

If only it were true!

"The more data you have, the more ignorant you are," explains our friend Michel. "If, for example, you get quarterly reports of corporate earnings, rather than annual ones, do you know more? No, because it's easier to manipulate quarterly returns. Imagine that you got returns every month . . . or every week . . . or every hour. You'd have much more data, but actually much less knowledge of what was going on. You'd suffocate under all the data."

But in the world of finance and economics, confidence increases with data. If stocks go up one year, people are happy, but not confident. If they continue to go up . . . year after year . . . confidence increases with every passing year. Thinking scientifically, they reason: If stocks have gone up for so long, odds are that they will continue to go up.

As confidence grows, the odds become exaggerated, skewed by emotional inertia. Unpredictable by real science . . . risk is under-priced. Eventually, a collapse comes, as it always does.

It has been a long time since the world's money system—or its reserve currency—has fallen apart. The event happens so rarely, it is practically unimaginable to most investors. They believe the current system will live forever. Consequently, insurance against its demise is extremely cheap. We don't know, but it may turn out to be one of the best investments ever made . . . when the funeral is finally held.

The Whacky World of Modern Economists

October 8, 2004

Economist: One who is exiled from dinner parties; a recluse, trapped in his own deluded sense of wishful thinking, unconcerned with debt . . . the people who manage the entire world's finances . . .

Most economic theories have little practical use in the real world.
—Walter Williams

Pity the poor economist.

He is a pariah at dinner parties. His conversation is dull. His face has no expression. His opinions are commonplace. He might as well be on reality TV. And so what if the world's economies need to be "rebalanced?" Not only do we not know what it means, we can do nothing about it anyway.

If you spend 15 minutes a year trying to figure out the world economy, Peter Lynch used to say, you've wasted 10 of them. Peter believes in buying stocks. Keeping it simple, he believes in buying the stocks of companies he knows. That way, he figures, what he doesn't know can't hurt him.

Lynch ran a major equity fund in a bull market. He was lucky enough to get out before the bull market was over and smart enough to write books for people who were dumb enough to believe that stocks always go up in the long run. You didn't need to convince them this was so. Their gains were proof enough. You didn't need macroeconomics, either; you just needed a bull market.

The poor macroeconomist gets no respect. Which is the way it should be; typically, he deserves none.

Generally, his employer determines the economist's opinions. And typically, he is bullish. Neither the City of London nor Wall Street make money by helping people get rich. They make money by selling them financial assets. Economists are put to work persuading clients that assets will go up in price. Abby Joseph Cohen, for example, is paid millions of dollars each year because she is reliable, not because she is accurate. Her forecasts are always the same—shares will go up! Even government economists usually have a bullish bias; neither presidents nor prime ministers are re-elected on bad economic news.

What's more, honest economists have few insights that aren't obvious: You can't spend more than you make forever, the old-timers would tell you. The dollar will go down in price if you print too many of them, they figured. If something gets too far out of whack, they predicted, it is likely to come back into whack sooner or later.

These insights are hardly enough to command much respect, let alone a high salary. So early in the last century, ambitious economists set to work creating a set of propositions that were not based on ordinary common sense—but on wishful thinking. Economists do not manage their own finances noticeably better than anyone else. But if given the authority to manipulate short-term lending rates, bank regulations and money supplies, they offer to manage an entire nation's economy. And if central bankers of major nations are able to collude on policy, they believe they can manage the entire world!

These vaulting pretensions required undergirders at least as absurd as they were. Hurricanes blew across Florida in record numbers this autumn. Yet the prevailing wind among U.S. economists and ordinary citizens was delightful. Rebuilding would be good for the economy, they told us.

The price tag for America's "war on terror" and the war against Iraq rises almost daily. Estimates over $200 billion are current. Those, too, are thought to be good things for the world's largest economy. More defense contracts will be let. More people would be hired. More money would be spent on tanks, equipment, and all the other paraphernalia needed to kill or avoid being killed.

The oil price hit more than $50 per barrel for the first time ever at the end of September. Yesterday, it broke $53. But even that is considered good news, at least according to the economists at the *New York Times*.

Every cloud now has two silver linings. Every disaster brings relief even before it happens. Every attack is met by an overwhelming counterattack of growth and prosperity. Drought, pestilence, famine, and war—nothing is so awful that it doesn't bring on a new burst of something wonderful.

Of course, if destruction really were so beneficial, it is surprising that economists do not encourage it. We still wait for a pair of them, armed with the courage of their convictions and a jerrican, to burn down each other's houses.

"Stimulus," they will say.

"Arson," we will reply.

Nor have we yet heard an economist propose the elegant solution put forward by a *Daily Reckoning* reader: Instead of waiting for a natural disaster or an attack by foreigners, bring our troops home from Iraq and put them to work blowing up our own cities!

But *stimulus* is just one of the twisted beams that hold up modern economics to ridicule. The "disappearance of whack" is another.

If Peter Lynch had tried his approach in the bear market of the 1970s, for example, today he might be just another poor schmuck, rather than an investment icon. Bear markets take down the stocks you know along with those you don't; they maul the geniuses as well as the morons.

The mean, an economist will tell you, is something to which things tend to regress. Prices progress in a bull market. They regress in a bear market. If something is far from the mean—the ordinary state of things—the economist guesses it will have to come back. "This can't go on forever," he will say. And yet perverse and inexplicable trends have been known to go on for decades after the economist who spotted them reached room temperature. Still, the earnest economist of the past looked for things that were out of whack—either with the way they have always been . . . or with the way he thinks they ought to be.

But the new economists of the twentieth and twenty-first centuries began to lose interest in whack. Things were no longer in it or out of it. They were merely what other economists had made them! Economies might be well managed or mismanaged, they thought, but they couldn't be unmanaged. For they had no natural condition, but only a state of being engineered for them by other economists. If they wanted faster growth, they had merely to yank a little harder on the lever marked *growth*. If they wanted less inflation, they might want to ease off. It was all a matter of how you ran the great machine! And if something went wrong—well, some economist must have made a mistake. Whack disappeared altogether.

This is a convenient way to look at things now. Because if there still were a whack to measure against, the whole world economy would be further out of it than ever before.

The world's two most important economies sit at opposite ends of a shipping channel. In one direction, ships head east loaded to the gunwales with geegaws and gadgets. As they make their way across the Pacific, they pass other ships coming back—empty. On one end of the trade are a billion Chinese making things at a furious pace. At the other, Americans enjoy the extraordinary lightness of being that comes with acquiring things without having to pay for them.

Asians work and save. Americans borrow and spend. The U.S. current account deficit—a measure of how out of whack the world economy has become—approaches 6 percent of GDP. The home of Anglo-Saxon consumerism isn't much better. In the United Kingdom, the current account gap is moving toward 3 percent of GDP.

If you asked a dead economist, "Something's got to give," would probably be his judgment. "No nation can spend more than it makes forever," he might go on. "There must be a give for every take."

But we have been taking record amounts of goods from Asia—more than we can afford—and giving paper money IOUs in return. Asians have been giving all they can . . . hoping to recycle their IOUs into something valuable before the paper money sinks.

Living economists are not worried. It is just another thing to be managed, they believe. It does not seem to bother them that the Americans and the British are getting poorer. They do not concern themselves with the huge pile of debt built up by consumers and government; these too can surely be managed.

Here again, economists replaced the old, obvious insights of an earlier age with absurd new ones. Every previous economist who ever thought about it had come to the same conclusion: The way to wealth was to make sure outgoings did not exceed income. The self-evident corollary was that you needed to focus your attention on creating wealth, not spending it. It was production, not consumption, that made people rich.

Yet the new economists are not paid to worry . . . they are paid to flatter.

"America has the most dynamic, flexible economy in history," the lumps believed. "They sweat, we think," they said approvingly. "We are creating wealth at the fastest pace in decades," said their president.

What we are really creating is a world economy that is dangerously out of whack.

But who cares? When it blows itself up . . . imagine how stimulating that will be!

Disappearing on the Pampas

October 31, 2008

The average cab driver in Buenos Aires knows more about financial crises than Trichet, Brown, and Paulson put together. His training comes neither from Keynes nor Smith. . . . And what the typical Argentine has learned, the English and the Americans are about to discover for themselves. Bill Bonner explains . . .

Last week, at the annual convention of the nation's mortgage bankers in San Francisco, protestors used bullhorns to heckle attendees; they demanded a moratorium on foreclosures.

Meanwhile, south of the Rio Plata, a mob formed in Buenos Aires, too. Their gripe was that the government of Christina Fernandez de Kirschner was grabbing their pension money. "No way," replied the queen of the pampas. We are just going to "rescue" it from the wicked capitalists. Like a Doberman rescuing a hot dog, the Argentine government will swallow $26 billion worth of private pension funds. The federales say they are taking the money into protective custody. It will just "disappear," say protesters.

The signal on the flag here unfurling is that, compared to the Argentines, the American mob is a bunch of naïve chiselers. At least the gauchos can tell the difference between self-delusion and grand larceny. But the average cab driver in Buenos Aires knows more about financial crises than Trichet, Brown, and Paulson put together. His training comes neither from Keynes nor Smith. The great Anglo-Saxon economists may have laid out their theories of political economy. But they left some important holes. Argentina's presidents have filled in the blanks. And what the typical Argentine has learned, the English and the Americans are about to discover for themselves.

Leaving Argentina, our cab driver tried a familiar flimflam. Hearing a foreign accent, he said: "My meter is broken . . . but the fare to the airport is always a flat 200 pesos." On the pampas, no self-respecting taxi driver gives a sucker an even break. But then, rarely do markets or governments, either.

"What is the message that the government is giving to the people today?" asks Argentine economist Roberto Cachanosky. "That it is ready to take their revenues and their savings with no limit . . . and also, that they will continue to give out information and make announcements that, to say it gently, have no connection to reality."

"The only secure retirement is one backed by the state," said a member of the Peronist party, proving Cachanosky's point. As the country approached bankruptcy in 2001, its leaders followed the traditions of all Peronists, Democrats, Republicans, and National Socialists when they get themselves in a jam. First, they lie. Then they steal.

Argentina has a parallel system of state-owned and privately owned pension accounts. Its state system pension payments were cut by 14 percent in 2001, and then cut an additional 66 percent when the peso was devalued the following year. Now, the Kirchner government is nationalizing the private accounts. Set up in 1993, these funds must invest 60 percent of their money in Argentine bonds. Naturally, bonds backed by the Argentine government are not necessarily the strongest credits in the world. Argentine peso bonds—like pensions—are adjusted for inflation. But the government lies, with a measure of inflation that is less than half the real 30 percent rate. As to the dollar bonds, it steals. In 2001, it defaulted on $95 billion worth of loans made by overseas lenders. It didn't settle up until four years later—stiffing the foreigners for 70 percent. And now the government is in trouble again; it must make a big payment to overseas lenders in 2009. Its main exports—soybeans, gas, and oil—are down about 50 percent this year. And the country has more public debt than it did when it defaulted seven years ago. That's why the private pension accounts are being seized; the government needs the money.

Things have a way of disappearing in Argentina. After WWII, hundreds, maybe thousands, of Nazis arrived in Buenos Aires from Europe, never to be seen again. Whether people are wanted by the law, or not wanted by the lawmakers, they have a way of vanishing. In the 1970s, when the generals running Argentina wanted to get rid of their opponents, they called on the old Nazis to help "disappear" thousands of them.

Money disappears, too. More than a half century ago, Evita Peron posed as an angel. She set up charitable organizations to help the poor and handed out Christmas presents, personally. After the holidays, she went back to her tricks—making the money disappear from the charitable funds and reappear in her Swiss bank account. And then, after her spirit gave the world the slip, Evita's own corpse disappeared. People wondered what had happened to the husk of her, until it was retrieved by Juan Peron 16 years later.

Senora Fernandez is a practiced magician too. Her recent acts of larceny have included disappearing Aerolineas Argentina from its Spanish owners . . . and then disappearing the profits of the nation's farmers, first by preventing them from selling on the open market and then by imposing a confiscatory tax (later withdrawn) on exports.

"Nationalizing private pensions is theft," said Juan Domingo Peron himself. The Peronists say they are only acting in the public interest—like the U.S. Treasury and the Bank of England. We would never have done this had there not been a worldwide financial crisis, they explain.

"The question that many people ask themselves," continues Robert Cachanosky is: "What rate of interest do you need to compensate for the risk of keeping assets within the reach of a government desperate for more funds?"

Answering Cachanosky's question, today you can buy 8.28 percent Argentine bonds at 22 cents on the dollar—giving you a yield of 31 percent. By comparison, a U.S. 10-year Treasury note, at less than 4 percent yield, looks like a broken taxi meter to us.

Inevitable and Disgraceful, But Still Unpredictable

November 28, 2008

Here at the *Daily Reckoning,* we take the part of the underdog . . . the downtrodden and the despised. Who fits that description now? Who is held in lower esteem than child molesters? Who gets less respect than smokers? Who is in a lower caste than hewers of wood and drawers of water? We're talking, of course about the toilers on Wall Street. So today, we take their part, because no one else will.

Who's to blame for the worldwide financial meltdown, a crisis that has so far wiped out a notional $30 trillion dollars . . . give or take a trillion or so?

"Lax central bankers . . . reckless investment bankers . . . the hubristic quants," says Niall Ferguson, writing in *Vanity Fair.* "Regulate them," is the universal cry. "Tax them," say the politicians. "Hang them," say investors.

First, let us look at the charges:

They skinned millions of investors—with their outrageous bonuses, spreads, fees, incentive shares, performance charges, salaries, and profits— leaving the financial industry severely undercapitalized . . . and unprotected.

Guilty as charged.

They ginned up securities that no one really understood and sold them to unsuspecting investors, including widows, orphans, colleges, pension funds, and municipal governments.

Uh . . . guilty again.

They put the whole financial world in a spin—churning positions back and forth between each other in order to collect commissions . . . leveraging . . . flipping . . . stripping assets . . . securitizing . . . derivatizing . . . making wild bets based on flimflam mathematics. . . .

No point in going on about it . . . guilty.

Yes, the financial hotshots did all these things. And more. They sold the world on finance, rather than making and selling things. Then, it was off to the races. Everybody wanted to bet. Perfecta, place bets, odds-on . . . double or nothing. Of course, investors would have been better off at the racetrack. The track takes about 20 percent. In the financial races, Wall Street took 50 percent to 80 percent of all the profits.

Before 1987, only about one of every 10 dollars of corporate profits made its way to the financial industry—in payment for arranging financing, banking, and other services. By the end of the bubble years, the cost of finance had grown to more than 3 out of every 10 dollars. Total profits in the United States reached about $6 trillion last year; about $2 trillion was Wall Street's share. What happened to this money? Other industries use profits to build factories and create jobs. But the financial industry paid it out in salaries and bonuses—as much as $10 trillion during the whole Bubble Period. And now that the sector finds itself a few trillion short, it waits for the government to open its purse.

But Wall Street's critics have missed the point. Yes, the financial industry exaggerates. But so does the whole financial world. Both coming and going. It's madness on the way up; madness on the way down. Investors pay too much for finance when the going is good. And then, when the going isn't so good, they regret it. This regret doesn't mean the system is in need of repair; instead, it means it is working.

The financial industry was just doing what it always does—separating fools from their money. What was extraordinary about the Bubble Years was that there were so many of them. There is always smart money in a marketplace . . . and dumb money. But in 2007, there were trillions of dollars so retarded they practically cried out for court-ordered sterilization. What other kind of money would pay Alan Fishman $19 million for three weeks' work helping Washington Mutual go bust?

Whence cometh this dumb money? And here we find more worthy villains. For here we find the theoreticians, the ideologues . . . and the regulators, themselves, who now offer to save capitalism from itself. Here is where we find the bogus statistics, the claptrap theories, and the swindle science. Here is where we find the former head of the Princeton economics department, too, Ben Bernanke . . . and both Hank Paulson and his replacement, Tim Geithner. Here, we find the intellectuals and the regulators—notably, the SEC—who told the world that the playing field was level . . . when everyone could see that it was an uphill slog for the private investor.

"Six Nobel prizes were handed out to people whose work was nothing but BS," says Nassim Taleb, author of *The Black Swan*. "They convinced the financial world that it had nothing to fear."

All the BS followed from two frauds. First, that economic man had a brain but not a heart. He was supposed to always act logically and never emotionally. But there's the rub, right there; they had the wrong guy. The second was that you could predict the future simply by looking at the recent past. If the geniuses had looked back to the fall of Rome, they would have seen property prices in decline for the next 1,000 years. If they had looked back 700 or even 100 years . . . they would have seen wars, plagues, famines, bankruptcies, hyperinflation, crashes, and depressions galore. Instead, they looked back only a few years and found nothing not to like.

If they had just looked back 10 years, says Taleb, they would have seen that their "value at risk" models didn't work. The math was put to the test in the Long-Term Capital Management crisis . . . and failed. Their models went sour faster than milk. Things they said wouldn't happen in a trillion years actually happened while Bill Clinton was in still in office.

In the real world, Taleb explains, things are stable for a long time. Then, they blow up. Then, all the theories and regulators prove worthless. These blowups are inevitable, but unpredictable . . . and too rare to be modeled or predicted statistically. "And they are almost always much worse than you expect."

Gonoism!

December 5, 2008

The *Daily Reckoning* typically takes the part of the underdog, the despised and the downtrodden. Sometimes we do so because the calumnies are misplaced . . . and sometimes we just pick up the poor schmuck for the fun of knocking him down and treading on him some more. Gideon Gono is no exception.

The *Financial Times* tells us that sales of government debt will reach $2 trillion next year—led by the United States and Britain, each borrowing about 10 percent of GDP. For France, the borrowing will reach 8.6 percent of GDP. Yet, this week, the brightest star in the investment firmament burned brighter still: U.S. Treasury bond prices rose to levels never before seen. The 10-year T-Note, for example, yielded all of 2.67 percent (yields fall as prices rise).

It was as if the laws of nature had been suspended. The cost of the world's bailout efforts are said to be beyond $10 trillion already. Yet, the more bonds governments sell to finance the rescue, the more the demand for them grows. Remarkably, the further in debt government goes, the more people want to lend it money. Maybe, if the feds get away with this, gravity will be the next to go.

Central bankers, as everyone now knows, are rascals and scalawags. Gideon Gono is no exception. But there is something heroically imbecilic about the man. While most economists hedge and weasel, Mr. Gono goes boldly, recklessly forward—where no central banker has dared to go, at least not since the worst days of the Weimar Republic. Mr. Gono stands tall . . . a colossus of error . . . an Olympus of bunglement.

It is easy to criticize the chief of Zimbabwe's national bank. In fact, it is hard not to criticize him. Keynes warned that "there is a lot of ruin" in a nation. Mr. Gono's contribution to economics is to show how much ruin there is. That . . . and proving that the laws of supply and demand still apply to money.

The latest news tells us what he hath wrought and it sounds like Hell: The trash piles up in Harare and the water system no longer works. Vendors are selling bottles of water for $25 U.S. Cholera has broken out . . . and anthrax too. Shops are empty. People are hungry. Nothing works. This week, even the forces of law and order are on the rampage, breaking windows . . . looting what little remains in the shops. The soldiers and police haven't been paid, at least, not with real money.

Between August 2007 and June 2008, the Zimbabwean money supply increased 20 million times. Naturally, this led to the kind of spectacular increases in consumer prices that modern economists had only seen on newsreels. Consumer price inflation was clocked at 2 million percent six months ago. Now, it is said to have sped up to 230 million percent.

Of course, Mr. Gono rolled out all the usual inflation-fighting measures—all that is, except for the one that works. Prices have been controlled. Mr. Gono personally went around, found shop owners who have illegally raised prices, and had them arrested. Bank withdrawals have been limited to 500,000 Zimbabwe dollars per day. If you wanted to buy 2 kg of sugar, for example, you'd have to stand in line for four days at an automated teller. But at present rates, you could stand in line at the automatic tellers every day for eternity and never get enough money to buy a drink of water.

Last weekend was Gideon Gono's 49th birthday. We salute him. He may be a moron; but at least he's a useful one. Better than another bad theory, he has provided a bad example. In an age when central bankers all over the world are trying to avoid a decline in the cost of living, Mr. Gono has proven that there are worse things.

But despite Gono himself, Gonoism seems to be gaining admirers in the rest of the world because the alternatives don't seem to work. Keynesianism, for example. The Keynesians say that when people stop squandering their money, the feds have to step in and squander it for them. Right now, practically every government in the world is promising huge new spending programs. Deficits be damned! In the heat of the emergency, Europe waves aside the Maastricht limits and America prepares its first trillion-dollar deficit in 2009. By 2010, America's deficit could easily reach $2 trillion.

But will "Keynes on steroids," as one journalist put it, work? There's no evidence of it in the record. America tried it in the 1930s. Japan tried it in the 1990s. In neither case were the results favorable.

Milton Friedman saw the problem with Keynesianism—it led to rising prices . . . and then stagflation. He pointed to the lever marked *monetary policy*. Give that a pull, he said; just make sure the economy has enough money, everything else will take care of itself. Maggie Thatcher and Ronald Reagan both pulled on the monetary policy lever. And in the recession of 2001–2002, Alan Greenspan yanked it so hard the handle practically broke off. Milton Friedman was still alive at the time and actually approved of Greenspan's handiwork, saying that he had "spared the economy a worse recession," or words to that effect.

But now we face an even worse recession. And central bankers are running out of ammunition to fight it. The U.S. Fed's key rate is only 100 basis points from zero. His resources are "obviously limited," said Bernanke, in a speech in Austin, Texas. But then, while the Fed can't push interest rates below zero, "the second arrow in the Federal Reserve's quiver—the provision of liquidity—remains effective," he said. One option is for the Fed to buy "longer-term Treasury or agency securities on the open market in substantial quantities," Bernanke said.

Gonoism, in other words.

100 Years of Mismanagement

January 8, 2010—Baltimore, Maryland

There must be some dark corner of Hell warming up for modern, mainstream economists. They helped bring on the worst bubble ever . . . with their theories of efficient markets and modern portfolio management. They failed to see it for what it was. Then, when trouble came, they made it worse.

But instead of atoning in a dank cell, these same economists strut onto the stage to congratulate themselves.

"The Greatest Depression that could so easily have happened in 2009 but did not is the tribute that the world owes to economics," wrote Arvind Subramanian in the *Financial Times*.

We were lost from the get-go, trying to interpret the sentence. It is as tangled and puerile as the staggering conceit behind it. Then, Mr. Subramanian sets up the stage props:

"In 2008, as the global financial crisis unfolded, the reputation of economics as a discipline and economists as useful policy practitioners seemed to be irredeemably sunk. Queen Elizabeth captured the mood when she asked pointedly why no one (in particular, economists) had spotted the crisis coming. And there is no doubt that, notwithstanding the few Cassandras who had correctly prophesied gloom and doom, the profession had failed colossally. . . ."

He then brushes off the Queen's very sensible question:

> But crises will always happen, and even if there is a depressing periodicity to them as Professors Reinhart and Rogoff have catalogued, their timing, form and provenance will elude prognostication.

Of course, the record doesn't show that the crisis eluded prognostication; any dope could have seen it coming. But the prognosticators who had contributed so mightily to the crisis had blinded themselves with their own claptrap. Still, Mr. Subramanian figures that they "vindicated" the profession in the way they responded to the crisis.

On monetary policy, Bernanke was true to the word he gave to Milton Friedman on the occasion of his [Friedman's] 90th birthday: "Regarding the Great Depression, you're right, we did it. We're very sorry. But thanks to you, we won't do it again." Bernanke, the pre-eminent student of the Great Depression, found conventional and some very unconventional ways of not doing "it" again. At the peak of his interventions, the U.S. Fed came to resemble the Soviet Gosbank, more a micro-allocator of credit than a steward of macroeconomic policy.

It probably wasn't the point he intended to make, but the Fed does resemble the Soviet-era Gosbank—manipulating, meddling and micromanaging the economy toward destruction. Meanwhile, Congress is doing some Soviet-style management, too; it is now owner of the nation's largest automobile company and its largest insurance business: "They took their cue from the writings of the academic scribbler of yore—Lord Keynes—and provided massive public demand for goods and services where private demand had collapsed. . . ."

We were still gasping for air when, on the 30th of December, columnist Martin Wolf called upon Keynes's ghost again. He, too, shuddered to think how horrible things would have been if the financial authorities had not taken resolute action:

> We could not in such times, even take the survival of civilization itself for granted. Never before had I felt more strongly the force of John Maynard Keynes's toast "to the economists— who are the trustees, not of civilization, but of the possibility of civilization."

Is there any doubt that Keynes was a scalawag? Civilization flourished for thousands of years before anyone made a living as an economist. Crises came and went. In the nineteenth century, for example, there were panics followed by depressions in 1819, 1837, 1857, 1873, and 1893. Not one of the depressions seemed worthy of the *great* modifier. Hundreds of banks failed. Civilization didn't seem to care. The rich and powerful took their lumps along with everyone else; most people enjoyed watching them go down. Business went on.

In 1913, on Christmas Eve, Congress passed the Federal Reserve Act, setting up America's central bank. Only then did economists get their hands on the economy's throat. The dollar was worth about the same thing it had been worth 100 years before. Now, almost a hundred years later, it is worth only 3 cents. And only 16 years after economists took their positions at the Federal Reserve came a depression worse than anything the nation had ever seen—at least, it was worst after government economists finished with it.

The Great Depression may have been an accident, but the debasement of the dollar certainly was not. It was a matter of policy. Economists, led by Keynes, had the idea that they could spur the economy forward by creating phantom demand—in the form of additional units of purchasing power. The gold standard stood in the way; it was abandoned like a bad neighborhood. First, temporarily, then partially, then, in 1971, completely. The first consumer credit boom came in the 1920s . . . leading to the Great Depression. By the 1980s, 50 years later, Americans had lost their residual fear of debt. Consumer credit boomed again. Then it bubbled. Economists didn't understand what was going on. They rarely do. But they had created a hundred-year flood of consumer debt. Now they congratulate themselves; households sink . . . but civilization floats.

Three Out of Four Economists Are Wrong

July 30, 2010—Paris, France

Wdoes an economist think . . . when he adjourns to the local bar . . . or is hauled away to the asylum? In the dead of night or the quiet of a confessional, does he laugh sourly at having fooled most of the people most of the time? Or does he curse his trade and feel like hanging himself?

The thing economists said was nearly impossible actually happened last week. Yields on 2-year U.S. debt hit a record low just as the Treasury prepares for another record-setting deficit. The supply of Treasury debt and the demand for it hit new highs—together. Stranger things have happened. But the strangeness of this event has caused a furor loquendi amongst economists. Usually, there are only two major ways of misunderstanding current events. Now there are at least four of them.

Party economists take the party line; whenever the party flags, get out more gin. Now, they say the recovery is proceeding, thanks to adroit demand management. Unsurprisingly, since they are the authorities, they claim that record low Treasury yields mean investors have confidence in the authorities. Deficits don't matter, they add.

Another group—the Paul Krugman, Martin Wolf, Joseph Stiglitz wing of the neo-Keynesian faction—fear the recovery may stall, as it did in America in the 1930s and Japan in the 1990s. They say deficits do matter; they wish there were more of them. Low bond yields are cheap gin to them.

In opposition is a large group of *inflationistas*. (Marc Faber, Jim Rogers . . .). They believe the authorities have already added too much monetary juice. And now they're afraid the feds will run bigger deficits and add even more monetary inflation. Along with tightened supplies and demand pressure from the emerging markets, this will cause consumer prices to rise more than expected. The dollar and bonds will be crushed.

A small group of hardcore deflationists, meanwhile, believes falling yields prove the economy is sinking into a deep hole of debt destruction and depression (Robert Prechter, Gary Shilling). These Jeremiahs expect the main U.S. stock index—the Dow—to lose 95 percent of its value and the bond market to continue to rise.

Yet another school of thought confines itself to this *Daily Reckoning*. It acknowledges that nobody knows anything, but it doesn't mind taking a guess. Herewith is its view, beginning with a critique of its opponents. Fair-minded reader, you be the judge.

Mainstream opinion is contradicted by the facts. Fewer people are employed today in the United States than when the stimulus program began. Sales are down. Growth is falling. Credit is contracting. Even hairstylists and cab drivers know something is wrong.

As for the inflationistas view, it makes sense. The feds add money. Prices should rise. But in Europe and America, the rate of consumer price inflation is generally ebbing. That's what low bond yields are really telling us; they signal deflation, not inflation. Maybe the inflationistas will be proven right, eventually. But for the moment, prices in the developed world are going down; they should remain weak until this phase of debt reduction is largely complete.

Meanwhile, hard-core deflationists could be right, too. A big credit expansion typically gives way to a big credit contraction. The past is not prologue; it is an account payable. Now it's due. But there's room for negotiation. If the hard-core deflationists are right, credit will contract back to 1970s levels, and asset prices will correct as much. But a lot has happened since the Carter era. There's much more demand, for example, coming from all over the world. China is now a bigger energy consumer than the United States, and a bigger auto buyer, too. Demand for just about everything is growing. This new demand is bound to boost prices.

The supply side, too, puts a brake on deflation. The easy, cheap oil has already been pumped. Other resources—including food and water—require huge new capital investments before supplies will increase. Domestic inflation rates in China and India are already increasing. It's just a matter of time before the exporters put inflation in a shipping container and send it west.

But we don't need to rely purely on guesswork. We have an example right in front of us—Japan. The island has been deleveraging its private sector since 1990 — complete with ultra-low bond yields. Consumer prices fell. Between real estate and stocks, investors lost an amount equal to three years' total output.

Economists misunderstood it completely and gave consistently bad advice. And the authorities took the advice and squandered a whole generation's savings. But the world did not come to an end. Japan deleveraged while the rest of the world went on a buying spree. Now, the entire developed world deleverages, while the emerging world continues to shop.

Nobody knows anything. But readers should expect a long, soft correction just the same.

The Patsy Revolt of 2010

March 12, 2010—Mumbai, India

"**M**asked youths . . . attacked the head of Greece's largest trade union, who was addressing the crowd, and hurled stones at the police. GSEE union boss Yiannis Panagopoulos traded blows with the rioters before being whisked away, bloodied and with torn clothes."

The *Daily Mail* account put the blame for these disturbances on Germany's finance minister, who warned the Greeks that "the German government does not intend to give a cent." At least *Bild,* a popular German newspaper, was trying to be helpful. It suggested that Greece sell Corfu . . . and that Greeks get up earlier and work harder.

Meanwhile, from Iceland comes news that every voter with an IQ above air temperature has cast his ballot against a bailout plan. The Icelanders were slated to make good $5.3 billion in bank losses. But why shackle common voters to the banks' losses? The plan was so outrageous and so unpopular that Iceland's normally compliant prime minister called for a referendum. Given a chance to vote on it, 93 percent said no. The other 7 percent probably read it wrong.

Insurrection is in the air. In England, government employees are preparing the biggest strike since the 1980s. In America, dissatisfaction with Congress is at record highs; four out of five of those polled say, "Nothing can be accomplished in Washington."

Herewith, an attempt to deconstruct the rebel yell. By way of preview, it's not the principle of the thing, we conclude; it's the money.

There are more clowns in economics than in the circus. They invented an economic model that has been very popular for more than 50 years—particularly in the United States and Britain. It began with a bogus insight; John Maynard Keynes thought consumer spending was the key to prosperity; he saw savings as a threat. He had it backward. Consumer spending is made possible by savings, investment, and hard work—not the other way around. Then, William Phillips thought he saw a cause-and-effect relationship between inflation and employment; increase prices and you increase employment too, he said.

Jacques Rueff had already explained that the Phillips Curve was just a flimflam. Inflation surreptitiously reduced wages. It was lower wages that made it easier to hire people, not enlightened central bank management. But the scam proved attractive. The economy has been biased toward inflation ever since.

Economists enjoyed the illusion of competence; they could hold their heads up at cocktail parties and pretend to know what they were talking about. Now they were movers and shakers, not just observers. The new theories seemed to give everyone what they most wanted. Politicians could spend even more money that didn't belong to them. Consumers could enjoy a standard of living they couldn't afford. And the financial industry could earn huge fees by selling debt to people who couldn't pay it back.

Never before had so many people been so happily engaged in acts of reckless larceny and legerdemain. But as the system aged, its promises increased. Beginning in the 1930s, the government took it upon itself to guarantee the essentials in life—retirement, employment, and to some extent, health care. These were expanded over the years to include minimum salary levels, unemployment compensation, disability payments, free drugs, food stamps, and so forth. Households no longer needed to save.

As time wore on, more and more people lived at someone else's expense. Lobbying and lawyering became lucrative professions. Bucket shops and banks neared respectability. Every imperfection was a call for legislation. Every traffic accident was an opportunity for wealth redistribution. And every trend was fully leveraged.

If there was anyone still solvent in America or Britain in the twenty-first century, it was not the fault of the banks. They invented subprime loans and securitizations to profit from segments of the market that had theretofore been spared. By 2005, even jobless people could get themselves into debt. Then, the bankers found ways to hide debt . . . and ways to allow the public sector to borrow more heavily. Goldman Sachs did for Greece essentially what it had done for the subprime borrowers in the private sector—it helped them to go broke.

As long as people thought they were getting something for nothing, this economic model enjoyed wide support. But now that they are getting nothing for something, the masses are unhappy. Half the U.S. states are insolvent. Nearly all of them are preparing to increase taxes. In Europe too, taxes are going up. Services are going down. And taxpayers are being asked to pay for the banks' losses . . . and pay interest on money spent years ago. Until now, they were borrowing money that would have to be repaid sometime in the future. But today is the tomorrow they didn't worry about yesterday. So, the patsies are in revolt.

Several countries are already past the point of no return. Even if America taxed 100 percent of all household wealth, it would not be enough to put its balance sheet in the black. And Professors Rogoff and Reinhart show that when external debt passes 73 percent of GDP or 239 percent of exports, the result is default, hyperinflation, or both. IMF data show the United States already too far gone on both scores, with external debt at 96 percent of GDP and 748 percent of exports.

The rioters can go home, in other words. The system will collapse on its own.

Junk Science

November 15, 2010

"When I started my economics studies at 16," wrote Paul A. Samuelson not long before he died last year at aged 93, "Carlyle was right to call economics a 'dismal science.' Thanks to modern science and better economic knowledge, this Malthusian curse has been vanquished. Good modern economics make economics the Hopeful Science. At last!"

Lucky professor Samuelson! Like an apparatchik who joined the shades before 1989, he went to his reward with his delusions intact.

This week, the scientists began to have doubts. Like the Pope wondering about the resurrection, or the Mormons questioning the veracity of the angel Moroni, the head of the World Bank, Robert Zoellick, shocked the learned world. It's time to start discussing a gold-backed currency, he said. Maybe the crown of creation of modern economics—its centrally managed money—was not such a good idea after all.

Like Christianity, the dollar only has value as long as people have faith in it. But that is true of almost every trick up the modern economist's sleeve. If people stop believing, the spell is broken and they're worthless.

Two years ago, when the financial world was melting down, we were told that the volcano needed to be appeased. Without immediate injection of funds, the whole system would blow up, they said. Where was the science behind that? The financial system melted down countless times in the past. No central bank came to its aid before the 1930s.

Or how about the corollary article of faith: that the public had to rescue the big banks, a tout prix? It was practically a universal constant—like the Golden mean or Brownian motion. When bankers make profits, it is theirs to keep. When they lose money, the losses are moved on to the public. The United States bailed out its banks. Britain, Ireland, and Iceland did the same. But where was the evidence that bank failures were so horrible? During America's Great Depression, 9,000 banks failed. And history is full of the wrecks of banks that were "too big to fail."

A hick Congressman from one of the corn states once proposed to round off pi to 3 to make it easier for schoolchildren to remember. He must have been joking. In the world of science, water boils at 212 degrees Fahrenheit, at sea level, whether you believe or not. Pi is always a long string of digits. The mathematicians can sweat and shake all they want; it doesn't change. But modern economists take the joke seriously. They think they can command water to run uphill and reset the Periodic Table with fancier china. That's why they hate gold: They can't control it. And it reminds them that they are imposters, no more effective than witch doctors or marriage counselors.

As of this writing, it takes more than $1,400 to buy a single ounce of gold—a new record. Why? Isn't it obvious? People are losing faith. Last week, the U.S. Federal Reserve said it was creating another $600 billion to buy U.S. Treasury debt. That will mean a total of $2.3 trillion added to America's monetary footings since the Fed began its QE program almost two years ago. This will also mean that Ben Bernanke has added three times as many dollars to America's core money supply as *all the Treasury secretaries and Fed chairmen who came before him put together.*

"Easier financial conditions will promote economic growth," wrote Mr. Bernanke, in the *Washington Post,* ". . . higher stock prices will boost consumer wealth and help increase confidence, which can also spur spending. Increased spending will lead to higher incomes and profits that, in a virtuous circle, will further support economic expansion."

Where is the proof? Where is the controlled test? Where is the peer review? Such an extravagant assertion ought to be accompanied by extravagant evidence. But there is none at all. Throwing virgins into a volcano would be no less scientific. The virgins appeased the gods; that was the theory. Mr. Bernanke has a voodoo theory, too. He says all that new money will make people feel richer . . . and then they will act richer . . . and then they will be richer!

John Hussman, also an economist with a loyal following of his own, read Mr. Bernanke's explanation and pronounced judgment: "The most ignorant remarks ever made by a central banker." The latest $600 billion gamble may or may not increase stock market prices, he says. Even if it does, it is unlikely to produce the "wealth effect" that Ben Bernanke is counting on.

People spend and borrow when they think they have permanent wealth. World stock markets have suffered two major shocks in the last 10 years . . . with no net gains for investors. An increase in stock prices now—driven by the Fed's printing press—is unlikely to create the kind of expectations that lead people to spend money. Especially when they don't have any.

Which makes us wonder, too. If modern economists are scientists, it makes us suspicious of the rest of them. What about the physicists? The molecular biologists? The archeologists? Are they all quacks too?

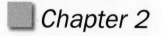 *Chapter 2*

The Maestro's Last Helipad

*The Conspiracy of
Greenspan and Bernanke*

Greenspan's Put Is Shot

December 8, 2000

Gentle reader, the whole world now turns its weary eyes to Mr. Greenspan. The financial press portrays him as the savior of the modern world. *Time* magazine, in fact, once put him on the cover, along with Robert Rubin and Larry Summers with this headline: "Committee To Save the World"—with no trace of humor. In Bob Woodward's book he is the "Maestro." *Fortune* ran a cover story: "In Greenspan We Trust."

And on Tuesday, Mr. Greenspan . . . the former jazz saxophonist and Ayn Rand devotee . . . seemed to live up to his billing. "Greenspan Arrests Wall Street Collapse," said the headline in *LA Tribune*. Greenspan had apparently done it. He had pulled out his put option and saved the day.

And yet . . . the dollar continues to fall. And the price of credit continues to rise. Either of these are probably sufficient to render Mr. Greenspan's put option worthless. "Euro continues to rise," reports the financial section of France's *Figaro* newspaper. The hapless European currency has defied almost every financial pundit in the known world by doing what none of them expected—it has gone up.

So delicately balanced—at the margin—is this international flow of funds that merely a small shift in sentiment away from the dollar could be devastating. In effect, if the dollar falls—it means that foreigners will demand a higher rate of return for buying U.S. assets . . . and the cost of credit will increase, not go down as the Greenspan Put requires.

Alas, Mr. Greenspan's put is shot.

Mr. Greenspan's only real weapon is central bank interest rate policy. But, as mentioned here in the last few days, that weapon only works when the enemy is in retreat. Lowering the price of credit does no more to alleviate credit problems than lowering the price of Jim Beam whiskey helps cure dipsomania.

In both cases, the problem is not the price of the elixir . . . but the use to which it has been put.

Over the last few years, every silly idea that came along could belly-up to the credit bar and imbibe almost as much as it wanted. Trillions of dollars worth of capital were raised . . . spent . . . and have now disappeared. What's left are IOUs, stocks, bank loans, and bonds. The quality of these debt instruments is falling rapidly.

"The junk bond market is suffering through its worst funk since at least 1990," reports the *Boston Globe*. "The market is cheap," according to Fred Cavanaugh, director of high-yield assets at John Hancock Mutual Funds. "The question is whether it represents value."

"The average junk bond mutual fund had lost 10.85 percent for the year through Tuesday," continues the *Globe* article. "In 1990, by any measure a disastrous year for junk bond investors, the average high-yield fund lost about 9.6 percent."

"So-called TMT companies, working in telecommunications, media, and technology, are the most worrisome creditors in the junk bond market. They borrowed huge sums to build out new communications networks and some are running into financial walls. ICG Communications Inc. had borrowed $2 billion by the time it filed for bankruptcy protection last month."

Falling prices for junk bonds means rising costs of credit for the borrowers—and not just TMT borrowers. J.C. Penny's bonds now yield 18 percent. . . . Tenneco Automotive's bonds yield 21.3 percent. And the gold producer Ashanti's bonds can be bought to yield 27 percent.

These are all troubled companies. But that is what you get after a credit binge—companies with problems . . . companies that have taken up too much capital and spent it too freely. You also get consumers with problems, for much the same reasons.

One company with trouble to spare is Bank of America. "They let credit quality get away from them and it's coming back to haunt them," said an analyst quoted by Bloomberg. "Loan problems are mounting at U.S. banks," the Bloomberg piece observes, ". . . as customers find it more difficult to pay debt. Bank of America expects to write off $1.1 to $1.2 billion in bad loans in the 4th quarter, compared to $435 million in the 3rd quarter."

BOA was the main creditor of Armstrong, the vinyl floor maker that went bankrupt a few days ago and Owens Corning, which filed for bankruptcy on October 5. Both companies were plagued by asbestos suits.

BOA wrote off a $500 million loan to Sunbeam . . . and also lent to Pillowtex and ICG—both of which went bankrupt on November 14.

A bank with this keen a nose for deadbeat borrowers could have hardly missed the movie business. In fact, it lent $1.2 billion to Regal Cinemas—the nation's largest theater chain—two years ago. Naturally, Regal defaulted and may also go Chapter 11.

When credit is too cheap, people treat it cheaply. The result is trouble. But it is not the sort of trouble that can be cured by even cheaper credit.

The U.S. economy is now at the end, I believe, of one of the biggest credit binges in history. The headaches and regrets cannot be dodged or ignored. And easier credit is not likely to make much difference—just as it has had no effect in Japan over the last decade.

The entire psycho-profile and attitude of the market is changing. Instead of dreams . . . there will be nightmares. Venture funds are being replaced with vulture funds. And hard-nosed, bitter-end investors and workout specialists are taking the places of naive amateurs. . . . The focus of serious investors will no longer be on cleaning up in the market . . . but on merely cleaning up.

Investors, who used to believe everything was possible and who accepted every fairy tale business plan, chapter and verse, are coming to believe nothing and accepting only Chapters 11 and 7.

Things can't be put back in order without cleaning up the trash and butt ends. This won't be done by quarter-point decreases in the Fed Funds rate.

God, Man, and Alan Greenspan

June 8, 2001—Paris, France

Tell me why do fools fall in love . . .

—Fragment of popular song from the late 1950s

Why must stocks fall in price?

I pose the question again today, dear reader, because I know it interests you, as it does me. If stocks do not have to fall in price, we could buy the big names of the S&P—even at 28 times earnings. Maybe they would rise higher . . . and stay higher . . . forever.

Stock prices rise from time to time—as if on an irregular, unpredictable ocean tide. Waves of bullishness rise up . . . between troughs of despair . . . and crash into the rocky shoreline. No matter how high the waves, nor how low the tide might ebb, sooner or later, as Jeremy Grantham reminds us—stock prices regress to sea level. The memory of man runneth not to the contrary.

Theory confirms experience, in this case as in others. After all, why should investors be willing to pay more for a dollar of earnings this year than they were five years ago? Why would they settle for a return of 5 percent on one investment when they could get 10 percent on another?

Stocks are nothing more than partial ownership of businesses. People rarely buy businesses for fun. They buy them for the income they will produce and let the price of shares rise and fall along with business earnings.

Over time, share prices tend to rise . . . but only in line with increased and accumulated earnings. If there were no competition and no alternatives, businesses might increase profit margins year after year. But that would be a different world than the one we live in. Without alternatives, there would be no stock market and no decisions for an investor to make.

As it is, competition holds profits down and directs investors' money so as to force all investment profits down to the same sea level of returns, adjusted for risk and other variables.

Over time, an article in this month's *Fortune* tells us, companies' earnings grow alongside GDP, inflation, and stock prices. Investors should expect only about 6 percent per year . . . plus dividends of, currently, only 1.2 percent.

But during a 17-year bull market, stock market returns rose far above the mean. A drop back to sea level requires either a long period of low or zero returns . . . as long as 10 to 15 years. Or, stocks could fall sharply — with the S&P down about 60 percent, estimates *Fortune,* reducing P/Es from 28 to about 10 — and then resume its normal rate of return.

But, look carefully. For there, standing on the beach, an aged, care-worn little man holds out a staff. It is King Alan Greenspan Canute, bidding the waters to hold fast. "Stay where you are," he commands. "Resist the tug of the business cycle, ignore the tilt of the credit cycle, and ignore the lunatic phases of investor sentiment . . . that inconstant moon of irrational exuberance and unreasonable gloom. . . ."

"It takes faith to believe in the invisible hand," said Mark Skousen at last week's lecture in Paris. "You can't see it. And yet, we know it works."

Everyone has faith in something, dear reader. Some have faith in Adam Smith's invisible hand of God. Others have faith in Mr. Greenspan's wrinkled mitts.

Some people believe they can think their way to the truth. Others wait for it to be revealed to them. But one way or another, we arrive at a truth we find convenient and hold to it . . . until the real thing finally falls upon us.

Houses without Moats

September 20, 2002

It is over. The Golden Age of Central Banking—when giants such as Alan Greenspan, Robert Rubin, and Larry Summers walked the earth—has come to an end. Now, day by day, Mr. Greenspan shrinks. Before the trend is over, he will be a midget.

We hear the hissing sounds already . . . other economists carping about his errors . . . investors whining about their losses . . . politicians eager to stick him with the blame.

There is also the hissing from his many bubbles. Stocks leak air almost every day. Bankruptcies reach record levels. Junk bonds get trashed and debts go bad in record numbers. And consumers' knees grow weak and weary from toting so much debt.

Consumers will be the last to catch on. As recently as a month ago, they thought they could borrow money without worrying about paying it back. Jobs would be no problem. The cash would keep flowing. Stocks may crash, they believed . . . but the housing sector is still growing and solid.

But yesterday brought news that the housing bubble may have found its pin. Housing starts fell 2.2 percent. Lumber cracked—dropping below the $10 limit.

Mortgage delinquencies at a record 5.7 percent . . . and foreclosures at the highest rates since they began keeping records . . . have begun to hammer away at both the builders and the lenders. Kaufman and Broad fell $3.26. Lennar dropped nearly the same amount.

And Fannie Mae—the greatest of the housing bubble stocks—slipped to $67.

Anecdotal evidence is beginning to show up too . . . and seems to be gathering a crowd. The smart money is selling, not buying:

"I bought this piece of land [near Middleburg, Virginia] about six years ago. I marked it up to four times what I paid for it and sold it before I even had it listed," reported a friend over dinner last night.

But in other areas, people say it is taking longer to sell houses. Rental rates are said to be falling off. Vacancy rates are increasing.

As reported here earlier, housing prices have risen 30 percent more than the inflation rate over the last seven years. Why should house prices increase faster than everything else? We have a partial answer: because you cannot import a house. Consumer price inflation has been coming down for two decades. But housing has bucked the trend in most areas. The Chinese are making more and more TV sets. They are making so many of them, so cheaply, that prices have been falling for many years. But the Chinese do not build houses for Americans. . . . Even in America, though, people can still make things—if there's money in it.

Years ago, your editor recalls that his cousin prepared to go into the construction business:

"What do you know about building houses?" was the question put to him.

"Nothing . . . what do you need to know?" answered the cousin.

"Don't you need a lot of tools and equipment?"

"I've got a hammer and a saw . . . what more do you need?"

And so the cousin went into the home construction business in 1972 and did well at it.

The typical American house is hardly a work of beauty or consummate engineering. In a matter of days, it can be hammered together out of pre-fabricated parts by a crew of illiterates. Over the long run, and making no allowances for local conditions, there is no reason for houses to be any different from other consumer items. They can beat the general rate of inflation for a while, but not for long.

Warren Buffett points out that the only way you can be fairly sure of protecting a profit margin is to own a business with a moat around it—a high cost of entry that makes it difficult for others to compete.

Some places have natural moats—mountain villages, such as Aspen, Colorado, with little available land . . . or islands, such as Manhattan . . . or seaside resorts, such as Naples, Florida, whose backs are to the ocean. Not surprisingly, these are the places where property prices have risen most quickly. In San Diego, for example, with its huge moat on the west side of town . . . stretching all the way to China . . . housing prices have been going up at 20 percent annually.

But there is no moat around St. Louis. Nor is there one around Baltimore or most other cities. As long as property prices rise faster than the cost of capital, builders will continue putting up marginal houses in marginal areas and selling them to marginal buyers with marginal financing.

That is the thing about a bubble that is almost indescribably wonderful. Things that people might have considered foolish and stupid begin to look reasonable. The housing development, for example, that was a loser at 10 percent mortgage rates, becomes a winner at 6 percent. People who could barely afford a double-wide find themselves with a mini-mansion with plastic siding and a maxi mortgage. And gradually the supply of houses catches up to even the most marginal demand.

And then a change begins. "For Sale" signs stay up longer. Foreclosures rise. Builders and lenders begin to lay people off. And suddenly, it begins to look as though the last of Greenspan's bubbles has popped.

Can Do Money

April 25, 2003

As long as you're pumping out money at a faster rate than demand for money is rising, you're going to stimulate spending. I think it would be kind of fun to fight deflation, actually.

—Robert "Let's hold hands and buy an SUV" McTeer

R obert McTeer must be something of an amateur magician. His idea of a good time, we guess from his remark from February, is creating money out of thin air.

We are not particularly shocked by this. For it has long been apparent that central bankers everywhere—McTeer is president of the Dallas Fed—must like inflating the currency, during working hours at any rate. We are pleased to see that Mr. McTeer enjoys his work.

What is shocking and new is that he would say so. Clipping coins used to be something bankers did when no one was looking, like going to the bathroom or sneaking into porno shops. John Law—when he still had his wits about him—threatened his subordinates with death . . . if they printed money without proper backing. He may not have had any particular interest in protecting the public's money. But he knew what was good for him . . . and if the public ever caught on to the fact that his bank's currency had nothing of value behind it, he would be ruined.

But now, it really must be a new era—of sorts. McTeer and Bernanke openly discuss the methods they intend to use to make sure the dollar does not rise in value. And the capo di tutti capi of central bankers, who is not coincidentally responsible for creating more money out of thin air than any central banker who ever lived—Alan Greenspan—has just been offered a new term at the head of the Fed. At 77 years, all he has to do is to keep breathing . . . and keep inflating . . . and he is assured employment.

Fed officials, from Greenspan on down, have made it clear that they will do "whatever is necessary" to avoid a Japan-style deflationary slump, including interfering with interest rates on both ends of the yield curve. If setting very short-term rates does not do the job, the Fed will distort the long rates, too. "If asset prices don't adjust sufficiently to stimulate spend- ing," explained Vincent Reinhart, of the Fed's Open Market Committee, "then open market purchases of long-term Treasuries in sizable quantities can move term premiums lower."

Here we yield to James Grant for a translation: "We take that to mean," writes Grant, "that if stock prices (or house prices, or other prices yet to be named) don't do what they're supposed to do, the Fed will cap the yields of longer-dated Treasuries in a bid to depreciate the value of the dollar."

And now one further translation: "The Fed will keep interest rates low—no matter what it takes."

Meanwhile, half a world away, another government employee brings the same spirit of optimism and determination to the sands of Mesopotamia. Jay Garner, proconsul, says he will stay "as long as necessary" in order to prevent things from regressing to their natural state in Iraq, while his boss, George Bush, affirms that his administration will do "whatever it takes" to bring peace and prosperity to the desert tribes.

In today's letter, we offer no critique of either department—Defense nor Treasury. We merely marvel at the can-do spirit that animates them . . . in the same way we once admired Evil Knievel for bouncing over the Snake River Canyon on a motorcycle. It was madness, but it was entertaining.

Here in Europe, people do not so much marvel as sneer. Where Americans see benefits, Europeans see problems . . . risks . . . dangers . . . complications. What if the whole Middle East is de-stabilized, they ask? What if more terrorists are incited to action . . . what if the Americans target us next?!

How the world has changed!

"We had our period of madness, too," Sylvie explained during our French lesson. "Ooh là là . . . if you had lived through that period . . . 1914 through 1945 . . . you wouldn't want to do that again."

Sylvie might have gone further. She might have gone back centuries. Every problem . . . every difference . . . every border in Europe seemed to lead to war. Catholic or Protestant . . . German or French . . . Fascist or Communist . . . no difference was so slight as not to be worth fighting over. It was the period of Machtpolitik . . . when Europe was strong militarily and every problem was thought to yield to the force of arms. For hundreds of years, armies marched in Europe . . . getting bigger and bigger, more and more deadly. Then, in the twentieth century, Europe's wars seemed to reach a level of such deadliness that it must have felt terminal.

In 1914 . . . and then again in 1939 . . . the Europeans marched readily into battle . . . each nation sure of itself, with a can-do attitude. Americans, meanwhile, hesitated. Not getting involved in foreign wars was thought to be a national virtue. Protected by two oceans, America's military was relatively weak. And so, the nation favored negotiation . . . hesitation . . . discussion. In World War I and again in World War II, Americans waited years—until the major combatants had already exhausted themselves, said critics—before getting involved.

During those years . . . indeed, since the beginnings of the republic . . . American can-doism was largely focused on commerce, religion, and other civil pursuits. Europeans marched . . . but Americans worked. And American factories from Trenton to San Diego profited by selling shoes, oil, guns . . . everything the Europeans wanted to buy.

But now it is the Americans who put their faith in machtpolitik and the Europeans—protected by an ocean of U.S. military expenditures—who sell them things. "Negotiate," say the Europeans . . . rely on the UN . . . talk . . . trade. The Europeans no longer have faith in can-do foreign policies; they barely have any foreign policies at all.

People learn more from defeat than from victory, we believe. Americans' military interventions have been, largely, successful. Europeans' have been mostly disastrous.

Likewise, too many devaluations . . . too many new currencies . . . and too much inflation have squelched the Europeans' can-do spirit in central banking. France has had two currencies and one 100-to-1 devaluation since World War II. In the 1920s, Germany suffered an inflation so severe that a thousand marks in the morning were almost worthless by the day's end. They do not want to do that again.

While the Fed cut rates 12 times—by 525 basis points—since the beginning of the slump, the European central bank has merely jiggled its rates up and down very cautiously. On the first of January 1999, the best ECB lending rate was 3 percent. Now it is 2.5 percent.

While the Fed program is aggressive, activist, and forward-looking, the European central banker reacts slowly and deliberately, as if he were less sure of himself . . . and more modest. And where Alan Greenspan is known throughout the world—a greater celebrity than Michael Jackson—who can cite the name of the ECB's chief, let alone identify him in a police lineup? Wim Duisenberg is almost a nonentity.

But his currency is rising.

The World He Lives In

May 2, 2003

Today we approach a serious and disturbing paradox: How could it be possible for an economy to slow down just when its central bankers and its central government push harder than ever on the accelerator?

If you would prefer something more lighthearted, you could read Alan Greenspan's address to Congress on Tuesday. More and more, we find we share the sentiments of Rep. Bernie Sanders, who remarked following a previous testimony by the Fed chairman:

"Mr. Greenspan, I always enjoy your presentation because, frankly, I wonder what world you live in."

We wonder, too.

As near as we can tell, it is a strange one. For in Mr. Greenspan's world, there are no paradoxes. It is a world as clean and dull as an actuarial table with only whole numbers. The Fed chairman is surrounded by such positive thinkers, the poor man must not get a chance to voice a doubt or doubt a voice. Ben Bernanke thinks he can make the dollar worth as much or as little as he wants, just by controlling the speed of the printing press. Robert McTeer says he can hardly wait to fight deflation; he thinks it will be fun. Alfred Broadus is probably the most cautious of the bunch . . . but still delusional. He says the Fed has proven that it can fight inflation, and now it has to prove it can fight deflation.

It is to this last point that we are drawn . . . as if to a crime scene. The Fed claims it came along just in time and chased off the miscreant. We look at Al Broadus and the rest of his gang and wonder: Who do they take us for, complete morons?

And yet, Americans' can-do optimism seems to depend on the ability of its central bankers to do what the Japanese could not—successfully wage war on deflation. All right, so the war on inflation was not the great success that Broadus thinks it was. (The dollar ended the year 1913 about where it was 100 years before. In that year, the Fed took up its mission—to protect the value of the nation's currency. Over the next 90 years, the dollar lost 95 percent of its value.) What the Fed has proven is not that it is a good inflation fighter, but that it is good at stabbing the dollar in the back. And since destroying the dollar is just what the times seem to call for, what are we worrying about?

If only there were not so many paradoxes, dear reader. Wouldn't life be much better if women meant what they said? Wouldn't it be nice if you could be happy by thinking of yourself and only doing what makes you happy? Wouldn't it be grand if the investments that made people rich last year would make you rich this year?

Or, more to the point, wouldn't it be just peachy if the Fed really could control the money supply . . . so that people would have money to spend when the Fed wanted them to spend? But therein hangs a tale, which is the subject of today's letter.

But here, hardly having moved forward a single inch, we must arrest our progress. Alert readers may already be looking ahead, with an objection:

"Hey, I know where you're going with this. You're going to say that the Fed will be as incompetent at destroying the dollar's value as they were at protecting it. But haven't you been saying that the dollar was going to collapse?" (And sotto voce: "I've been buying gold and euros thanks to you . . . the dollar damned well better collapse!")

Ah . . . but you expect too much, dear reader. If you want consistency or simplicity, you will have to pay for it. Dearly.

Many, if not most, of our friends have taken the Fed at its word, and on its record. If there is one thing the Fed can do, they say, it is inflate the currency.

"Buy gold," they say. Consumer price inflation is on the way . . . with higher interest rates and falling bond prices. But an odd thing: even as the dollar lost value . . . and the trade deficit hit 5 percent of GDP . . . and federal deficits soared . . . long T bonds, recently, went up. Why would people lend money for 30 years, at paltry rates of interest, to a government openly declaring that it intends to inflate?

We don't know. Perhaps people need the income, as small as it is. But, whatever the reason, the bond market is unconcerned about inflation. Not only did long T-bonds go up, the differential between regular Treasury bonds and those whose return is adjusted for inflation narrowed.

The bond market seems to anticipate not a rerun of the inflationary 1970s . . . but something else; perhaps America will follow in Japan's footsteps after all. For the last eight years or so, the U.S. economy and its stock market have done a fair imitation of the Japanese trendsetter . . . with a 10-year time lag. When the Japanese economy boomed, so did the U.S. economy—10 years later. Then, Japan entered its bubble phase, followed by the United States, 10 years later. Then came the bear market in Japan, again trailed a decade later by a bear market in America.

At first, no one paid any attention to the Japanese situation. It was just a blip, said economists; Japan will come back fast.

That was 14 years ago. And last week, the Nikkei Dow sank to new lows—down 80 percent from a high set back in the final year of the Reagan Administration. After Reagan, Bush the Elder took over in America, upchucked on Japan's Prime Minister . . . and it has been downhill for the Japanese ever since.

But the Japanese did not go gently into that good night. They fought the dying light just as the Greenspan Fed would do—10 years later. Rates were cut . . . and cut . . . and cut some more, until they reached zero. Nor did the Japanese shirk from government spending . . . public works projects of all manner and description were begun. Never before has so much concrete been mixed and poured in such a small place.

But it didn't work. The money supply fell anyway . . . and Japan became the first major nation to experience outright consumer price deflation since the Great Depression. Twenty years of stock market gains have been wiped out. Unemployment edges up as the economy experiences multiple recessions. Consumers seem unwilling to spend—guessing that they will get more for their money next week than they would this one.

How could it be, we ask ourselves? How could a central bank be unable to do what central banks do best?

We remind readers that when the Fed creates money out of thin air, it does not create any corresponding wealth. The world's supply of services or swimming pools does not magically increase when Ben Bernanke turns up the dial on the printing press. What it does create is an illusion of wealth; people with more dollars imagine that they are richer . . . and begin to act the part.

Kurt Richebächer describes this as "pseudo or phantom wealth," the effect of which is, paradoxically, to make people poorer. In the boom phase of an economy, the phony money goes into stocks, or real estate, or some other asset.

"What the rising asset values effectively create," Richebächer explains, "is a corresponding rise in claims on the economy at the expense of those who do not own such assets. But this is wealth redistribution, not wealth creation. More importantly, this kind of wealth creation involves no gain in current incomes and productive capacity. To the extent that it actually boosts consumption at the expense of investment and foreign trade balance, the net result from a macro perspective is overall impoverishment."

Poor people have less money to spend . . . and less money to repay their debts. Unless the central bank delivers the new cash along with the daily paper, money creation takes place through credit. The new money is lent out. If the borrower cannot repay, the cash disappears.

Curiously, money "created out of thin air" tends to disappear even when the loans are paid back. As explained in a recent issue of the Mogambo Guru's, which we would quote if we could find it, when a man lends out his savings, he can expect to get paid back, with interest, and all is well. No change to the money supply.

When money is created out of thin air, on the other hand, the money supply is enlarged when it is lent out. It didn't exist before it was borrowed. Then, when it is paid back, naturally enough, the money supply shrinks! The money goes back to its maker; it exists no more. Thus, the more new credit the Fed has created . . . the greater the measure by which the money supply will eventually fall.

The only way to avoid this inevitable deflation would be to either to give the cash away on the streets . . . or to keep the supply of credit expanding forever. The first solution would be worse than the problem it was meant to solve; the second is impossible.

Meanwhile, the world's apparent wealth—and implied spending power—expands and contracts as the assets, bought on credit, go up and down in value. About 7 trillion dollars were wiped out so far in the stock market decline of the last 3 years. If U.S. stocks follow the Japanese plan— falling 80 percent over 14 years—another $8 trillion or so, in America alone, will disappear.

Is it any wonder that cash and wealth created out of thin air returns whence it came—no matter what its creators would like? There is some elegant justice to it, we think, reminding us once again that we do not get what we want from life, nor what we expect . . . but what we deserve.

Poor House II—The Miracle of No-Sweat Equity . . .

October 10, 2003—Paris, France

Today, we return to our courtroom drama.

You will recall, dear reader, we are arguing that the typical house is not what it appears to be. It pretends to make its owner rich; instead, it makes him poor.

Practically every sentient being with a U.S. passport believes the opposite—that buying a house is a nearly risk-free/reward-guaranteed proposition. Taking the other side of the argument clearly puts us in a very small minority. We look around, and we are practically alone. So, the burden of proof is on us. Last week we carried the load a short way. Today, we pick it up again and teeter on.

Your editor begins by disclosing a prejudice: He is a sucker for real estate. He likes the feel of dirt beneath his feet and under his fingernails. He is comforted by the notion that—should the world go to Hell as he has been predicting—at least he would have a place to live. He even imagines himself living well—eating the fruits of his own garden. In extremis, he might even slaughter his wife's obnoxious horses and roast them over an open fire while swilling his own homemade hooch out of an old jar. For luxuries and heating oil, he could dig up a gold coin or two when needed.

On the whole, the end of the world might not be so bad.

Since he is making disclosures, your editor might also confess a mixed record when it comes to real estate investing. He has spent the week down in Nicaragua, scouting real estate investment possibilities. But this is not the first time he has been a pioneer in the Third World. Two decades ago, he bought a house in a bad neighborhood in Baltimore. He paid almost nothing for it and restored it himself. Back then, he felt he was building sweat equity in the property. Only later did he discover that his perspiration was not worth very much. He could improve the house, he discovered. But not the city around it. When the final tally was made, he found that he had lost money on an actual cash basis. For all his sweating, he had earned not a penny.

Typically, our experience was at odds with the rest of the world. In a sea of rising property prices, your editor managed to find a leaky boat.

But the real tidal increase in property prices began later . . . about eight years ago. In that period, house prices rose three times faster than rents. Not since The Flood has there been such a lift. Prices rose nearly 50 percent in nominal terms, almost 30 percent more than the increase in inflation. Without lifting a finger, the nation's homeowners found themselves $2.7 trillion richer—about $35,000 extra for every one of them. Where did the money come from, we wondered last week?

In almost every community, the story was much the same. You could toss a Congressman out of a helicopter almost anywhere in the country; it was very unlikely he'd fall upon a house that had not gone up in price.

But we contend that houses have not really made people wealthy at all. In fact, they've made them poor. How can that be?

Last week, we established an important point: that the house itself— the physical thing—couldn't possibly increase in value. All its components deteriorate, depreciate, fade and decay—just like everything else.

And now we call our star witness.

"Mr. Alan Greenspan, would you step up to the witness stand, please?"

"Mr. Greenspan, you have sworn to tell the truth, the whole truth and nothing but the truth, isn't that right?

"Of course, you wouldn't tell lies, we just wanted to make sure . . .

"Now, isn't it true you have said many times that your lower interest rates were a big help to consumers? In fact, wasn't it as recently as a few weeks ago that you testified before Congress that consumers were in 'better shape,' since they had been able to refinance their debts at lower rates?

"Now, to tell you the truth, you might as well have gotten down on all fours and barked . . . it would have made as much sense to us. As near as we can tell, consumers have never been in worse shape.

"Of course, as chief of the Federal Reserve System, you are well aware of the numbers. The old rule was that lenders insisted that monthly mortgage payments not exceed 28 percent of gross income. They called that the 'back-end ratio.' But as people came to believe that real estate always goes up, both borrowers and lenders began to loosen up. Now, in expensive markets such as Boston and San Diego, the percentage of income devoted to mortgage payments has risen to more than 43 percent. In San Francisco, the average family spends 47 percent of its pre-tax income on mortgage payments.

"San Francisco must be the Nasdaq of real estate markets, wouldn't you agree? The median house there sells for $515,000. Only 14 percent of the people in the area can qualify to buy a house . . . and those who do spend 5 to 6 times their annual income on it. Thirty years ago, the median house cost 2.1 times median income.

"Much of the reason for the increase in real estate prices must simply be that it is easier to borrow money, wouldn't you guess? Even very poor credit risks are routinely cleared for mortgages these days, aren't they? Because everyone is so sure house prices will keep going up. As long as prices are rising, why worry? If the homeowner runs into trouble, he can always sell his house for a higher price. Or, the bank can resell it for him.

"But isn't it true, too, that lending to the marginal credit risk is a little like introducing your daughter to a marginal sports star? If you make it too easy for him, there is almost sure to be trouble.

"Thanks to your policies, and the innovations of the financial industry, credit has never been easier to come by. As a consequence, debt has increased for the last 30 years . . . and it has continued to increase even through the recession of 2001 . . . and right up to the present. In absolute terms, as well as by most relative measures, Americans are more in debt than at any time in history. And after record levels of mortgage refinancing, never before have they owned so little of their own homes.

"In light of all that, would you care to explain what you meant by consumers being in 'better shape'?"

[Unintelligible response.]

"Well, let's approach it in another way.

"Do you read the papers, Mr. Chairman?

"You do?

"Good. Well, have you seen an advertisement offering an equity line of credit? It has a drawing of a house with bags of money under it. 'Go ahead . . . it's yours . . . you have a right to it . . . take it out . . . spend it . . .' the ad says, or something like that.

"Well, now . . . there wouldn't be any ads like that if rates hadn't been cut so dramatically, would there?

"Of course not.

"And there wouldn't be a refinancing boom, either, right? And if there were no refinancing boom, consumers wouldn't have been able to keep spending, could they?"

Refinancing boom; what equity?

"Now we understand that you regard all this as a good thing. If consumers had not been able to keep taking the 'equity' out of their houses . . . the whole world economy would have fallen into recession, wouldn't it? Americans wouldn't have had any money to spend. Foreigners wouldn't have been able to sell their products. Nor would they have been able to accumulate hundreds of billions of dollars or to reinvest them in U.S. Treasury bonds. There wouldn't be such a huge trade deficit . . . and no way to finance the federal deficit or the war against Iraq . . . at least not at current interest rates.

"Wouldn't you agree?

"You would? Good.

"So, you would say that the whole world economy depends on the rate cuts and on consumers' willingness to continue taking out 'equity' from their houses, right?

"Yes, it is fairly obvious. But now a more difficult question. Are you ready for this, Mr. Chairman? Here goes:

"What exactly is this 'equity'? We understand money you make from working. Or profits you make in your business. Or money you've saved up. But this no-sweat equity is something different, isn't it? It seems to come out of nowhere, almost magically. Houses are supposed to provide a sort of dividend for their owners; they give them a roof over their heads. But isn't it a bit peculiar that they should produce extra cash, too?

"What is this money? We've put the question to others. No one has had a good answer. We were counting on you, Mr. Chairman. As the best-known central banker since John Law, we thought you might be able to tell us what this money—this money that the world relies upon so heavily—really is.

"Well, let us jog your brain a bit.

"Isn't it possible that there really is no money there? A house is a house is a house, after all. It is a consumer item, not a capital asset. What is really happening is that the house owner is merely borrowing against the inflated value of it. And isn't it possible that the house is subject to the same fits of 'irrational exuberance'—as you put it—as the stock market?

Isn't it true that the mortgage industry is merely acting like the brokerage industry in a bubble market—lending money on the inflated value of the asset? And isn't it correct to say that this lending is itself contributing to the bubble in prices?

"You know how it works; you watched the same thing in stocks three years ago. You said you couldn't tell it was a bubble back then. But now that you've seen one up close, maybe you are better able to see the next one? A fellow sees his house going up at 10 percent per year. He figures he'll buy another one. How can he resist? It's easy money, isn't it? Especially since, as everyone knows, house prices never go down.

"But you remember Hyman Minsky? He pointed out that 'stability produces instability,' didn't he? The idea was that the more people come to believe something is sure, the less sure it becomes. As everyone came to believe that house prices only go up, lenders lent more freely and buyers spent more freely. Naturally, prices rose. This convinced other buyers that they should get in while the getting was good. Before you knew it, real estate prices had taken off, rising far faster than the incomes of the people who were to buy them.

"And isn't that exactly what has happened in America? The average after-tax, after-inflation income is barely rising at all. And yet, house prices are going up at 10 percent per year and more. Yesterday, we read that house prices in Minnesota have risen 50 percent in the last four years. And last year alone, in places as diverse as Topeka, Kansas, and Providence, Rhode Island, they were up nearly 20 percent. In Nassau County, New York, they were reported rising at an unbelievable 26 percent. How long can that last?

"You don't know? Well, we don't know either, but it definitely can't last forever, can it? There must come a time when the average person can no longer afford the average house and when some people need to sell. Then what?

"Of course, we're not blaming you, Mr. Chairman, we're just trying to get to the bottom of it . . . to understand what is going on.

"Now let me ask you another question. If house prices can stop rising, they can also go down . . . isn't that correct? And isn't it also correct to say that, in fact, sooner or later, they will go down? Isn't this exactly what happened following every stock market bubble of the last 70 years—in Japan, Korea, Hong Kong, the Philippines, Thailand, Indonesia, Mexico, and Brazil?

"And what do you think will happen to homeowners who have taken out the equity in their houses? They will still have to pay interest on it, won't they? In fact, at some point they will even have to put the equity back in . . . right? When they sell, for example?

"And now, here's something interesting. Even in a bad economy, most people will be all right, of course. Most won't have to sell. So, you might assume that property prices will stay fairly stable. But that's not really true, is it? In Japan, residential properties have fallen 23 percent since 1991.

"Prices are set by the properties that sell, not by those that don't change hands. In a crunch, all it will take is a few desperate neighbors and your house could decline in value by 10 percent . . . 20 percent . . . or even more.

"Yes, but? What but?

"We're not asking you to predict the future. We are talking about the present. We just want you to admit that a homeowner who takes 'equity' out of his house is actually poorer than the one who does not. And since low interest rates and rising real estate prices are an invitation to 'take out' this 'equity,' it might also be correct to say that the boom in the real estate market has actually made the marginal homeowner poorer. Am I wrong about that?"

[Unintelligible response.]

"You may step down, Mr. Greenspan, we have no further questions for you. . . ."

And now, let us call our final witness: you, dear reader.

Let us begin with the same question we've posed to our other witnesses. What is this no-sweat equity people take out of their homes? Is it really any different from any other promise of something for nothing?

And like every other promise of something for nothing, won't it more than likely end in more nothing than something?

And won't millions of homeowners end up sweating their equity after all?

Take It Away, Maestro

January 26, 2006—London, England

In the spring of 2005, the American economy had been in "recovery" for over 24 months. It was an odd recovery. No one was quite sure what it was recovering from. There had been a recession in 2001 and 2002. But it was a curious recession. GDP growth went negative. Yet consumer spending and credit continued to expand. If recessions were meant to correct the mistakes of the previous expansion, this one was a failure. Consumers should have spent less and increased savings. Then, after the recession was over, they should have had money to spend in the following expansion and a pent-up desire to buy what they had not bought during the recession.

The expansion was doomed from the beginning. Consumers had never stopped spending. So, when the economy turned around, they had saved no money. The only way they could continue spending was by borrowing more. The Fed helpfully dumped more alcohol in the bowl—lowering rates to make it easy for them. But by this time, the whole economy had become so woozy that the extra consumer spending had a much less positive effect on the real economy than had been hoped. Americans borrowed and spent. But, in the new globalized economy, much of what they bought came from Asia, particularly China, which could turn out consumer goods at a lower cost than the United States.

What America really needed was not a consumer binge, but a capital-spending boom. It needed to invest in new factories, new plants, and new jobs. The jobs would have given consumers real new income, with which to buy more goods and services and sustain the expansion. But gross investment—which had averaged 18.8 percent in the pre-Reagan years—had begun dropping the year Reagan entered the White House. By 2004, it had fallen to 1.6 percent—even dipping below zero periodically. People were spending, but on consumption, not future production. The gewgaws and gadgets bought from China merely put Americans further into debt.

Neither jobs nor incomes improved. Typically, at this stage of a recovery (June 2005), 10 million more new jobs should have been created. Likewise, incomes went up $300 billion less than they should have, based on the pattern of previous recoveries.

Many economists—including Alan Greenspan—maintained that the lack of jobs was a sign of something good happening. "Productivity," they said, "accounts for most job losses, not outsourcing."

"Over the long sweep of American generations and waves of economic change," explained the maestro, "we simply have not experienced a net drain of jobs to advancing technology or to other nations." Could something be different this time? Could this be a kind of new era in American economic history? The answer we give is "yes," but we will give it later. Here, our burden is more modest, and our proof comes more readily to hand. For here, we argue only that America's leading economic and political policy makers are either rascals or numbskulls.

Major tops in the credit cycle seem to correspond with major bottoms in economic thinking. From high offices all over the nation come the explanations, excuses, rationales, and obiter dicta; we don't know whether they are corrupt or merely stupid. But when the guardians of the public financial mores begin urging people to acts of recklessness, we cannot help but notice. Buy more, says one Fed governor. Borrow more, says another.

Don't worry about debt, interest rates, or the loss of jobs, says the captain of them all. It is as though the National Council of Bishops had come out with a public statement, urging wife swapping. The experience may not be unpleasant, but it is unseemly of them to say so. "Go out and buy an SUV," urged Fed governor Robert McTeer. Seventeen million people heeded his call each year, from 2001 to 2005.

On February 23, 2004, the Fed chief urged Americans to switch from fixed rate mortgages to ARMs—mortgages with adjustable rates, which left them much more exposed to interest rate increases, at the very moment when the Fed was increasing them.

If anyone could be held directly and immediately responsible for the record level of America's foreign and domestic debts, it was Alan Greenspan. He had brought about a binge of borrowing by lowering interest rates down to Eisenhower-era levels. But spiking the punch was not enough; he was urging consumers to have another drink. Even the press was beginning to notice.

"Alan Greenspan is essentially lending money at a loss," began a surprising editorial in the *International Herald Tribune*. "This cannot go on indefinitely, and it should not go on much longer. . . . It increased corporate profits and prompted consumers to refinance their mortgages and to spend their way into plenty of other debt. . . . Many homeowners, and consumers in general, are borrowing recklessly, betting that rising housing prices and easy credit are here to stay. . . . Americans may be in for a rude shock when the real estate market levels off, and when millions discover that the adjustable rates of their mortgages and other loans can be adjusted upward."

The Fed chairman had an uncanny way of arriving at ideas at a time when they would be of most benefit to his own career and of most danger to everyone else. To Greenspan, the conservative economist, the stock market looked "irrationally exuberant" in the mid-1990s, until a member of Congress pointed out to him that he would be better off keeping his mouth shut. A goldbug in the 1970s, Greenspan has now become the biggest purveyor of paper money the world has ever seen. Similarly, large federal deficits seemed at odds with his creed until it suited him to think otherwise. The new American empire needed easy money and almost unlimited credit: Alan Greenspan made sure they got it.

Markets make opinions, say old-time investors. Mr. Greenspan's opinions neatly corresponded with the market for his services. As the debts and deficits mounted up, Greenspan underwent an intellectual metamorphosis. An article in the *New York Times* explained:

"Many mainstream economists are worried about these trends, but Alan Greenspan, arguably the most powerful and influential economist in the land, is not as concerned:

"In speeches and testimony, Mr. Greenspan, chairman of the Federal Reserve Board, is piecing together a theory about debt that departs from traditional views and even from fears he has himself expressed in the past. In the 1990s, Mr. Greenspan implored President Bill Clinton to lower the budget deficit and tacitly condoned tax increases in doing so. Today, with the deficit heading toward a record of $500 billion, he warns more emphatically about the risks of raising taxes than about shortfalls over the next few years.

"Mr. Greenspan's thesis, which is not accepted by all traditional economists, is that increases in personal wealth and the growing sophistication of financial markets have allowed Americans—individually and as a nation—to borrow much more today than might have seemed manageable 20 years ago."

And here the article strikes gold:

"This view is good news for President Bush's re-election prospects. It increases the likelihood that the Federal Reserve will keep short-term interest rates low. And it could defuse Democratic criticism that the White House has added greatly to the nation's record indebtedness."

Out of convenience, rather than ideology, Mr. Greenspan came to see goodness in all manner of credit. Since he became head of the Federal Reserve system, debt levels rose from $28,892 for the average family in 1987 to $101,386 in 2005. Mortgage foreclosure rates, personal bankruptcies, and credit card delinquencies rose steadily and are now at record levels. Mortgage debt rose $6.2 trillion during his tenure at the Fed. By January 2005, it had reached $8.5 trillion, or approximately $80,849 per household.

But none of this seemed to bother the chief of America's central bank, nor its chief politicians.

Incredible Threat

August 6, 2010—Ouzilly, France

Last week, Mr. James Bullard was being both cagey and clairvoyant. The president of the St. Louis Federal Reserve Bank noticed what everyone else has seen for months: The U.S. economic recovery is a flop. GDP growth was last measured pottering along at a 2.4 percent rate in the second quarter, less than half the speed of the last quarter of 2009. At this stage in the typical post-war recovery, GDP growth should be over 5 percent with strong employment. Instead, the "Help Wanted" pages are largely empty. Homeowners are still underwater. And shoppers are still largely missing from the malls that once knew them. Whatever is going on, it is not the "V" shaped recovery that economists had expected. Many now worry that the recovery might have a "W" shape—a double dip recession form, with GDP growth dropping down below zero in this quarter or the next.

Mr. Bullard told a telephone press conference he worries that the U.S. economy may become "enmeshed in a Japanese-style deflationary outcome within the next several years." That is exactly what is likely to happen.

But it is a little early for the Fed economists to throw in the towel. They still have some fight left in them. If they were really on the ropes, for example, they could throw their widow maker punch—dropping dollar bills from helicopters. This would make sure that the money supply increases, even if the normal distribution channel—bank lending—is broken.

In a celebrated speech on November 21, 2002, Mr. Ben Bernanke, then a recent addition to the Federal Reserve Bank's board of governors, explained why deflation was not a problem:

> Like gold, U.S. dollars have value only to the extent that they are strictly limited in supply. But the U.S. government has a technology, called a printing press (or, today, its electronic equivalent), that

allows it to produce as many U.S. dollars as it wishes at essentially no cost.

It was that technology to which Mr. Bullard referred when he ceased being prescient and began being cagey. He was not advocating dropping money from helicopters, not just yet. He was hoping he wouldn't have to. Instead, he was raising the menace of inflation, in the hopes that that would be enough.

By increasing the number of U.S. dollars in circulation, or even by credibly threatening to do so, Mr. Bernanke had continued, "The U.S. government can also reduce the value of a U.S. dollar in terms of goods and services, which is equivalent to raising prices in dollars of those goods and services. . . . We conclude that under a paper money system, a determined government can always generate higher spending and hence positive inflation."

There's the problem right there. The threat must be credible. Ben Bernanke's speech title left no doubt about his intentions: "Deflation: Making sure it doesn't happen here." Back then, the reported consumer price measure stood at 1.7 percent—slightly below the 2 percent target. Perhaps it was that 0.3 percent undershoot that set Ben Bernanke to thinking about it. If so, we wonder what he must think now. Today, the Fed is off-target by 75 percent, which is to say, the measured inflation rate is just 0.5 percent. It is beginning to look as though Ben Bernanke's reputation as a deflation fighter is more boast than reality.

The Fed's Open Market Committee meets on August 10th. On the agenda will be more direct purchases of U.S. Treasury debt—bought with money that didn't exist previously. This is what economists call "quantitative easing." It is a way of increasing the money supply. But quantitative easing is not the same as dropping money from helicopters. If you drop money from helicopters there is no room for ambiguity, and no doubt about what happens next. In a matter of seconds, your currency will be sold off, your loans called, and your credibility ruined for at least a generation. Quantitative easing, on the other hand, is a much more subtle proposition. It allows the central banker to maintain his credibility, at least for a while, because it doesn't necessarily or immediately work. When the private sector is hunkering down, the money doesn't go far. Prices don't rise. Japan has done plenty of quantitative easing, with no loss to the value of the yen or to the credibility of its central bank. Europe has done it, too.

And so has America. The U.S. Fed bought $1.25 trillion worth of Wall Street's castaway credits in the 2008–2009 rescue effort. But instead of losing faith in America's central bank, investors bend their knees and bow their heads. Incredibly, the United States now announces the heaviest borrowing in history while it enjoys some of the lowest interest rates in 55 years.

A threat to undermine the currency, we conclude, is only credible when it is made by someone who has already lost his credibility. That is, someone with nothing more to lose. Bernanke, Bullard, et al., are not there yet.

Plumbers Crack

November 05, 2010—Delray Beach, Florida

Poor Ben Bernanke. There was a strange glow on his face as it appeared in Monday's *Financial Times* . . . like a bearded St. Joan of Arc; his hands were clasped together as if in prayer, and his eyes seemed to reach up to the gods, if not beyond.

He made his reputation as a master plumber in Princeton, New Jersey, interpreting drippy money supply faucets and deconstructing clogged fiscal drains. And now, he has become the hope of all mankind. Or at least that part of mankind that hopes to get something for nothing.

How came this to be? The answer is simple. The plumbers who came before him botched the job. Applying their wrenches to the recession of 2001, they let too much liquidity into the system. Everything bubbled up. The subprime basement overflowed in 2007 . . . Ben Bernanke has been on the job ever since.

And this week the financial world held its breath. It waited. It watched. Ben Bernanke was hunched over . . . sweat on his brow . . . easing on his mind. Commentators, economists, and the public wondered if he could really create new money . . . new wealth . . . out of thin air? If this were true, it was a giant step forward for humanity, at least equal to discovering fire, creating Facebook, or blowing up Nagasaki. Jesus Christ multiplied loaves and fishes. But He had something to work with. The Federal Reserve multiplies zeros . . . creating money—out of nothing at all. If it can really do the trick, we are saved. The legislature can go home. It no longer needs to worry about raising taxes or allocating public resources. Government can now buy all the loaves and fishes it wants. And give every voter a quart of whiskey on Election Day.

During the course of the last three years, the plumbers have spent hundreds of billions of dollars. It's hard to know what the final bill will be, since so much money—more than $10 trillion—is in the form of guarantees and asset purchases. They've pumped. They've bailed. They've squeezed and turned. They scraped their knuckles and cursed the gods.

You'd expect they might think twice before spending so much money. But on the evidence, they haven't even thought once. Quantitative easing has been tried before. Has it ever worked? Nope. Never. Do you dispute it? Give us an example.

Japan announced its QE program in the spring of 2001. The Nikkei 225 was around 12,000 at the time. It quickly rose to 14,000 as investors anticipated a payoff from the easy money. Then, stocks sold off again. Two years later the index was at 8,000. Today, it is still about 25 percent below its 2001 level.

Did printing money cause an up-tick in inflation? Not even. Core CPI was negative 1 percent when the program began. It rose—to zero—briefly . . . and then fell again and now stands at minus 1.1 percent after going down 19 months in a row.

America's own experience with quantitative easing is similarly discouraging. Between the beginning of 2009 and March of 2010, the Fed bought $1.7 trillion worth of mortgage-backed securities, creating new money specifically for that purpose. Where did the new money go? Into the coffers of the banks. Did it stimulate the economy? Not so's you'd notice. The unemployment rate today is 200 basis points higher than it was when the program began. And despite the flood of cash and credit, core CPI in the United States is still only a third of its level in 2008.

Of course, there are other examples where central banks printed money with more gusto. In Germany, during and after World War I, the nation's real money—gold—was used to pay for the war and the reparations following. The central bank felt it had to create additional money—like the Fed—without gold backing. It added about 75 percent annually to the money supply, from the end of the war until 1922. By late 1923, the U.S. dollar was worth 4 trillion German marks. Still other examples—from Argentina, Hungary, Zimbabwe, and elsewhere—are fun to read about. But they are not exactly the sort of thing you'd want to try at home, either.

Even if quantitative easing were a precision tool in the hands of a skilled mechanic, it might be little more than a wooden club in Ben Bernanke's dorky grip. This is the same man who missed the biggest credit bubble of all time! There is no evidence that he could fix a bicycle let alone the world's largest economy. But there you have a more interesting question. What if economists were duped by their own silly metaphor? What if an economy were not like a bicycle? What if the gods were laughing at them?

Central planning and cheap fixes have been tried before. When have they ever worked? Give us an example. Perhaps an economy is too complex . . . like love or the weather . . . unfathomable . . . and largely uncontrollable, something you can make a mess of but not something you can improve.

We have no more information as to the fundamental nature of things than anyone else. A toaster oven is designed and built for a purpose. When it doesn't work, it can be fixed. But an economy? Who built it? Who can fix it? It is an organic, evolving system . . . whose purpose and methods are infinitely nuanced. Does it let banks go broke? Does it back up once in a while? Does it permit falling house prices . . . high unemployment . . . and deflation? Yes . . . so what? Does it always do what politicians and economists want? No? So what?

It has a sense of humor, too. Wait until it turns around and kicks the clumsy mechanic in the derriere!

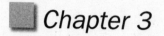 *Chapter 3*

No Clairvoyants Need Apply

More Perfect Unions

April 4, 2001

"Do you love him?"

"No."

"Was it better with him?"

"No."

"Then why did you do it?"

"Who knows?"

—Jean Anouilh, *Don't Wake Mother*

The subject was not roses. The subject was thorns: adultery, a staple of French literature . . . and perhaps French life.

"You seem shocked," said Sylvie last week. "Don't women in America cheat on their husbands?" We were reading a novel by Maupassant. I read out loud. Sylvie, a young woman who teaches yoga as well as French, corrects my pronunciation.

In the passage we were reading, a woman takes up with another man when her husband is out of town. In fact, she rents an apartment so they can conduct their liaison without being disturbed.

"I am not so much shocked by what they are doing," I replied, "as by the deliberate way they are doing it."

"I suspect that people in America are not so different," was her response.

"No, American women would agonize and feel more guilt. They would need to talk to psychologists and counselors."

"We French," answered Sylvie, "prefer to save our suffering for Hell."

Long-time *Daily Reckoning* sufferers know that we range far and wide—looking for the rare mushroom of insight that might have grown up overnight. . . . But new readers may be surprised. This is a financial service, isn't it?

Yesterday, I promised to tell you how to tell when the stock market bottoms out. And, oh yes, I also promised more—including how to find love . . . and how to have a happy marriage. Would it surprise you to learn that the secret is the same for all three?

The paradox of all three things is that you cannot get to them by a direct route. No road sign on life's highway offers "Love—Exit Here!" Nor will you find a "Last Exit Before Bear Market" signposted on your way to work. And don't bother to look for "Happy Marriage" on a map. Even with GPS, you will not find it.

If only it weren't so, I thought to myself as Jack and Mimi exchanged wedding vows on Saturday. I take some tiny portion of the credit for bringing them together. Both worked for my company . . . at least until one was fired. But by then it was too late—the gravity that was to bring them into mutual orbit had already captured them.

And now, what would happen to them? I feel toward them as I do to my own children: If only I could protect them from the mistakes I've made. If only I could protect myself from the mistakes I am about to make!

That is the problem with age and wisdom—it merely shows you how helpless you are. The wiser you become, the more you learn to keep your mouth shut, until eventually the grave silences you forever.

What a pity there is no Federal Reserve System of the heart—a group of wise old graybeards who could protect the currency of love . . . and keep Jack and Mimi's union in perpetual expansion, like the U.S. economy, with only an occasional, mild correction. If only there were some way to help them keep their stock rising!

Alas, gentle reader, some things are beyond our comprehension. Others are simply beyond our control.

All across America, investors, TV presenters, and analysts are watching, waiting, and wishing for that big bottom of their dreams.

"As stock prices have gone down," reports *USA Today,* "36-year-old Greg Reinhard has looked for opportunities to buy good companies at cheap prices."

"I'm happy with this type of market," he says. "This is when you have to step up to the plate."

Meanwhile, Lisa Jiminez and Jay Maxwell, who share a home if not a name, have "sold nothing during the downturn. As a result, their losses are only on paper."

Roger Pyle, who plans to retire in six years, says, "I still have a substantial amount in technology, because I believe it's going to come back."

And Simon Richardson "plans to resume investing in stocks when the market recovers."

How will we know when the market finally finds its big bottom? It will not even be reported in the newspaper. *USA Today* will not ask people what they are doing with their stock portfolios. And no one will care.

The bottom will come when people stop looking for it . . . when investors have given up, and turned their attention away from stocks— maybe even away from their financial lives.

"Get Rich and Stay Rich Forever . . ." says the headline on *Worth* magazine. "The Next Big Money Maker" promises another. [Worth once called me a *genius,* so I am suspicious of anything I read in the magazine.] Those are not the sort of headlines you find at the bottom of a financial cycle. They are more likely signs of a top—when everyone is obsessed with making money.

Bear markets correct not only stock prices, but attitudes and philosophies. People turn away from the existential pleasures of getting rich *Now!* in favor of other things. They turn to gardening. They begin to think about history or read mystery stories. They begin to think about what real value really is.

In financial matters, their eyes drift from the credit side of their personal ledgers to the debit side. They look for costs they can cut . . . and worry less about getting rich than about avoiding becoming poor.

The big bottom, when it finally comes, sneaks up on them . . . and passes unnoticed.

What should a prudent investor do? He cannot know when the market will go up or down. Should he take advantage of whatever hot opportunity comes along—like a faithless wife when her husband is out of town? Will an investor's performance be improving by chasing every big bottom that crosses his path . . . and hopping from one investment liaison to another?

It sounds like fun. But it is not likely to be rewarding.

"Come now. Think about it," urges Mark Rostenko. "Do you really believe that the majority of folks are going to identify the bottom when it shows up? How many times have you picked a stock's top or bottom successfully? How many people do you think are good at it? Do you have any idea what the statistics are for market timers? I'll give you a clue: they are aren't so good."

But if you can't find a big bottom by looking for it, how can you find it?

By not looking for it, of course.

Warren Buffett, the most successful investor who ever lived, wastes no time looking for bottoms or tops. Instead, he explains that he just wants "great companies at a fair price." But, as prices go up and down, they are not always fair. In the late 1960s, for example, Buffett found prices had gotten too high. He explained to his clients that he could find nothing worth buying—and returned their money. Coincidentally, Buffett had found the top. Stock prices peaked out soon after and didn't begin to recover until 12 years later—at which point, Buffett found many good companies at prices that were more than fair. Without looking for it, Buffett had found the bottom too, as a by-product of sticking to his tried-and-true principles.

Is that the way to find love and happiness, too—as a by-product of simply sticking to the basics, the rules, and the important principles? I don't know, dear reader, but I am naïve and sentimental enough to hope so.

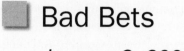 # Bad Bets

January 3, 2003

> God does not play dice.
>
> —Albert Einstein

Einstein upset the world with his Relativity Theory. All of a sudden, there were no fixed positions; everything seemed unhinged . . . loose.

"It's all relative," people said. Nothing was absolutely this or that, right or wrong, here or there.

And then Heisenberg's Indeterminacy Principle came along, and even Einstein had had enough. Not only are there no absolutes, said Heisenberg, but you couldn't know it even if there were. Everything was in motion, he pointed out; you could figure out where an object was . . . or its speed . . . but not both. And the process of trying to figure it out can't help but change the readings!

After Einstein and Heisenberg, the world had begun to look like a giant crap game. You throw the dice and hope for the best; what else can you do?

The idea of an uncertain, unknowable universe did not please Einstein; he spent the rest of his life trying to prove it was not so.

But today, we hear the rattle of dice everywhere. It is the end of one year and the beginning of another. People are regretting what they did last year . . . and warming up the dice in their right hands for another throw. What are the odds of this . . . or that . . . they wonder, as if they could know.

To give you a preview of our conclusions; we guess that this is a bad time to buy stocks.

The odds of a huge meteorite destroying lower Manhattan, we assume, are fairly low—as remote as the odds that Congress will pass a sensible law or that Jack Grubman will win a Nobel Prize for his investment research. Anything could happen, but some things are more likely than others. But, as Heisenberg warns us, as soon as we try to figure these things out, we distort the odds.

That is the strange perversity of the marketplace. As people come to believe that something will happen, the odds of it coming to pass go down. Likely as not, it has already happened. As people come to believe they can get rich by buying stocks, for example, they disturb the universe—they buy stocks and run up prices. Then, the higher stock prices go, the more people believe in them . . . and prices go still higher. At some point, because this cannot go on forever, stocks reach their peaks—at almost precisely the point when people are most sure they can get rich by buying them.

This point was reached in the United States somewhere between the fall of 1999 and March of 2000—about three years ago. Since then, the Dow has fallen 37 percent. The Wilshire Index, a broader measure, has lost 43 percent. It is has been the worst bear market since 1929, with the leading mutual funds down an average of 27 percent in 2002 alone. In terms of money lost, it has been the worst bear market ever. The total loss so far has equaled 90 percent of GDP, compared to only 60 percent of GDP for the two years following the 1929 crash.

Almost all market forecasters were wrong during this period; they overwhelmingly thought stocks would go up, not down—especially in 2002, because stocks "almost never go down three years in a row." Abby Cohen, Ed Yardeni, Louis Rukeyser, James Glassman, Jeremy Siegel—all the big names from the 1990s—still believe that stocks will go up, if not last year . . . certainly the next. They seem completely unaware that their own bullishness has tilted the odds—against them. Talking up the bull market year after year, they helped convinced Mom and Pop that stocks for the long run were an almost foolproof investment. Now, the fools are having their way—proving that nothing fails like success.

In the last quarter of the twentieth century, nothing seemed to succeed better than American capitalism. Stocks began rising in 1975 . . . and continued, more or less, until March of 2000. By then, all doubt had been removed. Americans had become believers in the stock market.

"To believe that stocks will be rotten again, . . . " wrote James Glassman early last year, "is to believe that they will buck a strong tide that has been running in the same direction for more than 60 years."

Glassman doesn't criticize our metaphors, but we can't resist criticizing his. Tides do not run in a single direction forever. They ebb and flow in equal amounts and opposite directions.

Glassman seems to believe in tides and weather, but never looks out the window. "It rains, but the sun comes out again. Stocks fall, but they always recover to a higher ground," he wrote. And then, he failed to mention, it rains again! And when the sun shines long enough, people stop noticing clouds on the horizon.

Who noticed, on those perfect days of early 2000, that odds had changed; the stock market had become very different from the stock market of 1975 . . . and that the few investors who bought shares in 1975 were very different from the many Moms and Pops who put their money into stocks in 2000? Who noticed, as Buffett put it, that these people may have bought for the right reason in 1975 . . . but they bought for the wrong ones in 2000? Warren Buffett has another helpful dictum: If you're in a card game and you can't figure out who the patsy is, you're it. Millions of patsies had entered the stock market in the last 25 years . . . lured by Buffett's example, Rukeyser's spiel, and the appeal of getting something for nothing. Hardly a single one of them carried an umbrella.

It is now three years since it began raining on Wall Street. On paper, more money has been lost than ever before. And yet, the little guys still believe. They believe the reasons why stocks are likely to rise . . . because they hardly ever go down four years in a row! On the little evidence available (since it so rarely happens) after stocks have fallen three years in a row, the odds are about 50/50 that they will fall again in the fourth year.

This year, the odds may be distorted—but not in the way investors hope. Stocks rarely go down four years in a row because—usually—after 36 months, they have almost always hit bottom. But this year is different. The patsies are so confident that they have not been willing to sell their stocks and take their losses. At the beginning of 2003, stocks were still selling at prices more typical of a top than a bottom. Based on core earnings, S&P stocks were priced at 40 times earnings. Or, as *Barron's* calculates it, based on last year's reported earnings, they sell at a P/E of 28. Either way, they are expensive.

While earnings are subject to interpretation, dividend yields are not; stocks yielded only 1.82 percent in dividends at the end of 2002.

But maybe the patsies will get lucky in 2003. Maybe the U.S. army will catch Osama bin Laden . . . and maybe stocks will go up. Maybe it is just luck, after all.

Imagine the roar of laughter when Einstein arrived in heaven and God explained, "I don't have any plan . . . I just roll the damned dice!"

God can do what he wants, of course. But made in His image, we will do the same. We don't presume to know God's plan or his method. We know that history is full of myths and lies, that the present is impossible to fully understand and that the future is unknowable.

But so what? As the existentialists tell us, we still have to get up in the morning and make decisions. Recognizing that we can't know whether stocks will go up or down in the year ahead, what do we do?

We take a guess . . . we make a wish . . . and we say a prayer.

We guess that stocks are a bad investment, for very simple reasons:

"The place to find a safe and remunerative investment is usually where others aren't looking for it," writes James Grant. Everybody is looking on Wall Street. So we will look elsewhere.

"Buy low, sell high;" the old chestnut practically pops out of the pan toward us. For the last 100 years or so, the average stock has sold for less than 15 times earnings (which used to be calculated more honestly). Almost any measure you take puts them about twice as expensive today.

"A bear market continues until it comes to its end—with real values," says long-time observer Richard Russell. Stocks are real values when they sell for 8 to 10 times earnings, not 28 to 40 times. If stocks are destined to sell for 10 times earnings some time in the future, why would we want to buy them today?

Of course, stocks could go up. And maybe they will. But it is a bad bet. Not that we know the odds any better than anyone else. What we know that many others don't is only that we don't know them. . . .

Misleading Knowledge, Part I

November 24, 2006

R eaders will recall from what we said last week at the New Orleans Investment Conference that rules are what we turn to when we don't know what to do. And most often we don't know what to do. Hence, our investment approach—like our philosophy of life—is founded on a bedrock of ignorance. Sure. Constant. Unyielding. Ignorance is something you can count on. A man is wise, and here you may quote us, only to the extent that he is aware of his own ignorance. The wiser he is, the more he sees himself as an ignorant fool. The real fool, on the other hand, thinks himself wise; he thinks he knows things he cannot possibly know. It is not given to man to know his fate, said the ancients. We can never know what the future will bring—neither in our investments nor in our private lives. Since we cannot know the future, we cannot hope to improve it . . . except in the most marginal, modest ways. "We will be better off," we say to ourselves, peeking ahead just a few seconds, "if we don't step off the curb quite yet; let us let the bus pass first." But will we be better off next year if we buy Google today? Will the world be a safer, better place in 10 years if we bomb Tehran today?

The gift of clairvoyance is not something you can give at Christmas. But what an awful gift it would be. Yes, we could read tomorrow's newspapers today. And yes, we could see what direction the gold price was going, for example, and adjust our investments accordingly. We could read about natural disasters . . . strikes . . . revolutions . . . and make sure we were somewhere else! But what a boring life it would be. There would be no pleasant surprises. And no chance to improve or achieve. You might win a Nobel Prize, but so what? It was foreordained. All of your striving, sweating, and stretching would make no difference; the whole thing was in the bag even before you began.

And imagine the tediousness of it. Day after day, going through the motions of life without the serendipity . . . the sheer chanciness . . . of it. Every action . . . every word . . . every event . . . already written out for you in bold relief. And you, just muttering your lines like a brain-damaged celebrity, not even bothering to think about what they mean; for what does it matter? The whole show would go on anyway with or without you . . . you are just playing a bit part in it.

You could look ahead, too, and foresee your last gasp. You hope for, at least, a small crowd of weeping friends and woebegone relatives . . . gathered 'round your bed . . . as you bid them farewell. Perhaps you will even get to do a grand deathbed oration: "The evil that men do lives after them," you will remember from Julius Caesar, "The good is oft interred with their bones." You will look at your children . . . grandchildren . . . your wife . . . your mistress . . . your creditors . . . your drinking buddies . . . and say: "Please remember the good that I was . . . the good that I did . . . and the affection I have had for all of you. And remember . . . I'll be waiting for you all, with open arms . . . on the other side."

At this suggestion, the grandchildren will get quizzical looks on their faces. They won't know where the other side is . . . but they have no intention of getting there any time soon . . . and the thought of grandpa's hairy arms waiting for them will not make them want to hurry.

But what's this . . . you turn to the future . . . you look ahead . . . and you see yourself crushed by the same cross-town bus you avoided today! Or done in by a jealous husband in Santa Monica. Darn, no deathbed scene! "I never get good scenes," you complain to yourself. And at that moment, you will be tempted to do a little rewriting. "Ah," you say to yourself . . . "I think I'll stay out of Santa Monica."

But could you? Even if we could know what the future will bring, we probably still could not reach ahead and improve it before it happened. There are simply too many possibilities. Change one today, and tomorrow's lines don't make any sense. Soon, the whole performance changes in ways even the fortune teller cannot foretell. Even if you could look into the future as it will be . . . you couldn't possibly look into all the futures that could be. In other words, as soon as you departed from the script, the ending would change in a way you couldn't predict. You would have lost the power of clairvoyance . . . and will pop right back into the same impromptu low comedy you're in now . . . ad-libbing from one day to next, ignorant of how thing will turn out, but hoping they sort themselves out better than you have any right to expect. You will have your appointment in Samara, no matter how far you think you are from fate.

If you look at the many mistakes and bamboozles of history, what you find is that the leading characters were misled not by ignorance, but by knowledge. What they thought was so . . . turned out to be not so. Hannibal knew the Gallic and Lombard tribes would rally against Rome. Hitler knew his master race could beat all the rest of Europe. Investors in 1929, 1966, and 2000 knew that stocks always went up in the long run.

No one has ever been let down by ignorance, on the other hand. Because ignorance forces upon a man a kind of modesty that rarely fails him. He has to retreat to the few things he really does know best . . . and follow rules that keep him from getting into too much trouble.

"I always tell the truth," Congressman Andy Jacobs once told us. "That way I don't have to remember what I said."

Likewise, a man who follows rules neither has to remember what he did . . . nor wonder about the consequences.

"Did you kill John Brown?" the prosecutor asks him. "I don't think so," says our modest hero, "It's not something I would do."

"Why not?" the lawyer follows up.

"Because I would never know how it might turn out."

If you knew that you would be better off by telling lies or killing people . . . you would go ahead and do so. If you could look into the future . . . and if you had the power to improve it before it happened . . . why wouldn't you? Imagine that it was 1920 . . . and you, for some unexplained reason, had the entire history of the twentieth century in your brain. You are traveling in Bohemia and happen to be sitting in a railway car when a young man, recently discharged from the German army, enters the car. His name, you discover, is Adolf Hitler . . . and you have a loaded gun in your pocket. Pull the trigger. Why not? Whatever happens, it is not likely to be worse than what did happen.

Alas, we have no histories of the future—ignorance is all we can count on . . . and rules are all we have to go on. We do not kill . . . we do not steal . . . and we do not lie. We follow rules because we are ignorant. Nor do we buy investments that are overpriced. They might go up, of course. But we can't know that. So, we stick to the rules.

Little Big Bubbles

December 1, 2006

On November 27th, a story appeared in the *Financial Times* telling readers that rich investors were having to resort to underhanded means and special favors in order to get into the best hedge funds.

Somewhere in the dark mush of our brains came a flicker of light . . . and the ringing of a bell. We recalled how hard it was to get in on the initial public offers of the late 1990s. All a fellow had to do was to put together a plausible dot.com story and take it to the financial wizards of Wall Street or the City. A few months later, actual shares of this hypothetical business would hit the streets. And since managers found it convenient for the shares to rise quickly following their release, they were normally priced at a level where they were bound to go up, even though they were already selling for far more than they were worth. This meant that getting in on the early stages of the IPO was almost guaranteed money-in-the-bank. And it is why Barbara Streisand, to cite a famous example, would send tickets to her shows to IPO managers, hoping for more than a round of applause.

Of course, the dot.coms blew up in January 2000 . . . and investment bankers stopped getting the free tickets. Now, they're going to hedge fund managers.

But the average fund has not been doing well; so far in 2006 you could have done better by accident than by hedge fund. The typical fund is up only about 7 percent. The FTSE has risen 9 percent and the Dow is up 15 percent. This seems only to have made investors desperate to get into the tiny group of funds that are doing well.

Well-established and top-performing funds are often closed. They already have plenty of money. And smart managers know that they cannot accept more without degrading their returns. When too much money chases a limited number of good investment ideas, investments regress to the mean. Still, "people are quite flabbergasted, especially very wealthy people, when you send their money back," said the *FT* source.

Last week, another bit of news reached us: The derivatives market, in which hedge funds tend to speculate, has reached a face value of $480 trillion . . . 30 times the size of the U.S. economy . . . and 12 times the size of the entire world economy. Trading in derivatives has become not merely a huge boom or even a large bubble—but the mother of a whole tribe of bubbles . . . dripping little big bubbles throughout the entire financial sector.

And now our friend Simon Nixon reports that the hedge fund industry is transforming the "social geography of Britain. Fortunes have been created on a scale and in a time frame that we have not witnessed for 100 years, if ever before. According to the *Daily Telegraph,* the average age of buyers of old rectories—those quaint country houses favored by the new-moneyed classes—in Britain has fallen by 10 years to people in their early 30s."

Societies go through major trends and minor ones, small fads and big ones, cute little peccadilloes and major public spectacles. Before the Renaissance, societies were besotted with religion—a passion that burned itself out in the Crusades, the wars of religion, and the Inquisition. Then, they took up politics—and became so wrapped up in *isms* that, by the twentieth century, they were killing each other at the fastest pace in history. More than 100 million people died in the twentieth century—victims of Bolshevism, national socialism, communism, nationalism, or some other excess of political enthusiasm.

And now it is finance that has the world's attention. China says it is a communist country. But it seems not to care. Nor does anyone else care what the Chinese call themselves. The only thing anyone seems to care about is that China is open for business. They could throw vestal virgins into Vesuvius or tear the beating hearts out of their enemies so long as their economy grew at 10 percent per year. The Chinese are the envy of the entire world. Politics has yielded to money.

The fashion for politics peaked out in the United States during the Kennedy Administration. Kennedy's inaugural remarks—"Ask not what your country can do for you . . . ask what you can do for your country"—marked the all-time high. That was before the war in Vietnam came a cropper, and before the war on poverty and the war on drugs were launched. People believed in those wars and were sorely disappointed when victories weren't forthcoming. Now of course, we have a war on terror . . . but few people talk about it at all . . . and no thinking person mentions it without an ironic smirk. In fact, the war on terror is hardly a political war at all—but a campaign designed to protect the flanks of the great financial empire. If it were discovered that it diminished consumer spending or raised mortgage rates, for example, it would be stopped tomorrow.

Now, it is money that counts. And mommas now want their babies to grow up to be hedge fund managers. They know where the money is. There's no money in religion—unless you're a TV evangelist . . . and those slots are hard to get. Besides, they are more business than religion, anyway. A good politician, meanwhile, even if he is slick, can only skim off a certain amount without getting caught with his pants down. The Clintons, for example, were only able to pull off a shady land deal . . . and operate a penny-ante cattle-trading account—besides the book contracts, of course. It might have been serious money, but it took a whole career of sordid dissembling to pull it off. The Bushes have done better, but it has taken them a couple of generations and a few CIA contracts. And in any case, it is nothing compared to the kind of loot a hedge fund manager takes in while he is still young enough to enjoy it.

In this late, degenerate imperial age, no one gets richer faster than hedge fund managers. Last year, Edward Lampert, of ESL Investments (a hedge fund business), set the pace with $1.02 billion in compensation. Compared to him, James Simons of Renaissance Technologies Corp. must have felt like a charity case, with only a bit more than $600 million in take-home. But he still did better than Bruce Kovner, at Caxton Associates, who earned $550 million.

The *New York Times* provides a list: Steven Cohen of SAC Capital Advisors, $450 million; David Tepper of Appaloosa Management, $420 million; George Soros of Soros Fund Management, $305 million (Soros was number one in 2003, with $750 million); Paul Tudor Jones II of Tudor Investment Corp., $300 million; Kenneth Griffin of Citadel Investment Group, $240 million; Raymond Dalio of Bridgewater Associates, $225 million; and Israel Englander of Millennium Partners, $205 million. Poor Richard Fuld; the man earned only a paltry $35,257,099 for his work running Lehman Brothers. And E. Stanley O'Neal, at Merrill Lynch got even less: a miserly $32,134,673.

We do not report those figures out of jealousy, but simply puzzlement and amusement. Every penny had to come from somewhere. And every penny had to come from clients' money. Investors in leading hedge funds must be among the richest, smartest people in the world. Still, with no gun to their heads, they turned over billions of dollars' worth of earnings to slick hedge fund promoters.

What do you need to do to get that kind of work? Well, it helps to be good with complicated math. Then, you can join other hedge fund managers who trade derivative contracts that the clients cannot understand, such as the recently launched CPDO, the Constant Proportion Debt Obligation. According to Grant's Interest Rate Observer, the CPDO may be an innovation, but it is hardly a new idea. It is remarkably similar to the CPPI, or Constant Proportion Portfolio Insurance, which made its debut 20 years earlier.

The CPDO is meant to protect investors against the risk of investment-grade credit defaults. CPPI was meant to protect investors from a stock market crash, using a complex formula that clients also couldn't quite understand. Then in 1987, only about a year after the CPPI was introduced, the stock market crashed and investors finally figured out how they worked. Sifting through the debris, analysts determined that CPPI had not protected investors; instead, its fancy programmed trading features actually magnified the losses.

We don't know how the CPDO will hold up under pressure, but we can barely wait to find out. Whenever the higher math and the greater greed come together, there are bound to be thrills.

The twitty quants at big investment firms invent the complex derivative contracts . . . give them a jolt of juice . . . and then the abominations spring to life. The next thing you know, the hedge fund whizzes are building big houses in Greenwich, Connecticut—and there are billions of dollars . . . no trillions . . . in CPDO and other contracts, in the hands of buyers who don't quite understand the elaborate equations behind the contract . . . and (here we are just guessing) who will be surprised when they find out.

If you are good with figures, you can at least partially protect your own investments. But it usually means taking a position on the opposite side of the great weight of investment capital. You can also find ways to make more money than your slower-moving peers, again, by doing things a bit differently. But neither financial wizardry . . . nor any complex instrument . . . can protect a whole market. The whole market can't protect itself from itself. The more people climb on to an investment platform—whether it is derivatives, dot.coms, dollars, or dirigibles—the more it creaks and cracks, and the more damage it does when it finally gives way.

But buyers of CME (the Chicago Mercantile Exchange) don't seem to notice. Google, the newest, hottest technology stock of late 2006, trades at a forward P/E of 36 . . . CME trades at an astounding 51. CME is where futures and derivatives trade. The stock came out three years ago at $39. Since then it's gone up 14 times, to more than $550. In New York, meanwhile, the NYSE gets half its daily volume from hedge fund trading. Its stock too, has been on a roll, now trading at 10 times sales, 119 times trailing earnings, and 46 times forward earnings.

If you want to profit from hedge funds, the best way is to become a hedge fund manager. Or, if you want really want to get into hedge funds, but wish to retain your dignity, you could consider investing in a hedge fund company. At least two hedge fund companies have sold shares to the public on the London market.

But hedge funds are supposed to be able to produce superior returns for both investors and managers. If they could do so, why would they wish to trade their shares for cash? What will they do with the money; invest it in someone else's hedge fund? But with returns falling . . . and customers beginning to ask questions . . . more hedge fund impresarios are likely to want to get out while the getting is good. As the funds become less profitable, in other words, more will probably be sold to strangers who don't know any better.

And then, someday—perhaps someday soon—a peak in the credit cycle will come. The mother of all bubbles will finally pop and then the little big bubbles in the financial industry will pop. The Dow will come down—the dollar, too. Junk bonds will sink. Builders in Greenwich will notice that their phones aren't ringing as often. NYX and CME will crash. And 5,000 hedge fund managers will be on the streets . . . looking for the next big thing. When will it happen? How? We don't know. But our guess is that when the history of this bubble cycle is finally written, derivatives will get a special tipping point place . . . like the Hindenburg in the history of the Zeppelin business . . . or the Little Bighorn in the life of George Armstrong Custer.

The Best Kind of Wealth

June 11, 2007

I s the great worldwide bubble still expanding?

We checked our usual sources this morning.

And yes . . . after a few days of uncertainty last week when the Dow fell 400 points . . . the leak was quickly repaired and the bubble continued to expand. On Friday, just before the end of the session, the Dow pumped up 157.66 points, or 1.19 percent, to 13,424.39. Gold fell to $650. The dollar rose.

It is now the sixth month of the twenty-fifth year of this historic expansion . . . and all is well.

Meanwhile, we got word, via Bloomberg, that there are still plenty of people eager to get into the party before someone calls the cops. Sales of CDOs (collateralized debt obligations) hit a record in the first quarter of this year. At $251 billion for the three months, they're running at more than $1 trillion per annum.

Bloomberg reports, "Sales of CDOs pooling asset-backed securities increased 21 percent from the previous quarter. The derivatives are typically backed mainly by subprime mortgage bonds, or securities created from loans to homeowners with poor or limited credit histories."

And yesterday, an old friend brought up another old friend,

"You remember Catherine?" he asked. "You know, she collects photographs. I mean, photographs from well-known people. Well, guess what? The market for photographs has gone crazy. Actually, all the collectibles have gone crazy. There's just so much money around, it's stirring everything up. She had a few photos that she'd paid $4,000 for, a few years ago. They're going on the auction block at Christie's this week. Guess what the guide price is? A half a million. It's really unbelievable."

See how easy it is to get rich, dear reader? Just buy something. Then, you wait a respectable interval, and then you sell it to someone. It's so easy an idiot could to it. In fact, many of the people who are doing it are idiots. They're dumb enough to believe that asset prices always go up. And they're getting rich because they don't know any better. Oh, to be an idiot.

But what kind of wealth is that you get without working or saving? "The best kind," say most people. But to us, it seems more like a case of false pretenses. It's like a man who marries a rich widow . . . and then discovers that she's as penniless as he is. Maybe it will work out; but, maybe it won't.

Here at the *Daily Reckoning* headquarters, we confess that we're too rich to steal . . . too dumb to lie . . . and too humble to profit from a credit bubble. To get rich in today's whacky markets, you have to believe whacky things. We don't mind believing whacky things, but the problem is the whacky things you need to believe today scratch uncomfortably against our sense of humility.

Today, you have to believe not only that over-priced financial assets are going up, but that you alone know which ones will go up most. And you also have to believe that you know better than Mr. Market. Because, when you buy at the market price, you're wagering that Mr. Market has made a mistake and missed something. And then, you have to believe that when he gets around to noticing what he's missed, the asset you just bought will have gone up in price.

The staggering arrogance of it is too much for us. We don't buy things because we think Mr. Market has bungled. We only buy things we think are of real value. But right now, where can you find a real value? In the stock market? In the property market?

How about Paraguay? Maybe. That's where the Bush clan has bought a ranch. We think perhaps they were looking ahead to the time when they'd have to flee an angry American mob. They've probably made a deal with the Paraguayan government, letting them skulk down there after people get wise to what they are up to here. Or, maybe they were just looking at values. According to *International Living*'s reports [at Internationalliving.com]—there is no place where you can get more for your money than in Paraguay.

Who wants to live in Paraguay, you ask? We don't know, but we'll check it out. You see, we just learned that we're being exiled from France, so we too will soon need a place to hide out. We'll give you a report when we get down there.

But let us return to the world's first worldwide bubble. We notice one other thing—in addition to gold—that did not bounce up on Friday. That was the 10-year U.S. Treasury note. It's going down. Which means, the price of credit is going up—despite the glorious gush of cash and credit from central banks, CDO investors, and others. Now, if the cost of debt goes up enough, of course, the credit bubble will blow up.

According to classical economic theory, an expanding credit bubble takes more and more credit to expand and keep output increasing. That is what we have seen for the last few years—higher debt and GDP. Economists now warn that the housing slump may have a longer-lasting effect on GDP growth than previously thought and that (according to the most recent reading) actual GDP growth has fallen below the rate of population growth. As a credit bubble goes on, it becomes less effective at producing wealth . . . and more effective at producing what was most lacking in the first place—humility.

If this trend continues, Americans will eventually be sneaking across the Rio Grande to look for work.

Maybe the Mexicans will build that wall before we do.

Our *New* Trade of the Decade!
January 4, 2010—Bethesda, Maryland

Well, that was it for 2009. Whew!

Another great year for gold. But it wasn't a bad year for stocks either. The Nasdaq rose 45 percent. The Dow went up about 20 percent.

As we guessed back at the beginning of the year, stocks bounced. What we didn't guess was that they would bounce so much for so long. All over the world, stocks went up . . . and continued to go up. A bounce is inevitable, following a stock market drop. And it's impossible to say how big a bounce it will be . . . or how long it will go on.

But a kiss is still a kiss . . . and a bounce is still a bounce. No kiss lasts forever. Neither does a bounce. Looking ahead, we have to anticipate that it will come to an end . . . probably in 2010.

If you've profited from the 2009 runup in stocks . . . bravo! Now, sell them. . . . Yes, the bounce could continue. But it's not worth the risk.

And how 'bout the gold market! Gold has risen every year of the decade. It was the surest, safest place for your money—by far.

Does that mean gold will go up in 2009? Does that mean we will stick with our Trade of the Decade for another 10 years? Not to brag, but our trade was a big success. Even we were surprised by how well it did.

As long-suffering *Daily Reckoning* readers will recall, we announced our Trade of the Decade in 2000: Sell stocks; buy gold.

"It turned out to be a good plan," observes colleague Merryn Sommerset in a recent *Financial Times* story. "In 2000, you could buy an ounce of gold for $280 (the average price over the year). Now, it will cost you about $1,100. At the time, Bonner saw what most others did not. He saw the United States not as an economy carefully and cleverly managed by then–Federal Reserve chairman Alan Greenspan and his passion for low interest rates, but as a massive credit bubble waiting to burst.

"He also saw the massive and growing national debt, the trade and budget deficits, and fast growth in the money supply as factors that would naturally debase the dollar over the long term. He also saw the credit bubble as global rather than peculiar to America. So it made sense to him to hold the only non-paper currency there is—gold."

So what's next? What's the trade of the coming decade? Well, your editor has decided not to double-down on the identical trade. Gold will remain in our core holdings, but not in our Trade of the Decade for the next 10 years. Why? Because we think the U.S. economy is going the way of Japan.

Japan went into a slump in 1990. It has come out . . . and gone back in . . . and come out again . . . and gone back in again. In terms of the amount of wealth destroyed—at least, on paper—it was the worst disaster in human history. The value of real estate went down 87 percent in some cities. Stocks fell from a high of 39,000 on the Nikkei down to the 7,000 range in 2009 . . . their lowest point in 27 years.

Why such a bad performance? As we keep saying, if you really want to make a mess of things you need taxpayer support. The Japanese put more taxpayer money into the effort to prevent the correction than any nation theretofore ever had. The result: the correction was stalled, delayed, and stretched out over more than two decades.

And now, U.S. economists are looking at Japan . . . not with alarm, but with admiration. They are beginning to believe that the Japanese model is the way to go . . . because it prevented widespread unemployment and a deeper slump.

Here's our best guess:

Now that the U.S. economy is caught in the same sort of de-leveraging process that gripped Japan, the same sort of remedies will inevitably be employed . . . leading to the same results, more or less.

We'll skip the details for this morning. You'll hear plenty of them in the days, weeks, and months ahead—promise!

Instead, this morning, we'll turn to our Trade of the Decade for the next 10 years. There are, of course, two sides to this trade . . . the long side and the short side. We had no trouble finding things to put on the short side. In a de-leveraging period, almost everything goes down. We could have stuck with U.S. stocks, for example. They'll probably continue to come down . . . just as they did in Japan.

But who knows? U.S. stocks just had their worst decade since the 1930s. What are the odds that they'll have another bad decade? We don't know. But what we look for in our Trade of the Decade, for the sell side, is something that has just had its best decade ever . . . something that has been going up for so long people think it will go up forever . . . something that everyone wants.

What does that describe? Well, the thing that comes closest is U.S. Treasury debt. Yields have been going down (meaning, the price of debt is going up) since 1983. And now, despite a supply that seems to be going off the charts, demand for Treasury bonds, notes, and bills has never been stronger. What's more . . . if our analysis of the U.S. economy is correct . . . the supply of Treasury debt is going to continue to rocket upward for many years. Deficits of $1 trillion to $2 trillion per year are going to become commonplace.

How long will it be before the market in Treasury debt crashes? How long will it be before hyperinflation . . . or a debt default . . . sends investors running for cover? We don't know . . . but it seems a likely bet that it will happen sometime in the next 10 years.

So, on our sell side . . . we'll put U.S. Treasury debt.

How about the buy side? Ah . . . that is something we've struggled with. While there are many things that seem likely to go down, there aren't many that seem destined to go up. Let's see, what has been beaten down, dissed, battered, and abused for the last 20 years or more? What is it that people don't want? What is it that they expect to go down . . . possibly forever?

Of course . . . Japanese stocks!

So there is our Trade of the Decade: Sell U.S. Treasury debt and buy Japanese stocks.

Crazy, right?

Maybe not. Treasury debt has been going up for the last 27 years. Japanese stocks have been going down for the last 20 years.

Does this mean we're giving up on gold? Not at all. We're sticking with gold. Aurum aeternus, or something like that. The yellow metal is what you buy when you think the financial authorities are making a mess of things. We have little doubt about it. So we'll continue to buy and hold gold . . . until the financial system blows up.

But gold at $1,100 an ounce is fully priced. It is not cheap. It's been going up for the last 10 years! At this level, it is insurance against a monetary catastrophe and a speculation on when and how the blow-up will finally come. It is definitely worth having. And holding. And using to protect your wealth.

But the Trade of the Decade is a way of making money . . . by buying and selling two opposing assets that are at extraordinary valuations. It is not a speculation on what *might* happen. It is merely a bet on the phenomenon known as "regression to the mean." Things that are out of whack tend to go back into whack. . . .

If we're right, over the next 10 years, the most popular investment of 2009—Treasury debt—will go out of fashion. The least popular investment of 2009, on the other hand—Japanese stocks—will surprise everyone by finally showing signs of life.

In any event, the trade is fairly low risk. What are the odds that U.S. Treasury debt will go up? What are the odds that Japanese stocks will go down? Of course, we don't know . . . things that are out of whack can get further out of whack. But we count on time to sort it out. And hope we live long enough to be able to say, "We told you so."

The Great Correction . . . Still Pending

April 6, 2010—Baltimore, Maryland

For more than a year, the recovery bounce in the stock market has refused to give up. The indexes have recovered more than 50 percent of what was lost. Technically, they look pretty good. What's more, the S&P sells at more than 21 times normalized earnings, according to Robert Shiller's latest tally. It seems like nothing can stop stocks now.

Then there's the Treasury market. Overall, yields remain remarkably low. It is almost as if Treasury buyers are unaware that they are being asked to finance the biggest increase in sovereign debt ever. It doesn't seem to matter either that many of the applicants for money will be incapable of repaying it. Several sovereign debtors, including the United States, have already reached the point of no return, according to professors Rogoff and Reinhard.

Still, the financial press is optimistic. Economists are irrationally confident. Investors and advisors are overwhelmingly bullish. And the American public seems willing to add a trillion-dollar health care program to its burdens—a sign of remarkable faith in the nation's prospects.

So, let's go back and re-examine our basic position. Is this really the Great Correction that we think it is?

If there is one lesson we've learned over the years, it is that we need to be patient. Things that have to happen generally do, sooner or later. You just have to wait. And when they happen, they generally happen much faster than you expected. Even when you've been expecting something for years, it can come and go before you realize what is going on.

You get used to being wrong . . . or at least premature. You wait. You watch. You think the time has come . . . and then: whoops . . . not yet.

Pretty soon, you are overcome by anticipation fatigue. Then when the real thing finally does start to happen you don't believe it. You wait to be sure . . . you hesitate . . . and then it's over!

Just what am I waiting for? I'm anticipating more evidence of this Great Correction, including another big swing down in the real price of stocks, bonds, and commodities . . . further deterioration in the real estate market . . . a falloff in consumer spending . . . and a higher savings rate.

I'm also expecting higher yields from government debt . . . and a dangerous intensification of financial problems in both the private and public sectors. If I'm right, those things must happen eventually. So far, we're still waiting.

But this week the long-awaited turnaround in the bond market may have begun. Rates are rising along the entire yield curve, especially at the long end. "The bond market is now very close to saying, 'We've had enough,'" predicts the octogenarian stock market technician, Richard Russell. The 30-year T-Bond's recent decisive move above 4.80 percent marks the end of a 25-year bull market in bonds, says Russell. Rates will be moving higher from here.

Investors are starting to tune in to how sovereign debt works. And they're starting to realize that even governments can default. In fact, almost all of them do default eventually. Yes, even governments whose debts are denominated in their own currencies default. And even when they have the power to print the currency themselves.

How could that be? Well, it is very simple and worth spending a little time on. I want to make two points:

First, governments will usually choose to default on their debt rather than risk hyperinflation of their currencies. Second, when they reach a point of no return they have no choice. They cannot cut back spending. Because even the most drastic cutbacks will not do the job. That would simply result in lower tax receipts and an even bigger deficit. At a certain point, the multiplier effect becomes the divider effect.

I've made the point many times that democracy seems hell-bent on self-destruction. America's founding fathers noticed many years ago that when people realized that they could vote themselves money from the public treasury, democracy would be doomed.

Most people presume that if a politician offers benefits, someone else will pay for it somehow, someday. In practice, the money doesn't come from additional taxes. Taxes are already, at least theoretically, at their optimal level. Higher tax rates produce lower economic activity, which lowers tax receipts. So instead of raising taxes, governments borrow the money. Then sovereign debt loads become larger and larger until, as Greece has recently discovered, they are impossible to carry.

America also has public sector debt problems—of about equal measure to Europe—and she has huge private sector debt problems as well. For the moment, the skies over the American financial markets are clear. But out at sea a hurricane is spinning faster and faster. Another huge wave of debt defaults and foreclosures in the private sector will hit the markets soon. This wave, combined with record borrowing from the U.S. government, is bound to push up bond yields . . . making it harder than ever to get needed funding.

The situation with the U.S. government is more complicated than it is with private borrowers—or even with Greece or California. The federal government can print money. But it, too, is ultimately at the mercy of the bond market. Last year Uncle Sam borrowed $2.1 trillion. This year it will borrow $2.4 trillion. Without this money, U.S. government spending would have to come to a halt. The United States counts on lenders. It needs lenders. Without them, it would be forced to make cuts equal to about 10 percent of GDP. Think you've got de-leveraging now? Just imagine what that would do.

Typically, of course, government bond buyers don't cut off a lender altogether. They merely demand a higher rate of interest to offset what they see as an increased level of risk. The higher interest rate adds to the borrower's cost—increasing his deficit and forcing him to borrow more.

This is where it gets interesting. You might say that a government can print its way out—it can just print the money it needs rather than borrowing it. But what would happen if the United States chose to print $2 trillion this year? It would risk hyperinflation. Lenders would run for cover. Prices would shoot up. The damage to the economy would be severe . . . so severe that only governments under extreme pressure—think Weimar Germany or Mugabe's Zimbabwe—are willing to risk it. Instead, they try to muddle through, as Greece is doing now—promising budget cuts, making special financing deals and pushing up the rate of inflation a bit, but not so high as to cause panic in the bond market.

See, as long as the bond market permits it, debt levels continue to grow. But at some point—the point of no return—a government can no longer save itself from disaster. How does that work? Well, when deficit and debt levels are too high, the cuts necessary to bring the budget back in balance are so great that they squeeze the economy hard, reducing output and decreasing government's tax revenues.

In this case, the government cannot escape. It has to print money. Or default. Most often, it will choose default, because it is the less painful solution. Either way, the government finds that it will be cut off from the bond market. Hyperinflation is merely an additional and unnecessary aggravation. (That said, I agree with Nassim Taleb that hyperinflation remains an underestimated black swan risk.)

The underlying story of the economy has not changed. We are in a Great Correction. We don't know exactly what it is correcting . . . but it looks as though it will at least reduce some of the leverage that has been added to American and British households over the last 60 years.

So far, the process is tentative . . . and unsure of itself. From a peak of 96 percent of household income in 2007, debt has fallen to . . . 94 percent! The drop is so small that it makes you wonder if it is a trend at all. But if it is, it has a long way to go. Ten years ago—at the peak of the dot.com bubble—household leverage was only 70 percent of income. At the present rate it will take another 24 years to get back to 1999 levels.

Albert Edwards of Société Général has examined the non-financial leverage in the system. There is excess leverage of about 60 percent of GDP, he says. He calculates it will take a decade of "Japan-like pain" to eliminate it.

Either way, you're talking about a long process of getting back to normal.

The Great Correction is also what is keeping housing and unemployment down. When the banks aren't adding to the nation's credit, you just can't expect many new jobs or many new house sales.

Nothing has changed in the last week—except we have moved one week closer to whatever crisis lies ahead.

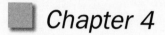 *Chapter 4*

War and Waste

All Quiet on the Western Front
November 11, 1999

> Like a wet, furry ball they plucked me up. . . .
>
> —Rupert Brooke

In August 1914, millions of young men began putting on uniforms. These wet, furry balls were plucked from towns all over Europe, put on trains, and sent toward the fighting. Back home, mothers, fathers, and bar owners unrolled maps so they could follow the progress of the men and boys they loved and trace, with their fingers, the glory and gravity of war.

I found one of those maps . . . with the front lines as they were in 1916 still indicated . . . rolled up in the attic of our house in France. I looked at it and wondered what people must have thought . . . and how horrified they must have been at what happened.

It was a war unlike any other the world had seen. Aging generals looked to the lessons of the American War between the States or the Franco-Prussian war of 1870 for clues as to how the war might proceed. But there were no precedents for what was to happen. It was a new era in warfare.

People were already familiar with the promise of the machine age. They had seen it coming, developing, building for a long time. They had even changed the language they used to reflect this new understanding of how things worked. In his book, *Devil Take the Hindmost,* Edward Chancellor recalls how the railway investment mania had caused people to talk about "getting up steam" or "heading down the track" or "being on the right track." All of these new metaphors would have been mysteriously nonsensical prior to the Industrial Age. The new technology had changed the way people thought and the way they spoke.

World War I showed the world that the new paradigm had a deadly power beyond what anyone expected.

At the outbreak of the war, German forces followed Alfred von Schlieffen's plan. They wheeled from the north and drove the French Army before them. Soon the French were retreating down the Marne Valley near Paris. And it looked as though the Germans would soon be victorious.

The German generals believed the French were broken. Encouraged, General von Kluck departed from the plan; instead of taking Paris, he decided to chase the French army, retreating adjacent to the city, in hopes of destroying it completely. But there was something odd; there were relatively few prisoners. An army that is breaking up usually throws off lots of prisoners.

As it turned out, the French army had not been beaten. It was retreating in good order. And when Galieni, the old French general, saw what was happening—German troops moving down the Marne only a few miles from Paris . . . he uttered the famous remark, "Gentlemen, they offer us their flank."

Galieni attacked. The Germans were beaten back and the war became a trench-war nightmare of machine guns, mustard gas, barbed wire, and artillery. Every day, *The Times* (of London) printed a list of casualties. When the generals in London issued their orders for an advance . . . the list grew. During the battle of the Somme, for example, there were pages and pages of names.

By the time the United States entered the war, the poet Rupert Brooke was already dead, and the life expectancy for a soldier on the front lines was just 21 days.

One by one, the people back at home got the news . . . the telegrams . . . the letters. The church bells rang. The black cloth came out. And, one by one, the maps were rolled up. Fingers forgot the maps and clutched nervously at crosses and cigarettes. There was no glory left, just tears.

In the small villages of France hardly a family was spared. The names on the monument in the center of town—to *Nos Heroes . . . Mort Pour La France*—record almost every family name we know: Bremeau, Brule, Lardeau, Moreau, Moliere, Demazeau, Thollet . . . the list goes on and on. There was a bull market in death that did not end until November 11, 1918 . . . at 11 A.M.

For years after . . . at 11 A.M., the bells tolled, and even in America, people stood silently . . . recalling the terrible toll of four years of war. Now it is almost forgotten.

We have a new paradigm now. And a new war. The new technology has already changed the language we use . . . and is changing, like the railroads, the world we live in. We think differently . . . using the metaphor of free-wheeling, fast-moving, networked technology to understand how the world works.

We are fascinated by the new technology . . . We believe it will help us win wars with few casualties, as well as create vast new wealth . . . and a quality of life never before possible.

And yet, we are still wet, furry balls, too.

I will observe a moment of silence at 11 A.M.

In Praise of Group Thinking

September 25, 2000

> Those who, standing their ground and closing ranks together endure the onset at close quarters and fight in the front, they lose fewer men. They also protect the army behind them. Once they flinch, the spirit of the whole army falls apart. And no man could count over and tell all the number of evils, all that can come to a man, once he gives way to disgrace.
>
> —Tyrtaios, *The Western Way of War*

The Greeks fought often. In two out of three summers the property owners, called hoplites, would be called out to do battle.

These were not professional soldiers—but farmers, artisans, philosophers, and traders. Nor were they just young men of draft age. Men were expected to fight until they were 60 years old. Of course, with so much warfare, many did not survive to retirement age.

The fighting was not high tech. In today's battles, soldiers may never even see the enemy. Bombs are dropped, missiles launched, cannons fired—at targets well over the horizon. And whole wars are fought for reasons that are even more remote.

But the Greeks formed up their phalanxes and marched straight at the enemy. Spears were used to jab. They were scarcely ever thrown. The idea was to press against the enemy . . . strike him down . . . march over him . . . and break up his formation.

In this, as in so many things, the Greeks were extremely successful.

"If crowd-thinking is so bad," you might want to ask me, "how come people do it?" Here is the answer.

The progress of man has been made by extending the division of labor. Instead of doing everything for myself—I can now go to the store and buy my bread, clothes, fuel, and everything else I need to live—and make my own very small, very specialized contribution to the commonweal of humankind in these daily letters.

As the division of labor extends, more and more people do more and more specialized tasks.

I know what you're thinking—not another essay on the division of labor! But please hang on . . . I am just warming up what could be an interesting point.

The division of labor requires trust and cooperation. I have no way of forcing the baker to bake bread or the roughneck to bring oil up out of the ground. Still, I can be reasonably confident that the bread will be better and cheaper than if I made it myself . . . and that the diesel fuel I put in my car's tank will be serviceable.

Progress, then, is a function of greater cooperation.

But force has played a big role in human affairs too. When material welfare, and even survival, depended on controlling good hunting ground . . . or good farming ground . . . a group of people could benefit enormously from using force. If they could expel or exterminate a rival tribe—they might flourish.

The Greek city-states were tribal. Each tribe—had its regional differences. They made war on each other . . . and came together to fight the Persians and others.

Throughout the ancient world, the Greeks were feared. They had no special technological or numerical edge. Their big advantage was the one thing I have been ranting against: group-thinking.

When the call to arms was sent out, the hoplites, young and old, notable and common, friends and relatives, grabbed their armor and formed up. They stood shoulder to shoulder, row upon row. Their polished helmets gleamed in the sun. The front row of soldiers held their spears straight ahead. The back rows held them straight up.

There was no skirmishing. No surprise. No tactics, other than the steady closing with the enemy until, toe to toe, they battled it out. The key to victory was solidarity.

Their enemies feared them. Because they knew they would not give way. The Spartans, especially, had a reputation for being willing to die where they stood rather than run.

"It was a sight at once awesome and terrifying," Plutarch described the slow, dreadful advance "as the Spartans marched in step to the pipe, leaving no gap in their line of battle and with no confusion in their hearts, but calmly and cheerfully advancing into danger."

Greek generals were usually on the front lines. When an army was beaten, its generals were almost without exception killed in the fighting.

Alcibiades, telling the story of Socrates' combat, comments: "Indeed, in war the enemy will not dare to press home their attack against men such as this; instead, they go after the ones who are fleeing away in complete disorder."

From the generals to the newest recruit, all the soldiers suffered the same fate. If they fought together and stuck together, their enemies might break and run. But if any one of them failed to do his duty . . . the whole formation was likely to disintegrate. Then . . . Tyrtaios:

> For once a man reverses and runs in the terror of battle, he
> offers his back, a tempting mark to spear from behind, and it is
> a shameful sight when a dead man lies in the dust there, driven
> through from behind by the stroke of an enemy spear.

Group cohesion was paramount. The whole phalanx had to think and act as one. Defecting was dangerous and shameful.

The Dark Years

September 12, 2001

. . . [B]ehind the doors of this ambitious day stand shadows with enormous grudges, outside its chartered ocean of perception misshapen coastguards drunk with foreboding, and whispering websters, creeping through this world, discredit so much literature and praise.

Summer was worse than we expected;

Now an Autumn cold comes on the water . . .

—W. H. Auden, *The Dark Years*

We will reckon again today . . . as we always do. But today we reckon with a heavy heart. For greed has been replaced by fear, and the comedy of the financial market has been replaced by the tragedy of politics.

Most of the people in our office raced home after work yesterday. The whole world watched television. But I felt like walking.

So, I made my way down to the Pont des Arts and crossed over to the Left Bank. On the bridge, couples stood together and stared at the river . . . the gray spires and apartment buildings silhouetted against the last evening light. They held hands, too . . . laughed and embraced, as the world grew dark.

I had come to see them, of course . . . to catch a glimpse of the world as it was yesterday . . . the bright lights and gaiety of the cafes, the somber elegance of the Louvre, the ordinary comings and goings of ordinary people in the world's most beautiful city. I wanted to remember it that way—just in case it would never be that way again.

Surely another bridge has been crossed, I thought, as I strolled along the Rue Jacob, looking in the antique shop windows. Things have changed. America—almost untouched by war for 136 years—is suddenly under attack.

We have been waiting for a defining event to conclude the twentieth century, as the assassination of the Archduke Ferdinand marked the end of the nineteenth. What tipping point event would close the book on the long period of peace and prosperity that America has so recently enjoyed, we wondered.

Nature was preparing some surprises. Something big was coming, we guessed. But not even in our gloomiest moments did we imagine such a bizarre and bloody trigger event. But now we have it.

"The New War!" screams the headline in today's *Figaro*. *"Terror Strikes America,"* proclaims a banner on the *International Herald Tribune*. All over the world, on live TV coverage, anyone can see—America is vulnerable.

The dollar plummeted yesterday. Markets all over the world collapsed, with the London exchange down 5.7 percent . . . Frankfurt off 8.6 percent . . . and Paris down 7.4 percent. The price of gold soared 5 percent . . . and then fell back in this morning's Asian trading. Crude oil also rose—$6.

In a radio broadcast earlier in the day a French commentator tried to put the catastrophe in perspective:

"It is simply unimaginable," he said, "it is as if the National Assembly had come under attack and the Eiffel Tower and the Tour Montparnasse had been completely obliterated."

The National Assembly building was closed. But armed guards were on alert. Clutching machine guns, they paced up and down the streets and studied me carefully as I walked along.

Then, at the base of the Eiffel Tower, everything seemed normal. It still stood. Tourists, though fewer in number than usual, milled around. Arab hucksters sold their trinkets. Life goes on.

In the next few days, weeks, and months . . . you will be told that everything is okay. Indeed, many will think it is better than okay. The Fed has already promised that it will provide more money. OPEC has pledged to provide more oil. The government will launch new anti-terrorist initiatives. Some will say that war is good for the economy. Defense stocks will rise.

Who knows, maybe markets will rally. But two years after the Archduke Ferdinand was shot, stocks in America reached their lowest level in history—trading for just four times earnings.

Nature still has her surprises. But it is likely that consumers and investors will hold their breath . . . and feel a cold new wind blowing. They will be less confident, less sure of themselves and of the future. They will tend to hold on to their money a little longer and worry about their debts a little more. This alone, as Dr. Richebacher reminds us, means the end of America's greatest boom.

The bells of St. Mary's are tolling this morning. They ring for the living and the dead, including the many thousands of brokers, analysts, clerks, firemen, policemen, and others—people who were in the very wrong place at a very wrong moment.

They also toll for another reason—heralds of something else we will all have to reckon with:

A strange darkness has settled over the world . . . a new era, finally, has come.

Tsar of Arabie

October 29, 2001

King Fahd rarely speaks. He is 82 years old and suffered a severe stroke in late 1995 that has left him incapacitated ever since.

Many presidents, kings, and emperors have lacked capacity, of course. Many have been mentally impaired, delusional, unreasonable, or merely profoundly stupid. The world would not be a worse place if they spoke less often . . . but Fahd's condition is the sort that would normally disqualify even a Republican from elective office.

"The King," reports an article by Seymour Hersh in the *New Yorker*, "with round-the-clock medical treatment, is able to sit in a chair and open his eyes, but is usually unable to recognize even his oldest friends."

Fahd is being kept alive and on the throne so that Prince Abdullah does not get the job. There is a delicate balance in Saudi Arabia . . . between oil revenue and Muslim fundamentalism. And Abdullah, 75, is a man with fundamentalist tendencies who doesn't mind throwing his weight around. The royal family is hoping that Fahd can continue breathing until Abdullah is out of the way.

We turn our eyes toward the desert this morning, dear reader. We recall that it was World War I that brought down the Hohenzollerns, the Hapsburgs, and the Romanoffs—the three great royal families of Europe. We have a hunch that the war on terrorism will bring down the house of Saud.

The fall of the European dynasties left an empty space—an opening for terrorists in Russia and Germany. The Bolsheviks quickly moved into the void left by the Tsar in Russia. And Hitler's Nazis soon squatted the vacant lodgings left by the Kaiser in Germany. Both succeeded by being more ruthless and single-minded than their opponents . . . murdering and bullying the social democrats out of the way.

If something similar were to happen in Saudi Arabia, no matter what befalls him personally, Osama bin Laden's trap will have served its purpose.

Even small, inept groups of terrorists can have huge, long-lasting effects on the world. Thirty years before the Bolsheviks, Russian terrorists killed Tsar Alexander II, in 1881. Alexander II was a reformer. It was he who had freed the serfs. Yet, the terrorists who tossed the bomb "got what they wanted," writes Gary North, "the ruthless oppression of Alexander III. He stamped out terrorist groups with a vengeance. Six years later, there was an attempt on his life. The government hanged the six conspirators. One of them was Lenin's older brother. This led to the overthrow of Czarist Russia thirty years later. The tactic worked. It just took time."

"Saudi Arabia," writes Christopher Byron in an MSNBC article, "teeters at the edge of economic and political chaos, imperiling the economic and geopolitical interests of not just the U.S., but of the entire world."

"Saudi Arabia, which is roughly one-fifth the size of the U.S., sits atop 25 percent of all known oil reserves on Earth," Byron explains. "It is currently pumping roughly 9.2 million barrels of crude per day, which account for about 10 percent of all oil consumed on the planet every day.

"It isn't an overstatement to say that the economic fate of the world revolves around the reliable and unimpeded flow of oil from the fields of Saudi Arabia. Indeed, that has been the case for more than 40 years."

If Saudi oil were suddenly taken off the world market, the world price of oil would soar—probably to $100 a barrel or more. The entire world economy—already barely growing—would be struck with a long, deep recession.

And it wouldn't be difficult for terrorists to shut off Saudi oil. Gary North cites a confidential study showing just how remarkably vulnerable the Saudi oilfields are. Yet, instead of going after an easy target close to home . . . the terrorists of September 11 chose a harder one far away. Why? Probably because some of the oil revenue ends up in the terrorists' hands.

There are about 6,000 Saudi princes, scattered all over the world, who have a keen interest in making sure the oil revenues continue to flow. Over the years, they've become as expert as the U.S. Corps of Engineers at diverting little streams of income in their directions. Thus do their corrupt viaducts of cash transport billions and billions of dollars worth of oil revenue flow out of the Saudi sands to various fancy apartments in Los Angeles, Mayfair, Manhattan, and the Avenue Foch . . . as well as to caves in Afghanistan . . .

Abdullah could be the Alexander II of Saudi Arabia, threatening reform. But things may have already gone too far for reform. Revolution is in the air.

Living standards in the kingdom are going down. Per capital GDP peaked out at $28,600 in 1981. Today, the figure is less than $7,000.

Much of the reason for this remarkable decline is a huge increase in population. Most of the country is barren, but its people are among the most fertile on earth. "Nearly half the country's population is younger than 15," reports Christopher Byron. "Public health services are poor, with the result that the nation's infant mortality rate of 51 deaths per 1,000 live births is not much better than Iraq's—60 per 1,000—and close to five times that of Kuwait."

According to a *New York Times* report, Byron continues, "all public high schools in Saudi Arabia teach mandatory classes in anti-Christian, anti-Western religious fundamentalism, with nearly 30 percent of all class time devoted to such instruction."

"It is compulsory for the Muslims to be loyal to each other," the *Times*'s piece quotes a textbook, "and consider the infidels their enemy."

"Not surprisingly," Byron concludes, "the country has become a breeding ground for terrorists. An estimated 50,000 boys leave high school every year only to find it impossible to land jobs. They become easy recruits for Osama bin Laden's Saudi-dominated al-Qaida network."

Sooner, rather than later, the Tsar of Arabie will sink into the sand. Then, many of these idealists may make their way back to the Saudi sands from whence they came and find themselves in control of much of the world's oil. Plus, they would come into possession of what Byron calls "a huge arsenal of some of the most advanced military weaponry in the world . . ."

"In the years since Desert Storm," Byron explains, "Washington and its NATO allies have armed Saudi Arabia with a staggering array of ultra-advanced weaponry," including hundreds of fighter planes and helicopters . . . and thousands of tanks, missiles, and other hardware.

But that is a story for another day. . . .

Pearl Harbor

December 7, 2001

We play with fire. We play with war. And then, fire and war blow up on us. America, until now, enjoyed the luxury of watching things from a distance. It offered its advice, lavishly . . . its homilies . . . its encouragement to the little people of the world. Now, America is in the bath along with the rest of the world. Now we will see. We will see if America is really the military, industrial, and social power that it claims to be. We're going to see if America really exists. Because it is no longer a matter of preaching, while taking orders and grabbing market share. It's no longer a matter of exhorting others to acts of heroism. Now, America must fight. And send Americans to risk their skins. Things have changed. We're going to see . . .

> —Marcel Deat, writing in the collaborationist
> French newspaper *L'Oeuvre,* December 9, 1941

Mr. Deat sounded skeptical.

My father wondered, too. The morning of December 7th, 60 years ago today, was a rude awakening for him. After a late Saturday night on the town . . . his head must have throbbed early Sunday morning. It was as if there were bombs going off, he must have thought . . . then, his eyes must have opened with a start; bombs really were exploding!

"All I remember is confusion," he once told me. "We didn't know what was going on. All I knew we knew was that we were under attack. We thought the Japs were going to land troops, so we got our rifles and got ready to fight back. Thank God, they didn't try to take Pearl Harbor. We were so disorganized, it was pathetic."

Disorganized, unprepared . . . America put aside its confusion and was soon fighting back. By dumb luck, perhaps, none of America's three Pearl-based aircraft carriers were in the harbor that morning. The Japanese hoped to put the U.S. Pacific fleet out of service for 18 months. But within just 60 days, U.S. forces were back in action. My father and thousands of other Americans had the pleasure of an extended tour of the South Pacific, courtesy of the U.S. Army. Maybe they were not the battle-hardened fighters of the Third Reich—with strong military traditions, iron discipline, and years of painful experience. But when the chips were down in 1941, they did their duty . . . sometimes well, sometimes not so well . . .

When Pearl Harbor was bombed, Americans knew the "luxury of watching things from a distance" would no longer be possible. Unlike the patriots of 2001, they prepared for sacrifice, not self-indulgence. They braced themselves for hardships and losses. Rather than buy a new Packard, they were likely to put the old one in the garage and walk to work. Gasoline was rationed. So was almost everything else. Stocks fell to a level never seen before—and changed hands for just six times earnings. Things had changed; America was "in the bath" with everyone else.

Men do stupid things regularly and mad things occasionally. And sometimes, the impulse to self-destruction is so overwhelming it overtakes an entire nation.

It is almost always madness to buy stocks at the peak of a bull market . . . or to buy a stock at 50 times earnings. (Note: currently, tech stocks in the United States are selling at an average P/E of 50 based on next year's earnings!) Ruin may not come quickly—as stocks may rise further. But it comes eventually.

The best a person can hope for when he goes mad is that he runs into a brick wall quickly . . . before he has a chance to build up speed. That is why success, in war and investing, is often a greater menace than failure.

My father did not realize it at the time, but he was witness to one of the stupidest, maddest acts in all of history. The Japanese had embarked on a campaign of conquest. Rampaging through China and Indochina, they found success easy. Encouraged, they sought to extend Japanese hegemony, by force of arms, throughout Southeast Asia.

"What was the point of the military expansion?" you may ask.

"To secure vital resources—oil, rubber, metals," comes the answer.

"Why did Japan need so many raw materials?"

"To supply its military expansion!"

The Japanese have little in the way of raw materials. They could buy them on the open market. But in the politicized world of the twentieth century, markets seemed unreliable. What if producers decided not to sell?

The idea was absurd. Why would producers not sell when it was in their interest to do so? In fact, the only reason they did not sell was to try to cripple Japanese military expansion! Thus did the Roosevelt Administration, in early 1941, cut off vital supplies—especially oil—to the Japanese war machine.

What were the Japanese to do? For nearly 10 years, they had been on a roll of military success. Were they not entitled to believe that their stock would always rise?

"The grandiose mood of the fascist powers in which no conquest seemed impossible, must be taken into account," writes Barbara Tuchman in her *March of Folly*. "Japan had mobilized a military will of terrible force which was in fact to accomplish extraordinary triumphs. . . ."

But attacking Pearl Harbor was a big risk. The Japanese knew what they were up against—a country far larger and with far more resources than their own. Admiral Yamamoto had attended Harvard and spent years in Washington as a naval attaché. Even so, he was no fool . . . he knew that Japan could not endure a long contest with the United States. "I have utterly no confidence for the second or the year," he told Premier Konoye.

Why did they do it? Why did they take "a gamble that, in the long run . . ." Tuchman asks, "was almost sure to be lost?"

"Fundamentally, the reason Japan took the risk," Tuchman answers her own question, "was that she had either to go forward or content herself with the status quo, which no one was willing or could politically afford to suggest. Over a generation, pressure from the aggressive army in China and from its partisans at home had fused Japan to the goal of an impossible empire from which she could not now retreat. She had become a prisoner of her oversize ambitions."

How much better off the Japanese would have been if they had been beaten in China! They could have gone back to their island, renounced the Tripartite Treaty with Germany and Italy . . . and they could have "taken the orders and grabbed market share"—selling tanks, planes, and ships to other combatants. Instead, a long string of battlefield successes led to one of the biggest strategic plunders of all time . . . and ultimately to complete ruin for Japan and her economy.

Before the attack on Pearl Harbor, Americans were deeply divided on the war. Most wanted nothing to do with it. A one-year draft law passed

Congress by a single vote just months before the attack. Japan could have conquered any Dutch, British, or French colonial territory in the Far East . . . without risking war with America. Of all the things Japan might have done, it chose the worst possible course of action. It did the one thing—and probably the only thing—that would bring America into the war as an active, determined combatant.

Admiral Yamamoto recognized his error almost immediately. "I feel that we have awakened a sleeping giant and instilled in him a terrible resolve," he said. Churchill was ecstatic: "To have the United States at our side was to me the greatest joy. Now at this very moment I knew the United States was in the war, up to the neck and in to the death. So we had won after all! Hitler's fate was sealed. Mussolini's fate was sealed. As for the Japanese, they would be ground to powder."

Three days later—on December 11th—Germans proved that they were at least as mad as the Japanese: Hitler declared war on America. He could have left the Japanese to their folly. Instead, in less than a week, the Tripartite Powers had managed to turn the war against themselves, by provoking the wrath of the world's largest economy. America, protected by two oceans, could turn out jeeps, tanks, planes, and C-rations faster than anyone. It could put millions of troops in the field, fully equipped, and bring to bear more bombs against a target than any nation ever.

But in 1941, Axis military power had been in a bull market for nearly a decade. People don't think clearly in a bull market. And their imaginations are dull. They can only see ahead of them what they've just experienced. It wasn't until the battles of Midway and Stalingrad, both in 1942, that Axis power peaked out. Then, the thinking began and imaginations began to work again. But by then it was too late.

"When we realized what had happened," said my father many years after the fact, "all I remember thinking . . . was that it would be a long time before I got home . . . if I got home at all."

He did get home, of course, three years later . . .

Too Big to Succeed

March 21, 2002—Paris, France

We are the indispensable nation. We stand tall. We see further into the future.

—Madeline Albright

A remarkable thought appeared on the editorial page of a recent *International Herald Tribune*. Your editor has lost the paper somewhere along the way, but he recalls the idea . . . the way he remembers a particularly bad meal.

Is there a risk that foreigners will stop financing the U.S. current account deficit, the writer wondered. Will they stop wanting to buy U.S. stocks and bonds? The rest of the world held $8.2 trillion worth of U.S. assets at the end of 2001 . . . up from $2.6 trillion in 1994. If foreigners decided to lighten up . . . just a little . . . the results would be devastating. The dollar, the stock market, the U.S. economy—all would enter a long, dark night . . . and who knows when the sun would shine again?

But not to worry, concluded the editorialist. The foreigners can't sell U.S. assets. The entire world economy depends on Americans' ability to continue spending money they don't have. For it is Americans who buy the world's production. America is the world's biggest consumer. If it ever stops spending . . . the whole world goes into recession. In short, the American economy has become too big to fail.

The sentiment is widespread in the United States: The nation has become so big, so powerful, so technologically, militarily, and economically advanced—nothing can stop it now. We Americans have a right to be proud. But pride is a challenge to the gods. We don't know whether it will be the god of the markets . . . or the god of war. But, to summarize today's letter—one of them is bound to take a swat at us before too long.

As we explained earlier this week, none of the world's armed forces can stand in the way of the U.S. military machine. It rolls wherever it wants . . . unstoppable, almost unchallenged. It has such an edge over its enemies that more casualties have been suffered at Olympic games than by U.S. soldiers in the War Against Terror (WAT).

The logic of continuing the WAT is simple enough that even a president can understand it.

1. Certain groups of terrorists want to destroy the United States.
2. They'd use nuclear weapons if they could.
3. They haven't used them yet . . . so they must not have them.
4. They must be stopped before they get them.
5. Where might they get them . . . Iraq.

This line of reasoning is so compelling that it seems to have brought even normally sensible people, such as columnist Fred Reed, to the edge of absurdity:

"We should perhaps remember that large wars happen," writes Reed. "Few wanted World War II or would have in 1932 thought it possible. Pearl Harbor, the 9/11 attacks, a nuclear bomb on American soil—all, before they happen, sound like the ravings of dementia. The world would be better off if these particular things didn't happen. . . . How can a convulsion be prevented?

"Answer: By taking any measures necessary—any measures at all—to prevent Iraq from building nuclear weapons. If it were not for the nuclear potential, one might argue about the President's policy toward Iraq. Or one might not. But Saddam Hussein cannot be permitted any possibility of having nuclear weapons. It's that simple. Whether we like it or not, we need to say 'no,' and we need to mean it. The potential consequences of not doing so leave no choice."

Our beat here at the *Daily Reckoning* is markets, not politics. But no matter what wandering path we take, we see the same telltale droppings— spoor from that strange animal, man.

Unlike other beasts, we are told, man is capable of rational thought. But whether you look at his behavior in markets or politics, you see the same thing: Rational thought yields to hysteria and wishful thinking as readily as a fat widow to a handsome gigolo.

The charm of man's intelligence is that it is so flexible; he can think himself into any position he wants to take. He is as ready to believe that stocks will rise—even though they are already two or three times higher than their long term mean—as he is that he needs to go to war. If he is not directly attacked by an enemy, he merely has to stretch his mind a little to find an abstraction . . . a jingo . . . that makes war sound, not only reasonable, but irresistible. Does the nation need more living room? Must it not help make the world safe for democracy? What about the threat of the domino effect? Napoleon, after securing all of Europe from Gibraltar to the Vistula, talked himself into attacking Russia—because it represented a threat to his Continental System by which he hoped to deny European markets to the British!

Wherever you look, logic follows desire like an inaugural ball after a rigged election.

And thank goodness for popular democracy! In the privacy of the voting booth, people fashion chains for themselves . . . and willingly drag around heavier balls of iron than a dictator or an emperor could ever put upon them. George III managed to squeeze out a tax rate of only about 3 percent from the American colonists. Since then, Americans have voted to raise the rate to more than ten times that amount . . . not to mention death taxes, capital gains taxes, excise taxes, sales taxes, property taxes, and so on.

The American colonists also complained, in Mencken's words, about "making poor people board and lodge a lot of soldiers they ain't got no use for and don't want to see loafing around." Now, the people of the American republic support an army that costs more than the next nine largest national defense budgets combined—about a third of the entire world's defense budget.

And the descendants of the people who had no use for soldiers eventually queued up—can you believe it—to risk their lives in some woebegone war far from home! What emperor or dictator could get that kind of cooperation?

Every war ever fought—like every bubble market ever—seemed like a good idea at the time. Measured in audacity as well as stupidity, Japan's attack on Pearl Harbor was the equal of Napoleon's march on Moscow. But, it seemed perfectly logical to the Japanese. They were trapped. They had far-flung interests throughout East Asia, but needed access to raw materials to supply its factories. The U.S. 7th fleet was all that stood in the way. Ergo . . .

Not that we know anything about foreign policy. It is a matter better left to others, we believe—such as mental defectives. Nor do we know whether the world will be a better or worse place following the WAT or an invasion of Iraq. That is not for us to know.

But both stock market and foreign policy float on tides of fortune. Beneath them run deeper currents of popular confidence. Readers are reminded: The currents sometimes shift. It is not man's power of reason that fails, but his power of imagination. He cannot imagine what will go wrong—until it does.

Your correspondent . . . stretching his imagination.

Imperial Over-Stretch Marks

March 5, 2004

T he Dollar Standard System—and perhaps American pre-eminence—
is on the way out. But you can't say we didn't tell you so. This *DR*
Classique was originally aired on October 14, 2002.

■ ■ ■

America remains the unrivaled leader of the world—the big
power . . . without which nothing good happens.
—Thomas L. Friedman, hallucinating

America is the "single surviving model of human progress," said George
Bush the younger, to the West Point graduating class, perhaps exaggerat-
ing just a little. He might have conceded, if he'd thought about it, that
there are elements to the American model that might not yet have attained
perfection.

The American model of human progress, it turns out, depends heavily
on the kindness (or naïveté) of strangers: America prints money; foreigners
make products. The foreigners send their products to the United States;
Americans send their dollars abroad.

Alert readers will notice the defect immediately . . . for what would
happen if foreigners changed their minds? Then who will pay so that
Americans can continue living beyond their means? And who will finance
the U.S. budget deficit, expected to rise about $400 billion thanks to
increased military spending? [Editor's note: This year, the budget deficit is
projected to reach $521bn. . . .]

The system survives as long as foreigners are willing to accept U.S. paper assets for more tangible ones. We don't know how long that will be, but we note that the value of paper tends to vary inversely with the amount of it available. No Fed chief provided so much American paper as Alan Greenspan. In fact, as reported here on several occasions (we keep mentioning it because we can barely believe it), Greenspan has increased the world's supply of dollars more than all the Fed chairmen and all the Treasury secretaries in U.S. history.

Still, the foreigners schlep and sweat and gratefully take surplus dollars in payment—about $1.5 billion per day. Typically, when a nation's trade deficit rises to 5 percent of GDP, something has to give. What usually gives is the nation's currency; it goes down, making imports more expensive and exports more attractive. So far, this has not happened, we are told, because the dollar is no ordinary currency—but an imperial currency, the leading brand of the world's only remaining super, superpower. How that protects it from the age-old cycles of over-stretch and regret, we don't know. More likely, the dollar will eventually do what all over-stretched currencies do, imperial or otherwise: It will snap.

"I see one possible way out," writes Stephen Roach, "a sharp depreciation of the U.S. dollar . . . a significant depreciation of the dollar—at least 15 percent to 20 percent on trade-weighted basis, in my view, would go a long way in cracking the mold of U.S.-centric global growth . . ."

"Oh no, I guess this means Mr. Bush will begin his war soon," said a neighbor this weekend. She was a woman of about 70, in a hunting get-up, with knee socks and a big brown sweater. Her low voice, mannish hair, and bright red face was slightly comical. But she was also carrying a 44-caliber pistol and waving it around the room. "But, heck, what's life without wars," she roared. "Every so often, maybe we need a war. I just hope the price of gas doesn't go up."

What set off my neighbor was the news that Congress has given the go-ahead, not by declaring war as required by the Constitution, but by passing the buck to the president; Bush is free to attack America's enemy du jour—Iraq. How Iraq achieved this honor is anybody's guess. But enemies come and go . . . along with models of human progress.

In the 1940s, Germany and Japan were our enemies and the Soviet Union was our friend. Then, the roles reversed for the 1950s and 1960s. And then, in the 1970s, Iraq was our friend and Iran was an enemy. And, of course, Cuba, North Vietnam, and North Korea . . . were our enemies at various times.

But who knows? Maybe a change of government will do as much good for Iraq in 2002 as it did for England in 1066. Today, we write not to criticize the president's war plans . . . nor Congress's pusillanimous dereliction—it may all work out for the better, for all we know. Instead, we merely wallow in the absurdity of it all.

The durability of Christianity, we thought to ourselves during this Sunday's sermon, comes not just from the enormous promise that it makes, but also from its adaptability. Christians believe that if they can just get God on their side, everything will work out. Even dying is nothing to worry about. "Even unto the grave, Hallelujah" we chant, with faith that death leads to a better life without mortgages or election campaigns. And in the meantime, people are free to do almost any lunatic thing they want.

Jean Mayol de Lupe was an army chaplain in the French army in World War II. He was wounded, held prisoner by the Germans and eventually decorated with the same award later given to Alan Greenspan—the Legion of Honor. Greenspan, a cynic might say, got his "cravate" for proving that you could inflate the currency and get away with it. . . . Mayol de Lupe proved that you don't have to be an analyst or a politician to be a fool.

The 1930s were a great time to be a fool. There was a bull market in foolishness such as the world had never seen. It seemed as though nearly half the world was keeping company with socialism, communism, or fascism. Mayol de Lupe was convinced that Bolshevism was a great threat to Catholicism . . . and that the only thing that might save it was Hitler's national socialism. After France had surrendered, he organized a voluntary corps of French soldiers to go to help the Germans in their war against the Soviet Union. Already 66 years old, he nevertheless went to the Eastern front himself along with his troops. The priest wore a SS Waffen uniform, ended his sermons with "in the name of our Holy Father Pius 12th and our Führer Adolf Hitler," and described the French volunteers' work . . . "what a beautiful mystery, a wonderful tale, that our boys write with the points of their bayonettes."

In Mayol de Lupe's eyes, the Soviet Union was the Iraq of the hour . . . and Nazi Germany the world's superpower. Many in Europe—including many in France and England—felt that the dynamic new Germany represented the force of the future, that it was "the only surviving model of human progress."

And so the poor old coot stretched on the Nazi uniform and went to war.

P.S. After the war, Jean Mayol de Lupe was arrested and jailed for notorious collaboration.

The Stain of Democracy
February 4, 2005—Paris, France

The Bush Administration sees the citizens of Iraq as lost souls, who just need something to believe in . . . so they bestowed on them democracy—even if they don't understand what it is they are voting for.

"If only I had been there with my army . . . I would have taught those Jews a lesson." Clovis, King of the Franks, recently converted to Christianity . . . referring to the crucifixion of Christ . . . and perhaps missing the point.

Our beat here at the *Daily Reckoning* is money. But there was never a dollar made outside the great comedy of human life. For every seller, there is a buyer . . . and for every one of them there is a vast web of sticky connections to everything else under heaven.

So we wander through the byways of the public spectacle as if working our way around the bar in a strip club . . . hoping to see things from a new and revealing angle.

What catches our eye today is the reports from the world's newest and most celebrated democracy—Iraq. We have never been to Iraq and have no particular desire to go. We have heard that it is hard to get a good drink and few places to dance, like many places in Texas or Arkansas. But if you were to listen to columnists such as Thomas L. Friedman and David Brooks, both given space in the *International Herald Tribune,* you might believe that the world is a much better place today than it was last week. Progress has been made; the Iraqis have voted, they say. Hallelujah.

Maybe it is true. But when you move away from the real, discrete, visible, understandable things of private life . . . it's hard to know. As things grow in size and complexity . . . ignorance and delusion increase by the square of the distance and the cube of the scale. A man may run a small machine shop and have a good idea of what it is worth. But put the company on the Big Board, and you will soon have shareholders 4,000 miles away without a clue. And as the company grows into a huge conglomerate, soon not even the CEO will know what it is worth. He'll watch the share price along with everyone else.

Likewise, there must be a million frauds and misapprehensions separating the Christianity of the Nazarene from the Catholic Church of the medieval and renaissance eras. And between the democracy of ancient Greece or a New England town meeting and the democracy of modern America or Iraq lay a million scams and false impressions. In both cases, what is lost in substance is replaced with rituals of solemn deceit.

A family might very well take a vote on where to go on vacation. A nation might vote on which flag it will fly over the capitol. In either case, people will get what they want . . . peacefully, tolerably. Civilization will be undisturbed.

But in Iraq, another form of evangelical democracy has been thrust upon the local bipeds. On Sunday, they stood in line to vote for people they didn't know, who would do things they knew not what, and—eventually—put in place a government that, if it holds together, that they probably will not particularly like. What the majority most wants in Iraq, according to press reports, is for the United States to leave. The locals, the Bush Administration has made clear, will not make that decision, no matter how many ballots they cast. And if the government elected by the Iraqis turns out to be disagreeable, as far as we can tell, the Bush Administration reserves the right to make another regime change.

Voting is supposed to confer legitimacy on the tyranny of the majority. But as democracy moves from the town meeting to the national election, it gathers frauds to it like con men to insurance claims. So remote is actual power and decision making that the voter no longer has any grasp of it. After a while, not even the majority gets what it wants. In America, for example, what majority wanted a government $55 trillion in the hole?

Like any public spectacle, democracy is full of the usual humbug. And Iraq's new democracy seems to have more than usual. It was a scam, said an editorialist in the *International Herald Tribune* who seemed to know what he was talking about. One of the largest tribes—the Sunni — boycotted it altogether. And those people who did vote—according to press reports—often didn't know what they were voting for. They thought they were electing a president (even though no one campaigned for president and most of the candidates on the ballot were completely unknown to voters.)

But so what? America has a faith-based currency. Now it has a faith-based foreign policy as well. We are in the modern age—the twenty-first century. Everything has changed. Politics have replaced religion. Baghdad has replaced Bethlehem. Humbug is all you can depend on.

When the Romans took Ctesphion, near modern Baghdad, the venture seemed a great success. Thousands of prisoners were taken who were sold into slavery. The proceeds went back to Rome.

When the Christians took Jerusalem, again, the captives were sold into slavery. That, combined with stealing everything that could be carried off, seemed to make the venture—if not profitable, at least plausible.

America has found no similar way to profit from its Eastern campaign. A few defense contractors, and a handful of Texas oilmen, have made money on the deal. But for the United States as a whole, the project has been a colossal financial drain . . . with a price tag of about $4,000 per American family so far.

But it would be a mean-spirited Ebenezer who would count the cost of such an uplifting campaign. This is a Holy Crusade, after all. Fourteen hundred U.S. dead . . . thousands more Iraqis . . . $200 billion . . . is any price too high for the benefits of the ballot box? Our defenders of the faith—George II and Tony I—have launched a crusade of sanctimonious idolatry worthy of the Borgia popes. The Sodoms of anti-democratic infidelity along the Tigris and Euphrates have been attacked . . . and largely destroyed. Insurgents are regarded as a cross between cannibals and the devil himself. They are "evil," says Brooks in the *New York Times,* no less. Had he lived in an earlier era he might accuse them of sorcery.

Like any crusade, the war in Iraq has its rituals, its saints, its sacraments, its relics, its holy writs, and its holy martyrs.

Last Sunday, Iraqis stood in line to take the sacrament. Instead of marking their foreheads with ashes, as Christians will do next Wednesday, they dipped their fingers in blue ink—as proof that they had come to the holy place and been sanctified. Whatever sins they had committed in that benighted era before the U.S. invasion were cast out. Now they were democrats, solemnly marking their sacred ballots with the sign of the cross.

Thus, the Mesopotamian tribes have been delivered from evil . . . at least for now.

Elections are hardly new to the Middle East. There was one in Palestine in 1996. In 2000, Egyptians went to the polls. Iranians voted in 2001 and Pakistanis voted in 2002. As it was convenient, the American government recognized the victors . . . or ignored them. Of course, not too many years ago, it also supported its key men in the region—Saddam Hussein and Osama bin Laden, neither of whose names appeared on the ballot on Sunday.

The nice thing about elections is that they represent a sort of imperfect progress. Political regimes are voted in and voted out. They are not necessarily any better than those chosen by other means—but at least the regime change is achieved without violence. That is the progress of politics of the last three centuries: Force is replaced by fraud.

But in bringing democracy to Iraq at the point of a gun, the Bush Administration seems to have missed the point. Voting is merely the form of a civilized society, not the substance of it. Democracy may be a good thing—but only to the extent it actually complements the charms of civilized life. It sits on a civilized society like a hat on a pretty girl. It may not be very elegant, but it is generally tolerable. But force the hat on the head of an Islamic fundamentalist . . . and the whole exercise seems pointless, costly, and ridiculous.

But the big day seems to have turned out better than expected. A few people died horrible deaths—but even they were martyrs to the cause of democracy.

"Salim Yacoubi bent over to kiss the purple ink stain on his twin brother's right index finger, gone cold with death," reports the *International Herald Tribune*.

"You can see the finger with which he voted," a friend volunteered, as he cast his tearful gaze on the corpse, sprawled across a body washer's concrete slab. "He's a martyr now."

"The stain marked the day the man . . . exercised his right to a free vote, and the day he paid for that hard-won privilege, with his life."

A neighbor reflected on what Election Day had meant for Iraq, "We were waiting impatiently for this day so we could finally rid ourselves of all our troubles."

We assume he exaggerated; even the Holy Eucharist promises less.

And now, the orthodoxy of modern democratic faith has been delivered to the Iraqis. The heathens have been converted. They may now save their souls any time they want—simply by dipping their fingers in blue ink and voting.

The holy sacraments have been given.

Saecula saeculorum.

The Good War

January 30, 2009—London, England

The *Washington Post* reports that the War on Terror is over. No armistice has been announced. No treaty has been signed. The whole thing is just being dropped quietly, like a burnt-out cigarette. Too bad. It was our favorite war.

In the few words that follow, we explain why. First, the background:

"The history of the world is but the biography of great men," was Thomas Carlyle's contribution to the genre. But here at the *Daily Reckoning* we are more of the "cometh the hour, cometh the man" school of history. When something needs doing . . . there is always found some clown dim enough to do it. Osama bin Laden was that man.

"Bleeding America to the point of bankruptcy," was what he was up to, he said in a videotape. He even did the math. "Every dollar spent by al-Qaida in attacking the U[nited] S[tates] has cost Washington $1m (£545,000) in economic fallout and military spending," said the report.

"We, alongside the mujahideen, bled Russia for 10 years, [in Afghanistan] until it went bankrupt. . . . So we are continuing this policy in bleeding America to the point of bankruptcy."

How many generations will still tell of bin Laden's triumph? He brought down not just one empire, but two. His band of terrorists leeched the Soviets so thoroughly, they fainted. It was no coincidence that the Soviets lost Afghanistan in the same year their empire disintegrated. Then, he delivered a challenge to the American's *amour propre*.

The attack on the World Trade Center incited a death wish. The feds flashed a red alert; Americans cowered in their houses and sealed their windows and doors against biological attack. The 9/11 attackers could have been pursued by the usual gendarmes—at negligible cost. Instead, in the general panic, the Bush administration decided to go all out. Thus it was that the greatest stimulus package since World War II began—in haste and in delusion.

The federal budget went from its biggest surpluses to its biggest deficits. Interest rates were cut too—to an emergency rate of 1 percent. Within 24 months, the bubble in the Nasdaq was replaced by much bigger bubbles—in housing, finance, derivative debt, art, private equity, executive compensation, student loans, and other forms of private debt. In effect, bin Laden suckered the fattest man on earth into having another éclair. The thunder coming from the financial markets for the past 18 months is the noise of his midriff exploding.

But we are not writing to complain about Osama bin Laden or the Bush Administration's reaction. When it comes to war and adultery, make-believe may be better than the real thing. Certainly, it is safer. In the War on Terror, the enemy had no tanks . . . no aircraft . . . no ships . . . no armies . . . no celebrated strategists . . . no famous generals . . . no sophisticated weapons . . . no military culture . . . no leather trenchcoats . . . no burnished helmets . . . no battle cries. . . . The problem was, it was hard to find the enemy at all. The Department of Homeland Security conducted 3 billion airport inspections looking for them. We remember getting patted down so thoroughly we felt we should leave a tip. But how many enemy combatants do you think they nabbed? Not a one.

There are two possibilities. The first is that the security procedures were so fearsome that terrorists dared not try anything funny. The second is that there weren't really many terrorists at large—at least, not in the United States of America.

But compare it to World War I or World War II . . . or even a penny ante affair like the Spanish-American war. The War on Terror mobilized the whole nation in a great national cause . . . at much expense, much damage to the Constitution, and much inconvenience, but without actually causing much real suffering. Sure, a few hapless Muslims, caught in the wrong place at the wrong time, were put on the rack. And yes, the cops in London gunned down a Brazilian electrician. Back in the United States, young couples did not embrace as they had in World War II—that is, as if there would be no tomorrow. Instead, they spent money as if there would be no tomorrow! No doubt, the desperate spending contributed to the bankruptcy of the whole system of bubble finance. But compared to the pain of a shooting war, the War on Terror was a delight. As far as we know, the Department of Homeland Security suffered not a single casualty.

Not even any self-inflicted wounds. No executions for treason. And hardly any reported cases, neither of fleeing in the face of the enemy . . . nor collaborating . . . nor sabotage.

What a shame to let such a marvelous war end without even a victory parade. Some of the agents should at least get medals for courage under fire . . . or exceptional valor.

Perhaps some special award [for those] such as the special agents who arrested Tamera Jo Freeman. A "Black Heart" medal might be appropriate. The woman was on a flight to Denver when her children got into a squabble. She spanked them both . . . and then Homeland Security agents put the cuffs on her. Charged with committing an "act of terrorism" she spent three months in jail and lost custody of her children.

And there ought to be some medal for the Pentagon flatfoot who put the long arm of American law all the way across the Atlantic and onto the shoulder of Gary McKinnon. Mr. McKinnon, as the mayor of London informed us on Tuesday, believes in UFOs. And to prove that the U.S. army is hiding information on extraterrestrials, he hacked into the Pentagon's computer . . . leaving his e-mail address and a message: "Your security is crap."

Rather than thank him for this useful observation, the Defense Department no doubt put out a billion dollar consulting contract for someone to tell them their security is crap . . . and put out a warrant for Mr. McKinnon's arrest on a terrorism charge. That kind of service above and beyond the call of duty should be recognized.

So form up the battalions of veterans! Assemble the legions of luggage inspectors and metal detector operators . . . and all the thousands of investigators, worn down by five years of following leads to nowhere! Dress them up in bright, clean uniforms . . . and give them their moment of glory. Pin medals on their chests. Then have a jolly march down Fifth Avenue. Line the streets. Give them a hearty hoorah as they march by. Throw out the ticker tape. Young girls . . . fling yourselves at them . . . and get a kiss! And then, send them home.

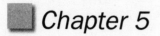 *Chapter 5*

Borrowing against the American Dream

Honor Insolvency

October 1, 2001

> Men, it has been well said, think in herds; it will be seen that they go mad
> in herds, while they only recover their senses slowly, and one by one.
>
> —Charles Mackay

"The struggle against terrorism," said French Prime Minister Lionel Jospin last week, "is not just the business of judges, the police, and the secret service. There is also a response that heads of business, investors, and consumers can give!"

I took the liberty of adding an exclamation point. Such a statement needed a little flourish at the end, I thought . . . as when a man claims to have invented a perpetual motion machine or been visited by spacemen in his backyard. The preposterous needs emphasis.

"Lionel Jospin invited the French to show their 'economic patriotism' by continuing to consume in order to avoid a recession," says the Associated Press report. "The head of government invited business leaders and consumers to 'resist intimidation' and to 'support economic activity'."

"Let's show, all together, our economic patriotism," Jospin urged.

I am not making this up. It would be impossible. I couldn't imagine that anyone outside of an asylum could say something so absurd. But there it is.

The French prime minister also gave assurances that economic fundamentals "remain favorable" and that "Neither the United States nor Europe is in recession; there is no collapse of production."

Jospin did not cite his sources. All available evidence suggests that the U.S. economy is presently shrinking, that is, in recession. And factory production has been going down for the last 11 months—one of the greatest collapses in history. But ignorance has never been a barrier to public office.

Despite the fact that no economic difficulty exists, according to Jospin, the government is nevertheless taking measures to deal with it. On one side of the Atlantic as on the other, politicians have the same idea—to find ways to keep the consumer spending.

It may come as a relief to many *Daily Reckoning* readers, but Americans are not the only ones made mad by the terrorists' attack. A kind of Esperanto madness—a common language of absurdities—seems to be spreading across borders and seeping into casual conversations between grown-ups. Everywhere, patriotism, nationalism, jingoism, militarism, religion, culture, and finance seem to have gotten jumbled up.

But I do not write to criticize. The day is long past when I attempt to tell the world how it should conduct itself. Instead, I write to honor those caught up in the madness.

Daily Reckoning readers may recall those dark and shameful events of the 1960s . . . when soldiers were sent off to Vietnam to risk their lives in a war they couldn't win . . . and then spat upon and reviled when they returned home. The prospects for today's economic patriots seem no better: For they are surely on a fool's errand. But, even so, they deserve recognition.

All over the world consumers and investors are being mobilized to fight the campaign against terrorism. They take up their credit cards and portfolios and aim at an enemy they can neither see nor understand.

It's madness, of course. Economies are not really helped by investors who make bad investments, nor by consumers who buy things they can't afford.

But madness needs to run its course.

So, there ought to be some form of recognition for the casualties. Soldiers—even those sent off on the most preposterous campaigns . . . such as the French attacks in the opening days of World War I, or the British Charge of the Light Brigade in the Crimea . . . were still able to come home (if they survived) and live in dignity. On appropriate occasions, they got to wear their campaign medals, to the delight and pride of all around them.

Surely, some medals should be prepared for people who blow themselves up in the name of "economic patriotism," too. Let me make a few suggestions:

For a man who distinguishes himself by running up huge credit card debt, for example, I suggest awarding a small pin, made of plastic . . . depicting a Visa card surrounded by a cluster of dollar signs.

And what of a man who loses his house in a bankruptcy proceeding? Maybe a pin shaped like a house would be appropriate. It should be made of an inferior grade of plywood—with the number 11 on it . . . or 7, for those who choose the liquidation route.

Shopping recklessly ought to be worth some kind of medal . . . something like a Distinguished Consumer Award. Anyone who increases his personal consumption through a recession should get at least a ribbon . . . maybe in dollar-bill green with red ink slashes.

And an investor who remains steadfastly bullish in a bear market also deserves recognition for his self-sacrifice. A small pin—of base metal— would be enough.

But a real hero, an investor who mortgages his house, his business, and his wife's engagement ring, in order to continue going long in the face of huge reversals, collapsing prices, and spreading panic—that person deserves something special. For he may lose everything for the Homeland, as it is now called: his house, his business, his money, and, most likely, his wife.

I suggest an Order of Economic Merit award—a medallion depicting a man in a barrel might be appropriate, with a flag in one hand and a credit card in the other. The medallion should be suspended from a red, white, and blue ribbon and worn around the neck on all state occasions . . . Armistice Day, VE Day, Veterans Day, and so forth. It should also be required at weddings and serve as a cautionary emblem for those just starting out in life.

What's more, this top honor should be bestowed, personally, by the Secretary of the Treasury, Paul O'Neill, with, perhaps, a kiss on each cheek . . . to give it the right preposterous flourish.

Playing the Game

December 27, 2001

E dward, Henry, and their friend from across the road, Nathaniel, were spread out on the floor playing "America," a board game I mentioned yesterday. The Monopoly-like game, festooned with the American flag and billing itself as "a game about our great nation," has recently become very popular in our family.

"What's the idea," I asked Edward. "How do you win?"

"The one who makes the most money is the winner!" Edward replied.

Money, money, money. That is, of course, the subject of the *Daily Reckoning*. Day after day, the game goes on. Once your family has food, clothing, and shelter, money is merely a diversion, an entertainment—like a board game or a newspaper's editorial page. For what difference does it really make if your wife carries a bag from Louis Vuitton or one from Kmart? Do they not render the same service?

Getting and spending may not make the world go 'round, but it gives it a good spin. And who are we to question it? Wanting more money is as natural as homemade hooch.

But sometimes people drink so deeply from the cup of financial ambition they nearly go blind and forget that it is just a game. During the great bubble of 1996–2000, for example, investors could not see that the stocks they were buying were worth only a fraction of the prices they paid. Nor could they make out the true dimensions of the debt they took on. Big debts looked small and loopy; spending seemed almost reasonable. "Last year," reminisces an article in the *Wall Street Journal*, "the well-groomed bankers—inspiration for Bret Easton Ellis' novel *American Psycho*—fed the city's economy with their fat bonuses. They easily dropped $200,000 at Gucci on a Saturday shopping spree and test-drove new BMWs with serious buying intent. It was the norm for a 28-year-old top associate at a bank like Goldman Sachs or Salomon Brothers to earn a $90,000 salary, topped off with a $210,000 bonus."

At the height of the bubble economy, dear reader, people played the money game as though it really mattered. Money seemed to mean everything to people . . . even though they spent it as though it were nothing. It has been three years since the mania reached its zenith. Times have changed. All across the economy, people are rubbing their eyes and straining to see what the future holds. And almost everywhere, they see earnings melting away like snow in Miami. Stocks are down with the broadest measure, the Wilshire 5000, off 27 percent from its high. Wall Street bonuses are expected to average about 30 percent lower than last year. "This year," continues the *WSJ* article, "the same associate will probably earn a total of $210,000, said banking sources. With bonuses slashed across the board, Wall Streeters have to—gasp—spend conservatively, especially in case the market doesn't rebound swiftly."

"Scrooge puts lid on pay raises in 2002," says a headline from Southern California. First year associates at law firms are getting only half the bonus they got last year, reports the *New York Times*. Bonuses are extremely important, explains the *NYT,* because young lawyers measure their success almost completely in terms of money and jump from one firm to another in search of the highest salary. The law firms have to play the game, too, or they will lose their talented associates. And between the two coasts, the story is much the same. Even assembly line workers in Elkhart, Indiana, are getting slimmed-down bonuses and less overtime if they still have jobs at all. Never before in U.S. history have so many people depended so much on the performance of U.S. companies. Over the last 10 years, a sizable portion of the workforce has moved toward incentive-based compensation plans. If the company does well, so do its employees. While profits and share prices were rising, the shipping clerks and marketing managers, as well as the CEOs, could anticipate an increase in earnings, often in the form of a big bonus at year end. But this year, as perhaps never before, the bonuses are smaller. Most people will regret the decline in revenue.

But here at the *Daily Reckoning,* as usual, we take a contrary view. "Money isn't everything," they say. "Everything isn't money," we add, pointing out that the financial gains most people thought they made in the late 1990s are turning out to be an illusion.

But what does it matter? The genius of America is not that it celebrates material success alone, but that it lets people worship whatever fool thing they want. Through the refracted bubble light of rapidly rising equity prices in the late 1990s, Americans could see only money. Falling incomes, we think, will help improve their vision. In the first decade of the new century, we predict, they will take money less seriously and spend it more carefully.

Your correspondent . . . just playing the game like everybody else.

Even More Unexplanatory

June 7, 2002—Paris, France

Excessive debt accumulation was, of course . . . a prime ingredient in
the financial condition that was to overtake a large sector of the economic system: illiquidity. It was, indeed, an illiquid, over-expanded
colossus of debts, rather than an excessive money supply, on which the
price structure of the late 1920s rested.

—Melchior Palyi, *The Twilight of Gold*

In death, all debts are paid.

—William Shakespeare

The world's most powerful group of price fixers is meeting this week in
Montreal. None were elected. But the public seems to prefer to leave
the world economy in the hands of unelected bureaucrats, rather than
elected ones; its admiration for democracy goes only so far.

Central bankers have a lot to talk about, we are sure—comparing perks
and publicists, for example. Still, between cocktails and dinner, the managers of the world's managed moneys might let the conversation wander . . .
over to the curious U.S. recession and even curiouser recovery.

"This downturn pattern has no precedent in the whole postwar
period," writes Dr. Kurt Richebacher. "Investment spending is unusually weak and consumer spending unusually strong. Yet this pattern has at
least one ominous parallel, but before World War II: the U.S. economy of
1926–1929."

Neither angelic economists, nor the archangels at the world's central
banks have an explanation. In today's letter, we rush in.

"Debts gotta be paid," we remember writing yesterday.

"Or otherwise settled . . ." we add today.

"Last year," explains Dr. Richebacher, "U.S. national income grew by $178.6 billion. Debts, on the other hand, increased more than $2 trillion. Debts of the non-financial sector were up $1.1 trillion, and debts of the financial sector by $916 billion. All in all, debts rose more than 10 times faster than income. Broad money, by the way, increased $882.7 billion. Consider that barely 9 percent of the total credit creation in 2001 turned into GDP and income growth.

"In the fourth quarter of last year," (Richebacher never lets up . . .), "the consumer increased this outstanding debt by $610 billion, but his spending on goods and services increased by only $120.6 billion. Businesses borrowed $377.65 billion while cutting their outlays on fixed investment and inventories by $163.3 billion."

Telecom debt alone now equals nearly as much as the combined total of the S&L crisis of the 1980s and the junk bond crisis of the 1990s—about 5 percent of GDP. Taxpayers ended up paying an amount equal to 3 percent of GDP to bail out the S&Ls.

We left off yesterday wondering why stocks are not going up. If the nation really were looking ahead to a recovery, shouldn't stocks be able to see it coming?

Instead, stocks seem to see trouble.

"I view the U.S. economy as being in the early stages of a post-bubble shakeout," writes Stephen Roach. "Most others see the context quite differently—as a fairly standard business cycle, dominated by a powerful, yet self-correcting, inventory dynamic. Only time will tell who's got this one right."

While we will wait for time to tell the tale, along with everyone else, we still can't help but wonder: What will become of all this debt?

There are only three possibilities. Sooner or later, debts are either paid off, written off, or inflated away. Taking up the third possibility, we note that the Founding Fathers defined a dollar as 371.25 grains of fine silver. Determining the value of gold coins, the Coinage Act of 1792 decided that an ounce of gold was equal to 15 ounces of silver.

Later generations found the legal connection between precious metals and paper money inconvenient. The issue was debated off and on for years—whenever some backwoods yahoo decided to make an issue of it. For example, Nebraska congressman Howard Buffett took it up in 1948.

"So far as I can discover," said the father of the world's second-richest man, "paper money systems have always wound up with collapse and economic chaos. If human liberty is to survive in America, we must win the battle to restore honest money."

More than half a century later, we look back nostalgically at 1948's dollar . . . and its liberty. Neither has survived. Back-of-the-envelope calculations tell us that today's dollar is worth only 5 percent to 20 percent of what it was worth when the Coinage Act was passed.

Almost no one misses liberty. And few would mind if the dollar kept waving a long goodbye. In fact, most economists, consumers and politicians count on it. They are betting that a gentle decline in the dollar . . . along with yet more money and credit from the Fed . . . produces yet another inflationary boom in the American economy.

But, "for the first time in history," concludes Dr. Richebacher, "the economy and stock market have slumped against the backdrop of rampant money and credit creation.

"These unprecedented experiences raise some highly critical questions: Why has the deluge of money and credit failed to boost the economy and financial markets in any significant way? And what, exactly, is behind the U.S. economy's miserable profit performance? These are the two most important questions to scrutinize."

Central bankers rule the globe, we are told. "One begins to see the global economy as a vast network of interconnected strings," explains William Pesek, "all being controlled from above by Greenspan, Macfarlane (central banker of Australia), and a handful of other monetary policy makers."

Yet, following the biggest pull on credit lines in history . . . the world's economy has barely budged. Central bankers, perhaps after dinner, might want to check their twine.

Land of the Free

July 4, 2003

> This is a society of true believers. The belief in democracy, market
> economics, and the importance of religion is far more pervasive here
> than Marxism ever was in Russia.
>
> —Michael Ignatieff, in *The Daily Telegraph*

It is the Fourth of July. Should we hang out the red, white, and blue bunting from our office balcony . . . or the black crepe? Should we whine about the America we have lost, or give a whoop for what we have left of it?

That star-spangled banner still waves, but does it still fly over the land of the free, we ask? Or over a country with a spy camera on every street corner . . . a nation so deeply in debt that freedom has become a luxury it can no longer afford?

Whatever direction we take, we trip over a contradiction. Things always seem to be black and white at the same time.

That is why we took up tango, dear reader. People who dance the tango or write poems don't let contradictions bother them. They glide across the floor and enjoy themselves. As far as we know, no serious tango dancer has ever committed suicide. It's the mathematicians and engineers who blow their brains out.

An ideologue or a mathematician cannot tolerate contradiction. His little world has to fit together neatly, like a crossword puzzle. It is cat in one direction and day in the other. Each intersection has to work perfectly.

But that is not the way real life or real people work. A healthy woman loves her husband, but often hates him, too. She has two eyes, and sees a slightly different view of him with each of them. What is wrong with that? Likewise, even a man with only a single eye cannot help but notice that the world is menaced by inflation and deflation at the same time . . . and that America is both free and un-free at exactly the same moment.

What we have come to dislike about the neo-conservatives is not that their view of the world is right or wrong—for how could we know, but that it is so small. They are true believers in a very tiny world . . . one with no room for mystery, contradiction, ignorance, or humility. It has to be small, otherwise they could not understand it.

Neo-cons think they can see what no mortal has ever seen: the future. That is the twisted genius of the preemptive attack; they stop the criminal before he has committed his crime!

They think they can know what no mortal has ever known: not only what is good for himself and his country . . . but what is good for the entire world. And they intend to give it to them, whether they want it or not. In today's e-mail box, for example, George W. Bush himself sends us the following message:

> . . . liberty is God's gift to humanity, the birthright of every individual. The American creed remains powerful today because it represents the universal hope of all mankind.

Here we will take a wild guess: There are probably more than a few bipeds hobbling around the planet for whom the American creed is not so much a hope as a dread.

But the president continues, "We are winning the war against enemies of freedom, yet more work remains. We will prevail in this noble mission. Liberty has the power to turn hatred into hope."

"America is a force for good in the world," continues the leader of the world's only super-duper power, "and the compassionate spirit of America remains a living faith. Drawing on the courage of our Founding Fathers and the resolve of our citizens, we willingly embrace the challenges before us."

America's citizens, meanwhile, are deeply in debt. They see little choice but to back the system, such as it is. Free or un-free, they could care less. Just keep the money flowing. They have come to rely on government. They need Fannie Mae . . . and unemployment insurance . . . and Social Security . . . and jobs . . . and the Fed . . . and fiscal stimulus. Or, at least, they think they do.

After 50 years of the Dollar Standard boom, the average American finds himself less free than ever. He is a slave to the highest government spending and biggest public debt burden in history . . . and to the heaviest mortgage and other private debt load ever. He has mortgaged up his house . . . he has taken the bait of credit card lenders. Now he has no freedom left; he must keep a job . . . he must pay attention to the Fed's rates . . . he must have an interest in George Bush's government (for now he depends on it)!

"July 4 should be about celebrating freedom and independence," wrote Richard Benson, published in this week's *Barron's,* "yet the bankers are the only people jumping for joy. Never have Americans owed so much in terms of their total debt, the ratio of total debt to income, and the amount of cash flow the debt needs to serve it. Americans used to believe that if they were debt-free, they were free. Today, Americans just want the freedom to borrow more, even if it means they are on the way to becoming enslaved by their debt."

The average citizen is only a few paychecks from getting put out of his house. He no longer has the freedom to step back . . . to reflect . . . to think . . . to wonder about things . . . or to enjoy the contradictions. Instead, he must listen to the words of economists as if they meant something . . . and bow before the politicians who control his livelihood . . . and place himself at the beck and call of every government agency with a dollar to spend.

The message from George W. Bush concludes with an endearing personal note, in which "Laura joins me in sending our best wishes for a safe and joyous Independence Day. . . ."

Laura who, we wondered? Oh yes . . . the First Lady.

How we got to be on a first-name basis with the woman, we don't know. We have never even met her. Why she should wish us a happy day, we don't understand. But these are the peculiar, baroque eccentricities of America that make it such an endearing place to its citizens and such a rich treasure for contemporary ethnologists and stand-up comics.

They, too, will wonder about the contradictions. Why do Americans celebrate freedom ever more loudly, while becoming ever less free . . . ? How can they crow about the "home of the brave" when they attack pitiful, Third World nations that can't defend themselves? How can they ballyhoo their own independence when their armies occupy two foreign nations?

Most people will ignore the contradictions altogether. Many will see them as hypocrisy. Some will be outraged. And a few will hear the off-tempo tango beat, and enjoy the holiday anyway.

Fantasies

December 19, 2003—Paris, France

I think we differ principally in that you assume the future is a mere extension of the past whereas I find history full of unexpected turns and retrogressions.

—Winston Churchill

The United States is fighting, we are told in the editorial pages, to make the deserts of the Mideast safe for democracy. George W. Bush, America's conservative president, is conducting what Thomas Friedman has called a "revolutionary" and sublimely "idealistic" war. "Nurturing," he tells us; that is what the 4th Army is really doing. At the same time, on the home front, the Republican Administration has put into place the largest budget and largest budget deficit ever . . . along with the most ambitious, most activist domestic spending program ever seen on this jolly planet.

Meanwhile, on the economic front, America's strong-dollar policy seems to include allowing the dollar to take a dive in the early rounds against its main rivals—the euro and gold—and to lie there looking dead for the rest of the match. That doesn't seem to stop central banks from betting on it; they see the gamble as a way to stimulate their own spectacles. We guess they think it is worthwhile to impoverish themselves so their nations can grow rich. How? By lending to people who cannot pay the money back . . . selling to people who cannot afford to buy . . . and buying assets that cannot be worth what they pay for them.

The American consumer not only keeps pace with the absurdity, he races ahead, as if he wanted to be first in line at bankruptcy court. He has convinced himself that the more he spends, the happier he will be.

A *New York Times* headline explains that he must continue spending—even if he has no more money. The economy depends on it, explain the geniuses at the *Times*.

Our head spins.

And along comes David Brooks, again in the *New York Times,* with more fantasy. He tells us that all these "positive trends" prove that government works! The *Times* really ought to include paper airplane bags for readers with sensitive stomachs and no sense of humor.

But we write today neither to put ourselves in earnest opposition to these trends, nor to offer constructive comment, nor even to throw up. Instead, we offer ridicule and nothing more.

First, we notice that the trouble with politics and economics is that the words lack precision. Talking politics with your neighbors is worse than asking a teenager about his personal life. The teenager gives you nothing you can use—just rough sentiment formed of half-shaped syllables interspersed with MTV groans. If you work hard enough, you can pry some useful data out of him—names, addresses, times, places. Given enough time and energy, you might even know something.

Not so with politics or economics. Almost all political statements are empty of meaning; nearly every word is a promiscuous lie. We know of no political leaders today—from the most craven to the most honorable—who do not claim to act in the name of prosperity, freedom, and democracy. Yet, no one has any idea what the words mean. And if you peel off the layers of humbug, what do you find at the center? Truth? Not at all; you find a mountebank masquerading as an imposter. It is not merely a fraud, but a compound fraud, in other words—so dense and impenetrable that there's practically no hope of making sense of it.

If by some accident, Saddam's goons had failed to rig his 2002 referendum properly, and it had gone against him, we doubt he would have given up power. But if Osama bin Laden were elected president of Iraq, tomorrow, we have little doubt but that the Bush Administration would demand a recount. Neither leader honestly believes in democracy.

But underneath, the lie is even more profound . . . for the idea of democracy itself is such a scam that only a fool would take it seriously. Suppose a majority of voters should decide we should all speak ancient Greek at home and tie our shoelaces together and hop to work each day? Would you go along, dear reader? Suppose they should vote to exterminate Presbyterians or force vegetarians to eat pork rinds?

The majority is merely a big bunch of dunderheads; you have only to read the papers and watch the stock market to figure that out. Why should they get to tell us what to do? Which is why nobody who has ever thought about it actually believes in democracy. When people say they believe in democracy, what they mean is that they believe in Western-style consensual government, in which the voter is only marginally involved.

What really count are the institutions, customs, habits, and manners of a modern, civilized society. The voter gets to cast a ballot from time to time, but he is only dimly aware of what the vote is all about . . . and generally makes his decision on the basis of which candidate has the more likable mug and promises to dig deepest into his neighbor's pocket. Despite him, government goes on its way—mismanaging the economy is the usual ways.

We only bring this up in order to reach for a point . . . not being too sure what we will grab: almost all discussion of political and economic issues is as futile as arguing with a goose about the Christmas menu. The poor goose is not likely to understand a word . . . and it doesn't matter what he says anyway.

Instinctively, people know this. The big words merely fill the empty headlines, the empty space in campaign speeches, and the hollow cavities in the lumpencrania. People do not waste their time talking to geese. But they still need to explain what they can't understand. They bring up GDP growth, democracy, and freedom from time to time. And when things go wrong, they lay it onto wicked men and incompetent managers. If the dollar declines too sharply, they will blame Greenspan or the Chinese. If the war in Iraq turns sour, it will be the fault of evil Mohammedans.

Not since the Enlightenment have people been ready to concede that many things happen beyond their ken and beyond their control. Nor can they admit that they often live in a fantasy world—where their own credulity . . . and their own desires . . . bend light and muffle sound, so that all they hear and all they see confirms what they most want to believe. "The economy is recovering," they say to themselves. "Somehow, it will all turn out all right."

"We are fooling ourselves if we think the world is going to wake up one of these days and merge the fantasy to the reality," writes Fred Sheehan in Marc Faber's *Boom, Doom and Gloom Report*.

"When it hits," Peter Bernstein goes on to describe the gathering storm, "and whichever sector takes the first blow, the restoration of balance will be a compelling force roaring through the entire economy—globally in all likelihood. The breeze will not be gentle. Hurricane may be the more appropriate metaphor."

What will happen, will happen. Somehow, the war in Iraq will run its course. . . . The deficits . . . debt . . . and dollar . . . will all meet in some fatal destructive collision. And one way or another, the goose will be cooked.

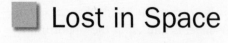

Lost in Space

January 23, 2004

We sense that we live in a time set apart.

—George W. Bush, State of the Union, 2004

N ever before has the nation been so deeply in debt. Yet, never before have any people been so eager to spend more. On the road to ruin- ation . . . they press down on the accelerator.

Here, from Bill King, are the average annual real increases in domestic discretionary spending:

LBJ	1965–1969	4.3%
Richard Nixon	1970–1975	6.8%
Gerald Ford	1976–1977	8.0%
Jimmy Carter	1978–1981	2.0%
Ronald Reagan	1982–1989	−1.3%
George H.W. Bush	1990–1993	4.0%
Bill Clinton	1994–2001	2.5%
George W. Bush	2002–2004	8.2%

Source: Club for Growth, based on U.S. Budget, Historical Tables, 2004.

We are talking, of course, of the usual slimy programs. George W. Bush, the conservative Republican, is increasing spending more than 300 percent faster than his predecessor, Bill Clinton, the liberal Democrat.

But that is the charm of politics. Its shifty sands cover the creepy tracks of countless crooks and connivers. No sooner has a man piled up a few corrupt positions, policies, and proposals . . . than the winds change, and his whole program is blown away. He re-invents himself as the opportunities present themselves.

"It's strange how you never know what you're going to get with a President," writes Doug Casey. "Few people remember that Franklin Roosevelt ran on what was almost a radical free market platform in 1932, decrying the tax, spend, and regulate policies of Hoover. One might have thought you'd have gotten fiscal conservative with Reagan . . . but his policies sent the deficit through the roof. It was reasonable to anticipate a socialist disaster with Clinton, but government spending grew slower than the overall economy. Baby Bush, few now recall, made noises about personal freedom, and no more nation building in foreign hellholes.

"I'm not sure what conclusion one can draw from all this, apart from the fact that the kind of people who survive in the game of politics long enough to become President are, almost necessarily, pathological liars."

We do not recall it, but according to legend, if not history, there was a time when Republicans still might have had a claim to some small measure of integrity. The lumpen Republican could hold his head high, for at least his party platform rested on what many took to be eternal verities—spend little, balance the budget, and mind your own business.

Murray Rothbard saw the sand get into the Republican gearbox more than 10 years ago. He wrote:

> In the spring of 1981, conservative Republicans in the House of Representatives cried. They cried because, in the first flush of the Reagan Revolution that was supposed to bring drastic cuts in taxes and government spending, as well as a balanced budget, they were being asked by the White House and their own leadership to vote for an increase in the statutory limit on the federal public debt, which was then scraping the legal ceiling of one trillion dollars. They cried because all of their lives they had voted against an increase in public debt, and now they were being asked, by their own party and their own movement, to violate their lifelong principles. The White House and its leadership assured them that this breach in principle would be their last: that it was necessary for one last increase in the debt limit to give President Reagan a chance to bring about a balanced budget and to begin to reduce the debt. Many of these Republicans tearfully

announced that they were taking this fateful step because they deeply trusted their President, who would not let them down.

Famous last words. In a sense, the Reagan handlers were right: there were no more tears, no more complaints, because the principles themselves were quickly forgotten, swept into the dustbin of history. Deficits and the public debt have piled up mountainously since then, and few people care, least of all conservative Republicans. Every few years, the legal limit is raised automatically. By the end of the Reagan reign the federal debt was $2.6 trillion; now it is $3.5 trillion and rising rapidly [Editor's note: $7 trillion as of today, January 23, 2004]. And this is the rosy side of the picture, because if you add in off-budget loan guarantees and contingencies, the grand total federal debt is $20 trillion.

Before the Reagan era, conservatives were clear about how they felt about deficits and the public debt: A balanced budget was good, and deficits and the public debt were bad, piled up by free-spending Keynesians and socialists, who absurdly proclaimed that there was nothing wrong or onerous about the public debt. In the famous words of the left-Keynesian apostle of "functional finance," Professor Abba Lerner, there is nothing wrong with the public debt because "we owe it to ourselves." In those days, at least, conservatives were astute enough to realize that it made an enormous amount of difference whether— slicing through the obfuscatory collective nouns—one is a member of the *we* (the burdened taxpayer) or of the *ourselves* (those living off the proceeds of taxation).

Since Reagan, however, intellectual-political life has gone topsy-turvy. Conservatives and allegedly free-market economists have turned handsprings trying to find new reasons why "deficits don't matter . . ."

Today, if you were to pose the question to the small-town Republican, you might still find a faint residue of the Old Religion. But the poor man has been betrayed . . . by his party . . . by his representatives . . . by politics itself . . . and by his own fatal urges.

Like investors, Republicans have gone a little light in the head. They no longer aim for balanced budget and modest programs; they aim for the stars.

"You can't have a war, cut taxes, have the economy in a garbage pail and spend billions going into space," said an American quoted in *The Economist*. But this old-school Republican is sadly out of step with the times. The new-school conservatives are on the march . . . headed to buffoonery.

It is fairly late in the day of what *Bank Credit Analyst* refers to as the *supercycle* of credit. The idea is fairly simple. All of nature works in cycles. You are born; you die. There are the seasons, the earth's annual movement around the sun, and its daily spin. Things go up and then they go down. The hog cycle—in which hog prices rise and fall with production—takes only about 18 months. The presidential cycle takes four years. A supercycle is merely a cycle that takes a long time and includes many other mini-cycles.

The key dates for America's supercycle of credit—also known to *Daily Reckoning* readers as the Dollar Standard Era—are 1913, 1933, and 1971. In 1913, the Federal Reserve was set up. In 1933, Roosevelt banned gold and brought European-style social welfare programs to America. And in 1971, Richard Nixon broke the last link with gold . . . creating an international monetary system based entirely on paper—or fiat—money.

Not entirely by coincidence, 1971 was also the year in which the space shuttle program was launched. Since then, in current dollars, about $150 billion has been spent on the program. That may seem like a lot of money to you, dear reader, but it is nothing compared to the cost of the next phase. President Bush plans to put up a permanent station on the moon . . . and to move on from there to Mars. "The sky's the limit," says *The Economist*.

Thus we see the full ambition of the new conservatives—to conquer not just this tired old ball we live on . . . but the entire galaxy.

"This development will open new worlds; and its consequences will go a long way toward cleaning up and vastly enriching the old one. It will not be merely revolutionary: It will be Promethean."

The writer is Rod Martin of *Vanguard,* a Republican political action committee, a man who seems to have spent too much time staring at the full moon. Now, he howls:

> The only real question is who will exploit it. Will America colonize those new worlds, controlling the economic life of humanity to a degree today's Arabs can only dream of, or will we allow others to dominate us instead?
>
> Will Washington and Madison's children continue to lead in science, military power, and political dominance, or will it

cede that to the socialists in Brussels, or even the totalitarians in Beijing? That question remains to be answered. But for today, while we wait for the new Orvilles and Wilburs to do their magic, George Bush is building—at a minuscule cost—the infrastructure to give America the early lead. The day may come when we and our children owe all we have to this single act of statesmanship.

Here we have what must be the new-Republican manifesto. Gone is any trace of Republican virtue: laissez-faire deference, humility, modesty, probity, and thrift. Instead, we are expected not just to get along with our fellow man, but to dominate him politically . . . to outdo him in science . . . and to outspend him. Forget letting him run his own life. We are going to control "the economic life of humanity."

They might as well be Democrats!

What words can stand up against this grandiose vision, dear reader? It is arrogant. It is audacious. It is proud and confident. It is loony.

Yes, that is it . . . or lunatic. Root = luna, the moon.

The trouble with the new Republicans is that they don't really believe in civil society or free markets. Orville and Wilbur Wright launched the airline industry without taxpayer money. Now, according to the Republican guardians of the modern capitalism, it will take more than a similar act of entrepreneurship to put us in to space . . . but an act of statesmanship.

"I'm struck by . . . the grand idealism of the crowds . . ." writes our favorite Martian, David Brooks, in the *New York Times*. "It's sort of inspiring in this cold Iowa winter to see at least some Americans who have preserved, despite decades of discouragement, a stubborn faith in politics . . ."

Yes, thank God the rubes haven't caught on!

Hoorah for Capitalism!

*February 27, 2009—San Jose
de los Perros, Nicaragua*

Everyone hates capitalism, so it can't be all bad.

"Poor of the World, Unite against Capitalism!" says a huge poster in Managua . . . featuring the largest picture of an accused rapist we've ever seen. No kidding. Daniel Ortega's stepdaughter said he had raped and abused her since she was 10 years old.

What is wrong with these people? Do they never learn anything? "Capitalism has failed," they say. "We need government to fix the problems . . ." The rich hate capitalism because it threatens to take away their money. The poor hate it because they think it keeps them from getting any money in the first place. And everywhere you look, the chiselers are offering bailouts, boondoggles, and bamboozles. With so many people trying to improve on capitalism, it's a wonder they've never come up with something better.

Danny Ortega makes it sound like capitalism is a system invented by rich people to keep poor people down. Instead, it's what happens when you leave people alone: Some people watch TV . . . some blabber about politics . . . and some build wealth. The rules are simple: Thou shalt not steal, it saith in the Bible. Do unto others as you would have them do unto you, Jesus added. Everything else—from hedge funds to derivatives—is merely an elaboration. People make deals with their neighbors in order to get what they want. One plants the wheat; the other bakes the bread. As long as they respect each other's deals and each other's property, everything goes tolerably well.

But the urge to larceny and slavery is as strong as rum punch. One man gets a bottle of Flor de Cana rum; another wants to punch him and take it away. And if he gets away with it, we're all in trouble. In the second half of the twentieth century, approximately two billion people participated in a bold experiment. The idea was to prove—or disprove—that central planning would do a better job of providing goods and services than people left to their own devices.

After Mao came to power, for example, China turned its back on capitalism for an entire generation. Millions starved or were killed outright in various hokums such as the Great Leap Forward and the Cultural Revolution. Then, Deng Xiaoping announced a change. "To get rich is glorious," he proclaimed. Since then, the comrade capitalists have been creating wealth at the fastest rate in history.

Too bad the Chinese weren't running things in Africa. But then, Africa had a big disadvantage, says Damisa Moyo: The rest of the world was "helping" it. Rather than allowing nature to take her course, Africa has gotten one bailout after another. Thanks to so many bailouts, it is now more busted and more desperate than ever.

"Think about it this way," says Ms. Moyo, "China has 1.3 billion people, only 300 million of whom live like us, if you will, with Western living standards. There are a billion Chinese who are living in substandard conditions. Do you know anybody who feels sorry for China? Nobody. Forty years ago, China was poorer than many African countries. Yes, they have money today, but where did that money come from?"

It didn't come from bailouts, she points out. And it didn't come from anti-capitalist claptrap-babbling demagogues. Russia, too, prospered only after it sent the Bolsheviks packing. Gorbachev introduced his perestroika program in June 1987.

In the control group, meanwhile, Americans made their own anti-capitalist mistakes. The central bank lent money at artificially low rates— distorting the value of all capital assets. Tax policies, government-backed lenders, and government's banking regulations stimulated the housing bubble. And the use of the dollar as an international reserve currency created what was effectively an all-night party with an open bar. Instead of having to settle up in gold, as they did up until 1971, the United States could pay its bills by emitting more pieces of green paper. Then, local economies had to put out great quantities of their own paper money just to keep up. This liquidity created a series of bubbles . . . leading up to the great bubble in finance and housing that blew up in 2007–2008. . . .

Late at night, after the party has been going strong, all credits are almost equally fetching. An Argentine bond? A house in Pomona? A share of Renault? All went up in value. But come the morning light, and investors begin to make distinctions: then, they want only the best credits.

A business that is losing money is like the Soviet Union—it is a wealth destroyer, not a wealth builder. It produces things that are worth less than the resources that went into them. Eventually, it needs a perestroika; propping it up with bailouts and boondoggles only deepens the losses. In the Soviet economy, businesses were taking valuable raw materials and working them up into shoddy finished products that no one wanted. In the capitalist blowout, valuable products and services were produced by the boatload, for people who couldn't really afford them. Naturally, the producers are worth a lot less than people thought. So are the houses their over-indebted customers live in. And so are all the debt-based instruments that their spending was meant to support. The wealth of the entire world is estimated to have a value of around $100 trillion. Capitalistic markets, in their wisdom, have judged about a third of that wealth as no longer viable.

"Today, it's America that must have a perestroika," says ex-Soviet boss Mikhail Gorbachev. "You don't have to be a Nobel Prize–winning economist to understand that it's not normal that the country with 20 percent of the world's GDP consumes 40 percent of the world's resources."

Yes, Gorbachev is right about a number of things. The Western, capitalist economies are in the midst of their own perestroika. They are being restructured. But not by the world-improvers. Instead, they are being restructured by capitalism itself. . . . Leave capitalism alone and it will do the job far faster and far better than the meddlers could ever do.

Ready for the Shovels

February 20, 2009—San Jose de los Perros, Nicaragua

The snowball that was Obama's bailout plan rolled downhill this week, gathering to it all manner of trash and stones. On Tuesday, President Obama signed the $787 billion bailout plan. In a Churchillian moment, he admitted that the end of the war on depression was not at hand, and more sacrifices would have to be made, but "today does mark the beginning of the end."

At least, he has the whole world behind him. America's mayors, for example, have enlisted en masse. Heeding a call from the White House, they came up with 18,750 projects that are "shovel ready," meaning, they can begin digging holes within hours after the cash hits their bank accounts. Las Vegas, for example, said it could use $2 million to put in more neon signs. Shreveport, Louisiana, said that if had $6 million, it would put in three new aquatic centers with slides.

Whee! These are the worst of times for many . . . but they are best of times for some. There is a bull market in claptrap; politicians haven't had it so good since the New Deal.

In France, the Sarkozy government recently announced a plan to bail out the nation's auto industry. The government will lend 9 billion euros to Renault, PSA (Peugeot), and their related finance companies. In return, the state hopes to collect interest and requires that the companies continue to employ French voters. Slovakian autoworkers don't vote in French elections; they can go to hell. In England, Gordon Brown announced yet another bank bailout this week—37 billion pounds, he says, will provide a "rock of stability" for the system. Traditionally, gold provides solidity to a banking system. But Gordon Brown, when he was

Chancellor of the Exchequer, sold off tons of British gold at barely a quarter of today's price.

When the going was good, people believed things that weren't true. Now, they still believe things aren't true—but in the opposite direction. Where they once believed they could get richer, eternally, by squandering money they hadn't earned, now they look to the government to do it.

Depressions are so rare that there is no statistically reliable evidence about them. They are like women who rotate their husbands' tires while preparing their dinners; they are so infrequently encountered that there is no point in making generalizations or trying to form them up into a baseball team. Each one is sui generis.

Hardly anyone is still alive who remembers the depression of the 1930s or what the feds' bailouts wrought. Here at the *Daily Reckoning,* we have already given our version of the story. A depression is not a pause; we recall explaining it as a time when debt is squeezed out of a saturated economy. Bailouts, handouts, and government stimuli actually retard the process.

But ours is a minority view. Only that great economist, Fidel Castro, seems to agree with us. The geniuses can't help, he says; structural change is needed: "Even if Kant, Plato, and Aristotle were resurrected together with the late brilliant economist John Kenneth Galbraight [sic], they would neither be capable of solving the more frequent and deeper antagonistic contradictions of the system."

But the burden of proof is on us. Which is too bad; Fidel is retired and we have no proof of anything. All we can do is marvel, and guffaw, at things so absurd they take our breath away.

In the bubble era, people spent too much money they didn't have on too many things they really didn't need. Then came the credit crunch. Now, they hallucinate that if they spend even more money they don't have, on things they hardly even want, they will get what they really need— jobs, growth, and inflation. Even respected economists say they believe in miracles. Resources have been made idle by the depression, they claim, like strong backs in an unemployment line. Government spending is just putting them to work. By this reasoning, things that were too expensive even in the boom years miraculously become cheap at any price. And things that weren't worth spending money on in the fat years become miraculously indispensable in the lean ones. It is like a man who didn't care for caviar when he had a good job; now that he is unemployed, he must have it every night. They are only taking up idle resources that would otherwise go to waste, explain the miracle workers. In their minds, an umbrella is useless unless it is actually raining.

But sometimes capital needs to take a break and hang on a coat-rack. Every banker, householder and investor needs a reserve against mistakes. Now, more than ever. Until the crisis is over . . . and a new economy takes shape . . . any investment of labor or capital is likely be another mistake.

In normal times, residents of Chula Vista, California, turned up their noses at spending a half a million on a public park for dogs. But now that the hard times are here, a place where dogs can run off the leash seems a fitting use for money the town doesn't have. In the best of times, Lincoln, Nebraska, was in no position to spend $3 million on an "environmentally friendly clubhouse for a municipal golf course." But cometh the worst of times, and the golfers suddenly deserve not just a clubhouse, but one that is pals with nature.

Things we used to take for absurd we now take for granted. But it is just one of the wonders of the human race that it is capable of believing anything. The sunny years have passed. Now, there are storm clouds on every horizon. And instead of protecting its precious idle reserves . . . the government turns them into dog runs.

Aughts Ruined by Wall Street

January 4, 2010—Bethesda, Maryland

W e're back in the USA after 15 years of living in Europe.

Bethesda is one of America's wealthiest suburbs. Money from all over the nation rolls this way. The playing field is tilted in Bethesda's direction.

"I was sitting in the Starbucks, having a cup of coffee," Elizabeth reported. "One man next to me was on the phone. He was talking about some deal he had done with the U.S. Army in Afghanistan. It sounded as though he was very happy with it. The man next to me on the other side was on the phone, too. He was a jollier fellow, talking loudly about how much money he had made. I thought he was a stockbroker or something like that. Then, I realized he was talking about a contract with the government."

While the rest of the nation has suffered a setback over the last 10 years . . . the Washington metropolitan area has boomed more than ever. Real estate prices are down . . . but less than in other areas.

And when we looked for a house to rent, we expected to be able to name our price. We thought it would be a buyer's market. Not so. Nice houses in Bethesda are still being sought after. How so?

Wars . . . bailouts . . . boondoggles—this area loves them. Federal employees' earnings keep going up . . . and a higher portion of the U.S. national income goes to Washington.

"Aughts Were a Lost Decade for U.S. Economy, Workers," says a headline in the *Washington Post*:

> For most of the past 70 years, the U.S. economy has grown at a steady clip, generating perpetually higher incomes and wealth for American households. But since 2000, the story is starkly different.

What was different about it?

There was zero net job creation in the first decade of this new millennium, compared to healthy job growth in each of the previous six decades.

No decade going all the way back to the 1940s had job growth of less than 20 percent.

How many jobs were created since 2000? None. Not a single one, net.

If new jobs are not being created, you can't expect working people to do very well. And they didn't.

The Aughts were the first decade of falling median income since figures were first compiled in the 1960s. And the net worth of American households—the value of their houses, retirement funds, and other assets minus debts—has also declined when adjusted for inflation, compared with sharp gains in every previous decade since data were initially collected in the 1950s.

Bummer.

The Aughts were a nasty decade for investors too. *Bloomberg* reports that the value of all the world's public companies was a bit more than $60 trillion at the end of 2007. Stocks were cut in half in 2008. In 2009, after the March low, the bounce began. They recovered roughly half of what they lost to end 2009 with a total value of about $45 trillion.

Bummer again.

What went wrong? According to the *Post* account, economists are scratching their heads wondering. What a bunch of morons!

Long-time sufferers of the *Daily Reckoning* already know what went wrong. GDP figures were positive throughout almost the entire period. But they were phony . . . they were a fraud. They just measured the rate at which Americans were ruining themselves—by buying things they didn't need with money they didn't have.

It was obvious to us and anyone who bothered to think about it for two seconds that you can't really get rich by spending money. It's *not* spending that makes you rich. It's savings. You have to save and invest . . . so that you can produce more. Everybody knows that.

But economists don't work for "everybody." They work for the government . . . or Wall Street. Both sectors have a keen interest in making people believe in what isn't so. "We live in the greatest, most flexible, most dynamic economy the world has ever seen," said the politicians. "Yeah . . . and it will only get better," added Wall Street.

But it was a fraud. It didn't get better. It got worse. And now, Americans pay the price. Ten years of work . . . and they're poorer than when they started.

The Aughts were ruined by Wall Street. Washington will ruin the next decade. It will take the lead in spending money it doesn't have on projects it doesn't need. It will lavish money on parasites: those fellows in the Starbucks . . . 39 million people on food stamps . . . AIG executives . . . much of Wall Street . . . most of the federal payroll.

Instead of competing actively in the world economy—providing goods and services to honest people who are willing and able to pay for them—these people depend on government.

And now, the whole U.S. economy depends on government, too—just like the Japanese economy. Now we need (or so we are told) big spending from Washington, or the economy will stop growing. But the growth we are seeing now is not real growth—it is growth in government spending. And like all government spending, it rewards parasites, not the people who actually add wealth.

But heck . . . it's a New Year. We'll look ahead. What's coming up? Another 10 years of backsliding? Or 10 years of real growth? Better? Or worse? We'll bet on the backsliding . . . keep reading.

U.S. Economy in a Self-Made Vise

June 16, 2010—Delray Beach, Florida

S tocks rallied yesterday. The Dow rose 213 points. Gold went up too—plus $9. So many people are buying gold coins that the storage vaults are getting crowded, says a *Bloomberg* report.

But since we don't trust the numbers anyway . . . let's return to words.

Vise is a funny word. It looks like it should be pronounced like *vies* . . . but it is actually pronounced like *vice*.

Whatever. The *New York Times* says it has a grip on Congress.

On the one side, the pols are pressured to cut deficits. On the other, they are pushed to create jobs.

Of course, the *Times* misses the point. It makes it sound as though Congressmen were just innocent, well-meaning schmucks, trying to do their best to resolve conflicting pressures.

Not at all. They're the ones who built the vise. On the one hand, they passed hugely expensive programs. They didn't have the money to pay for all the boondoggles and bailouts, so they had to borrow. The deficits, in other words, are a problem they brought on themselves. The pressure to cut deficit spending is merely reality raising a boot with which to kick them in the derriere.

On the other side of the vise is the pressure to create jobs. The idea is preposterous flattery. Congress never actually created a single additional job in all its history. Jobs come from productive effort. From making things or providing services—at a profit. One person pays another to cut his lawn. Another pays a person to fix his teeth. Both the lawn mower and the dentist have jobs. The government, on the other hand, is a job destroyer. It takes away resources that might have been used to hire a dentist or buy a lawn-mower. It can put people to work . . . but only by taking away resources, and real jobs, from the wealth-producing economy.

If it wanted to, government could force everyone to work digging holes or counting each other. It could increase salaries and report full employment. But no one would have a real job. And we'd all go broke.

American politicians are facing up to the phony challenge in a phony way. That is, they are pretending to create jobs. The Europeans, on the other hand, say they are cutting deficits. They have to; lenders said they wouldn't give them any more money. As Nouriel Roubini put it, in the Old World, "austerity is not optional."

Here at the *Daily Reckoning*, we're with the Germans. The euro feds are beginning to correct a mistake, albeit dishonestly. Americans are just adding on a new one.

Neither Americans nor Europeans are happy with each other's response. The U.S. Treasury Secretary accused the Europeans of threatening the recovery by withdrawing demand at a critical juncture. He insinuated that if there were another Great Depression, it would be the Europeans' fault. Claude Trichet, meanwhile, head of the European Central Bank, says it's the Americans who are to blame. It was they who came up with subprime mortgages and it was they who permitted Wall Street's reckless and greedy speculations.

At this point, most responsible journalists and economists would say something such as: "Both sides should put aside their differences, work together, and put the economy back in order." But you won't get that kind of earnest drivel from us! It's just mealy-mouthy nonsense. The Europeans should stop bailing out French and German banks (by guaranteeing the debts of Greece and the other PIIGS). The Americans should stop trying to bail out everyone. Both should stop bailing and merely get out of the way so the economy can collapse if it wants to.

Dear readers may find our opinions too radical. Everyone else does. But the evidence shows that collapse is actually a good thing. Free market economies are remarkably robust. They don't require the genius of politicians and bureaucrats in order to operate. And when they occasionally stumble and fall, it's actually healthy for them. It's how they shake off parasites. Bloomberg reports:

Currency collapses tend to spur a resumption of economic growth rather than fueling a decline in gross domestic product, according to the Bank for International Settlements.

Currency collapses are associated with permanent output losses of about 6 percent of GDP, on average, though the drop tends to appear beforehand, the Basel, Switzerland–based BIS said in its quarterly review yesterday.

"This suggests that it may not be the currency collapse that reduces output, but rather the factors that led to the depreciation," Camilo E. Tovar wrote in the study. "To gain a full understanding of the implications of currency collapses on economic activity it is important to carefully examine the full circle of events surrounding the episode."

The positive effects of a weaker currency on GDP, including making local products cheaper than imported goods, may outweigh the negative ones, such as rising inflation. Currency collapses occur when the annual exchange rate drops by about 22 percent, according to the BIS, which identified 79 such episodes, "more commonly in Africa than in Asia or Latin America," since 1960, Tovar said.

Why Debt Does Matter

July 6, 2010—Baltimore, Maryland

O n Sunday, we celebrated America's independence from Britain. Having just come from London, it's hard to see what the fuss was all about. The English seem like decent people. The queen still has her dignity. The British government seems no worse than its American counterpart. And David Cameron appears to have a much better idea of what he is doing than the Obama team.

Cameron is calling for austerity. He wants the British public to make sacrifices so that British public finances can be brought back under control. We have some doubt that he will succeed. As far as we know, no democratically elected government has ever been able to reduce its debt burden *during a credit contraction*. A number of governments—including the United States and Britain—managed to reduce their debt in the 1980s and 1990s. But that was when their economies were booming. As long as the economy is growing faster than the debt, the burden of debt will decline as a percentage of GDP. The 1980s and 1990s were boom years. Credit was expanding. People were buying more and more things they didn't need with more and more money they didn't have.

Obviously, that kind of boom can't go on forever. And when it came to an end in 2007, it changed the financial picture for governments as well as households and businesses. Tax revenues went down. Expenses went up. And so did the bailouts and boondoggles that they call stimulus spending.

As deficits rise, so does debt. And so do the voices who tell us that debt is nothing to worry about. Those voices—led by Paul Krugman at the *New York Times*—mention the debt decline of the 1980s and 1990s. They say we can "grow our way" out of debt this time, just like we did the last time.

Here at the *Daily Reckoning,* we don't rule out anything. The day is long past when we said anything with absolute, unshakable conviction.

Today, even when someone asks us our name, we check the initials on our undershirt just to be sure.

Might the United States and Britain grow their way out? Well, anything is possible. But two things make it unlikely. As we said before, we're in a credit contraction. It's part of what we call the Great Correction. Growth rates are going to be low . . . and occasionally negative. U.S. government deficits, on the other hand, are scheduled to be over 5 percent of GDP from here to Kingdom Come. And if David Stockman is right, they could stay over 10 percent of GDP for the foreseeable future. Stockman is the former head of OMB during the Reagan Administration. He predicts deficits as high as $2 trillion per year, thanks to a weak economy and strong spending by the feds.

The second thing that makes it unlikely that we will be able to grow our way out of debt is the composition of the economy. More and more of it is under the control of government. Growth in this economy is largely phony. It reflects activity. But not prosperity. The activity, therefore, is not the sort that you can tap to pay down your debt. Instead, it adds to the debt.

You can see how this works just by imagining what would happen if the feds hired a million census takers. The economy would appear to grow—maybe even faster than the debt. But the economy itself would be hollow and less able to sustain the debt burden.

The other example used by Krugman et al. is World War II. At the end of the war, U.S. debt was equivalent to what it is today, as a percentage of GDP. "Hey, what's the big deal? It didn't do us any harm then," they say.

But the federal government was actually in a much stronger financial position back then. While it had about the same official national debt, it faced almost no off-the-books unfunded liabilities, financial guarantees, and open-ended commitments. The last time we looked, these off-balance-sheet debt items—such as for health care programs—totaled more than $50 trillion.

And then, there's the private sector debt, too. That's about $50 trillion, too.

How much net private debt was there in 1950? Almost none.

In the post-war period we were in a different stage of the credit cycle. People were just beginning to spend. They didn't have a mountain of debt. They had a mountain of savings!

Yes, dear reader, people made sacrifices during the war years. They had put off consuming. Then, soldiers came back from Europe and the South Pacific with pent-up demand, and real savings that they could put to work.

So, the economy was ready for a credit expansion, not a contraction. People had lived through the lean years. Now they were ready for some fat ones. The economy too was ready to rock and roll. It had been converted to a war footing. Now it was ready to meet consumer demand.

This is the opposite of the picture today. Few sacrifices were made over the last 50 years. Instead, the last five decades were a time of increasing extravagance. That's why sacrifices are necessary today.

Households are only now beginning to cut back. Governments in Europe are cutting back too—or so they say. And under the sway of Krugman and other neo-Keynesians, the U.S. government continues to run huge deficits . . . hoping that the debt will be refinanced and repaid, as it was after World War II.

But probably the nicest thing about after World War II was that there was an *after* World War II. The war had a beginning and an end. When it was over, people were finally able to get on with their lives. The economy was ready to switch to a new phase, too—from making tanks to making hot water heaters. And, finally, governments could stop borrowing and begin repaying their debt.

The major trouble with today's struggle is that there is no end in sight.

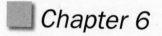

The Zombie State: When Government Fails

Wealth, Poverty, and Blithering Idiots

September 9, 2005

Politicians and bureaucrats are being wrongly blamed for the New Orleans debacle.

"When government fails," is also the headline of *The Economist's* latest piece on the subject. So great was the failure of government, according to *The Economist,* that it has resulted in "The shaming of America."

French citizens thought their government should have mounted its own rescue operation—pulling U.S. citizens out by helicopter as it had airlifted out French nationals during recent insurrections and civil wars in Africa.

British papers are appalled; they thought America was a civilized place.

Cuba offered disaster relief. So did Iran, and Honduras, the poorest country in Latin America.

The head of FEMA—a Bush appointee—was described by Maureen Dowd, who ought to know one when she sees one, as a "blithering idiot." *The Economist* suggests—attributing it to "Bush supporters"—that New Orleans Mayor Nagin, who is black, "proved more adept at berating the federal government than at implementing the city's pre-prepared emergency plan." And of course, Bush himself has been portrayed as lackadaisical, incompetent, uncaring, and stupid. The debate is about which officials—federal, state, or local—are the most incompetent.

Here, uncharacteristically and quixotically, we rush to defend our public officials as we would rush to the aid of a drunk trying to find his car keys.

First, we begin our defense with a long list of admissions. We do not dispute the basic facts. Yes, all of the named—and many more never mentioned—officials are numbskulls. We wouldn't trust any of them to drain our bathtubs, let alone rescue a city from floodwaters.

Also, we admit that they could have made a better show of it.

In today's *International Herald Tribune,* Simon Winchester compared the response of today's politicians to those 100 years ago.

On April 18, 1906, 400,000 people were in San Francisco—including one of the world's greatest opera stars—Enrico Caruso—and one of its greatest actors—John Barrymore. At 5:12 A.M., an earthquake struck the city. Buildings crumbled. Gas lines broke. Electric lines fell. In moments, not only was the city in ruins . . . it was ablaze.

But it took only moments, too, for the people of San Francisco and the nation to get themselves in gear. Just 153 minutes after the quake began, soldiers arrived in the city, with bayonets fixed, and presented themselves to the mayor, ready for duty.

"The mayor, who had previously been little more than a puppet of the city's political machine, ordered the troops to shoot any looters, demanded military dynamite and sappers to clear firebreaks, and requisitioned boats to the Oakland telegraph office to put the word out over the wires: 'San Francisco in ruins . . . our city needs help.'

"America read those wires and dropped everything . . .

"By 4 A.M. on April 19th, William Taft, President Theodore Roosevelt's secretary of war, ordered rescue trains to begin pounding toward the Rockies; one of them, assembled in Virginia, was the longest hospital train ever assembled.

"Millions of rations were sped in to the city from Oregon and the Dakotas; within a week virtually every military tent in the Army quartermaster general's stock was pitched in San Francisco; and within three weeks some 10 percent of America's standing army was on hand to help the police and firefighters. . . ."

The comparison is damning, we admit it. The New Orleans rescue operation could have been handled by the Three Stooges; it would have been smoother.

Still, "without a theory, the facts are silent," as Friedrich Hayek used to say. And the theory that holds that our Moes, Larrys, and Curlys in public office are responsible for the debacle on the bayous is misleading.

And here we would like to call our star witness, the media darling Thomas L. Friedman, not so much because he helps us make our case, but simply because we would like to make fun of him.

We had counted on him for an absurd opinion; he does not disappoint us. In today's column, Friedman blames our old friend Grover Norquist for the whole mess. Grover likes to say that the conservative agenda ought to be to reduce the size of government to the point where, "we can drown it in the bathtub." Humph! And ah ha! says Friedman, as if he had found the murder weapon with fingerprints on it. Now we see the consequences of George W. Bush's conservative philosophy: Big government was not there to help people when they really needed it. Typically, Friedman has found the theme that most appeals to the lunkhead masses.

The failure, columnists and foreign governments complain, is not merely that officials bungled the job; of course, they bungled the job. The criticism is deeper than that. It is that America not only fails to protect its poor people, it also fails to lift them up out of poverty so they can protect themselves.

Here, too, we concede the basic points of the argument. In fact, we have made this argument many times ourselves. The supply-side revolution was a fraud. Hourly wages have gone nowhere since 1971. The average man earns less per hour today than he did in the Nixon administration. The number of people living, officially, in poverty has increased.

It is also true that American society has congealed between the San Francisco earthquake and the New Orleans flood. Now, there are sub-communities of poor, shiftless, almost helpless people at the bottom in major cities throughout the country. It is harder for these people to leave one class and move up to another than it used to be. According to a recent study, America and Britain have the two most socially static economies in the developed world.

When you go into the houses of these poor people you don't find proper dinner settings or books with the words of Aristotle underlined. What you find are people with disordered lives and lifestyles more similar to those of the people of Kinshasa or Port au Prince than the Cincinnati suburbs. Their babies are much more likely to die as infants than are mainstream American children; their young men are more likely to die in violence (statistically, it is still safer for a young black man to serve in Iraq than to live in Washington, D.C.); and their old people are likely to need public assistance.

All of that is true.

It is also true that politicians and bureaucrats have not only failed to do anything about it; they have actually made the situation worse by targeting tax cuts to the rich, failing to put in place adequate public health and educational systems, and so forth. We not only concede that point, we embellish it, adding that even their efforts to alleviate poverty have increased it.

Friedman, Brooks, and other critics maintain that something must be done. But here is where we part company and make our stand against them. What would they ask be done? More of what has been done for the last half century? Who do they expect to do it? The same incompetents who failed to deliver New Orleans from its ordeal, and who have failed to lift the poor out of misery—federal, state, and local officials?

The government needs to do more, they say. Or, as James Galbraith put it, the government, "must be big, demanding, ambitious, and expensive."

Here, we object.

All governments of the United States—from the beginning of the imperial period during the reign of Theodore Roosevelt to that of George W. Bush—have been big, demanding, ambitious, and expensive . . . some more than others, of course. The federal government has gotten bigger and more ambitious almost every year. In fact, it grew bigger faster under the conservative George W. Bush than it did under the liberal William J. Clinton.

It's not that local officials are especially incompetent or corrupt in 2005; officials have always been corrupt and incompetent, especially in Louisiana, where voters appreciate it.

American society is not particularly evil or uncaring, as the European press alleges. The U.S. government announced an imperial War on Poverty nearly 40 years ago. It engaged the enemy in close fighting from Watts to Anacostia. It lost fair and square. If there were a lot of poor people in New Orleans, it wasn't for lack of spending or effort. It is because there are a lot of people who like being poor; it is easier and more agreeable to many than a disciplined work life.

In other words, it was not for lack of a big, expensive, and ambitious government that New Orleans sank. Government is far bigger and far more expensive under the second Bush than it was under the first Roosevelt. Yet, government responded in an exemplary manner to the San Francisco earthquake and in an inept way to the New Orleans flood.

No, dear reader, it is not right to blame the politicians and bureaucrats. But thank God there weren't more of them.

Said the Joker to the Thief

January 9, 2009

The year of our Lord 2008 died in disgrace. It was tossed in a hasty grave . . . and mud was thrown on its face as though on a dead dictator. "Good riddance," says practically everyone. But here at the *Daily Reckoning*, we're going to miss and mourn it. It may have been the worst year in stock market history, but we can't remember when we'd had such a good time. We barely broke a sweat the entire year; never were there more jackasses to laugh at or more con artists to admire. So, today, we hang black crepe . . . spread tea roses . . . and bid adieu.

Among the other milestones of 2008 came word that 1 out of 100 adults in the United States was in prison; but as the year progressed, that seemed like hardly enough. Each week brought new evidence that there were still many miscreants who should be behind bars. On January 11, 2008, one of the nation's biggest mortgage lenders—Countrywide Financial—went bust. On February 17, Britain's Northern Rock was nationalized. Still, U.S. rulers missed the calamity taking place right under their noses.

"I don't think we're headed to a recession," said George W. Bush. "I don't think I've seen any scenario where the American taxpayer needs to be stepping in with more taxpayer dollars," added Henry Paulson. Then, on March 11th, the Treasury secretary went on to explain that the fallout from subprime mortgages was "largely contained." From the report in the *Wall Street Journal*:

> Paulson, a former chief executive of Goldman Sachs Group, repeated his view that the U.S. economy is fundamentally on sound footing and would dodge a recession.

The very next day, Bear Stearns CEO Alan Schwartz told the world that his firm faced no liquidity crisis. In an exclusive interview with CNBC, he said the nasty rumors were unfounded: "We finished the year, and we reported that we had $17 billion of cash sitting at the bank's parent company as a liquidity cushion," he said. "As the year has gone on, that liquidity cushion has been virtually unchanged." That same week, SEC Chairman Christopher Cox added that his agency was comfortable with the "capital cushions" at the nation's five largest investment banks.

Four days later, the cushions seemed to have mysteriously disappeared. Bear Stearns faced bankruptcy brought on by collapsing subprime prices. In a desperate measure, the firm sold itself to JPMorgan Chase the next day for $2 a share—a 98 percent discount from its high of $171. (The sales price was later revised to $10 a share.)

But by May things were looking up again. On the 6th of the month, Cyril Moulle-Berteaux, managing partner of Traxis Partners LP, a hedge fund firm, wrote in the *Wall Street Journal*: ". . . it is very likely that April 2008 will mark the bottom of the U.S. housing market. Yes, the housing market is bottoming right now."

But by July, several things were clear: Housing had not bottomed out, the subprime problem was not contained, the banks did not have enough cash, and every official—public or private—who opened his mouth was either a joker or a thief.

On July 16th Fed Chairman Bernanke told Congress that troubled mortgage giants Fannie Mae and Freddie Mac were "in no danger of failing." The next day, ABC interviewed Fannie Mae CEO Daniel Mudd. Would Fannie Mae need a bailout? he was asked. "I think it's very unlikely" was the opinion of the top man. "And I think everybody that has described it . . . [says it's] a backstop in case things turn out different than everybody predicts."

If anyone knew what was happening in the nation's housing market, he wasn't sitting in the CEO's seat at Fannie or the Fed. By September, things were turning out differently than everybody predicted. On the 6th, the U.S. government nationalized both Freddie Mac and Fannie Mac, wiping out the shareholders. On the 14th, Lehman Brothers went broke. Lehman's main man, Dick Fuld, blamed the few people who actually seemed to know what was going on—those who sold the company's stock: "When I find a short-seller, I want to tear his heart out and eat it before his eyes while he's still alive." The day after, Merrill Lynch ceased to be an investment bank; it was taken over by the Bank of America. And the following day, the Fed bailed out American International Group Inc. in return for an 80 percent stake.

But by the middle of September, the financial authorities—who saw no evil nor heard any—were on the case. On September 18 the UK Financial Services Authority took the Dick Fuld approach; it banned short-selling financial stocks. The next day, U.S. Treasury Secretary Paulson took aim at the problem he never saw, calling on Congress to ante up $700 billion. Whence cometh the $700 billion figure? "It's not based on any particular data point; we just wanted to choose a really large number," said a Treasury Department spokeswoman.

Besides, who had time to look for data points? "If we don't do this, we may not have an economy on Monday," said Ben Bernanke to the U.S. Congress. Mr. Bernanke was as wrong about that as about everything else. Monday came. Monday went. The economy never seemed to check its agenda. But then, the U.S. House of Representatives rejected Paulson's rescue plan and stock markets all over the world crashed. The Dow Jones Industrial Average posted its largest point decline ever. "I believe companies that make bad decisions should be allowed to go out of business," opined George Bush.

By early October, however, the world's rescuers had their defibrillators plugged in; Congress approved the acquisition of up to $700 billion of Wall Street's toxic assets and the UK government announced a £400 billion bank bailout. "We not only saved the world . . ." began Gordon Brown's victory speech, before he was drowned out by howls from the Tories.

"I got to tell you," said Paulson on November 13th, "I think our major institutions have been stabilized. I believe that very strongly." Two weeks later, the country's largest bank and its largest automaker were on the verge of bankruptcy.

By year end, the thieves had been blown up by their own debt bombs and the jokers were in control of most of the country's major industries— housing, autos, banking, and finance. "The lack of specifics [in the bailout legislation]," explained a Bloomberg report, "gives President-elect Barack Obama plenty of leeway to decide who succeeds and fails. . . ."

And as 2008 began its death rattle, America's president managed to capture the zeitgeist of the whole remarkable period with just a few flagrantly absurd bon mots: We had to "abandon free market principles to save the free market system," said he.

Au revoir, 2008 . . . sniff, sniff.

In Gono We Trust

There it is, dear reader . . . the future of the United States of America.

This just in:

We have it from our usually unreliable source in Washington that Gideon Gono, now head of the Zimbabwean central bank, has been called in to aid the Obama Administration. In secret talks, Gono has agreed to replace the out-going Ben Bernanke, who is said to be going to work as a helicopter pilot. Gono will take over the Fed. And a new bill has already been designed—our source was able to sneak out a copy of the new note—for 1 million U.S. dollars. That's Gideon Gono's picture on it.

According to reports, Gono insisted on getting his face on the bill as part of the deal. "Dead presidents are a dime a dozen," he is said to have remarked. "And this is just the beginning; we can add zeros later."

Gono was in the news yesterday for other reasons, too. Zimbabwe has taken a couple of bold steps recently. First, it announced that henceforth citizens would be allowed to use currency other than the stuff produced by its own central bank. This came as a great relief to the people of the nation—who were already using U.S. dollars to replace the Zimbabwean brand. With 230 million percent inflation, the Zimbabwe dollar has not been so much a store of value but an incinerator of it. Second, Gono announced that he was taking 12 zeros off the Zimbabwean currency. Twelve seems like a lot. And it seems like only yesterday that Gono introduced the first note with 12 zeros on it—the 1 trillion Zim dollar note.

But that's the problem with zeros. They've got holes in them. You add nothin' to nothin' and you still got nothin'. Easy come. Easy go. You can as easily add zeros as take them off. At the end of the day, the extra zero gets you zilch.

Still, dear reader. . .

In Gono We Trust. Our economy is in a terrible mess. We need inflation; only Gono seems to know how to get it.

Yesterday, the report card on the economy came in. It showed growth in the last quarter of last year at *minus* 3.8 percent. "Could have been worse," say economists. It *will* be worse, we reply. This depression is just getting started.

The Dow fell 40 points yesterday. We're in February already. Investors look back and see that stocks have lost more than 8 percent so far this year—the worst on record. In 87 percent of cases, what goes down in January goes down all year long. Last year, we had the worst stock market performance on record. But what the heck . . . records are made to be broken. This year will probably be worse still.

Macy's said it laid off 7,000 people. California says it is kiting checks. And Republicans say they are digging in their heels about Obama's Bailout Boondogglization program. They favor boondoggles of their own.

Consumer spending fell last month—for the sixth month in a row. Consumers are exhibiting the quality that economists fear . . . "the propensity to save." Until last year, of course, they had a propensity to spend. Now, all the news tells us that what ought to happen is happening now; consumers are closing their pocketbooks.

According to mainstream economists, this "propensity to save" thing is as welcome as halitosis. It's a conversation stopper, for sure. One man's expiration is another's inspiration. One's spending is another's income, in other words. So when he stops spending, the whole system of consumer spending comes to a halt. Sales plummet. Incomes fall. Jobs are lost.

Hey . . . welcome to the Depression of 2008–? And get ready to welcome Gideon Gono to the Fed. We need him.

■ ■ ■

Yesterday, we promised to take up a theme . . . hmmmm . . . what was it? . . . Oh yes, the critical issue . . . when.

When? When what?

Oh yes . . . when will deflation turn into inflation?

You want a date, don't you, dear reader? You want to know exactly when you should switch out of Treasury bonds and into stocks, gold, and freeze-dried food. Alas, that we can't give you. Not even an approximate date.

This past weekend, we sat down in the Dr. Richebacher chair that we keep next to the fireplace. It's the chair where Kurt Richebacher used to do his heavy thinking. We inherited it from the family after he died.

We sat and we tried to channel Kurt. What would he think . . . we wondered.

"Imagine you are in a small town," we thought we heard him say. "Imagine that the banker printed up the town's money in his basement. One day, he went a little crazy and started making huge loans, even to unqualified borrowers, at very low rates of interest. You would soon have a boom on your hands, with everyone paying for everything with IOUs, all derived from the bank's easy credit policy. But, eventually, when it was discovered that people couldn't repay their loans, there would be a terrible bust.

"That is where you are now. (I say 'you,' because I am no longer among the living . . . but I have to say, heaven is not a bad place to be. . . . There is almost a total absence of economists, lawyers . . . and not a politician anywhere.) It is a period of price discovery in the credit market . . . because no one knows who can pay his bills and who can't. The IOUs are being marked down. Unemployment is rising, too, as the local economy slows down. Consumer demand has been greatly reduced as everyone has gotten poorer.

"Now, the banker sees what a mess the place has become. Naturally, he wants to do what he can. He tries to lend more money, but people have been down that road; they are reluctant to borrow. Then, he undertakes to build a new ballpark . . . you know, for playing baseball. And he decides to upgrade the town hall, too . . . printing up the money to pay for it, as necessary, and to pay for a variety of projects to keep his friends and relatives employed.

"But while he is trying to get the boom going again, the bust is still going on. For every dollar he puts back into the town economy, $2 or $3 is taken out. Instead, of spending money like they used to . . . citizens stuff it in mattresses and bank accounts (much of it comes back to the bank where it started!).

"This process can go on for much longer than you think. Because the banker is, in effect, standing in the way of what needs to happen. He is blocking the process of price discovery . . . by lending money to deadbeat debtors and propping up businesses that are no longer profitable. The baker, for example, had built a fancy oven to produce 200 pastries every day. When the boom was in full swing, he sold every one of them. But now that people are cutting back, he sells only half as many. His investment in the new oven is now a losing proposition. But it takes the market a long time to find out; because the banker gives him enough money to carry on . . . when he should have declared bankruptcy months ago. And so with the tailor and the hatmaker and all the rest.

"Eventually, the banker realizes that his efforts to restart the boom have failed. Instead of spending money, people use it to pay down their debts. They cut their expenses; they reduce their output; and they'll continue to use their cash surpluses to pay their debts until they are back down to where they usually are, he reasons. Even then, people are likely to save because they've gotten in the habit of saving; this could go on for a long time, he figures.

"And then, he realizes that the only way to prevent people from falling into the 'propensity to save' trap is to make them realize that the currency is not worth saving . . . that it is losing value. That is when he will turn to Gonoism. He will go down into the basement; print up stacks of $100 bills . . . and begin passing them out on street corners."

Inflation is needed. Not just more credit from the bank. But money . . . cash . . . free cash . . . piles of it.

The United States currently has about $1 trillion worth of spare output capacity. It has about $6 trillion worth of private debt—above and beyond what is traditionally considered normal. And unemployment is rising. As long as those things persist, prices are not likely to go up. First, because business has no pricing power—not when there is excess capacity. In our earlier example, for instance, the baker can double his output of pastries with no further investment nor additional costs. He cannot raise prices; instead, he'll probably lower them in order to compete with the baker down the street who also has excess capacity. Nor are labor rates going to go up—not when workers are still being laid off. The proletariat has no more pricing power than the bourgeoisie. And as for consumers . . . they won't go back to consuming until they've lightened their debt burden. With $6 trillion, more or less, to unload, it will be a long time before they're ready to spend again.

So don't expect miracles from the Boondogglization programs. Prices won't rise until central bankers "go Gono." And once they've gone Gono . . . things will really start to pop! Stay tuned.

■ ■ ■

Our friend, Nassim Taleb, author of the *The Black Swan,* told the Davos crew that "we should not trust these bankers. Look at their track record. The only way to stop the process is for the government to own those banks."

Yes, dear reader, everyone is jumping all over the bankers. There are two schools of thought. Either the bankers are evil. Or they are just very, very stupid.

Jamie Dimon, chief of JPMorgan Chase, joined the "they are stupid" camp.

"God knows, some really stupid things were done by American banks and by American investment banks," he said. But he went on to suggest that maybe the bankers weren't the only morons. "To policy makers, I say: 'Where were they?'"

The grammar suggests he really is stupid enough to be a politician. He probably meant to say: "To policy makers, I say: 'Where were *you?*'"

But the thought seems correct to us. Where were the regulators . . . the policy makers . . . the economists . . . the commentators . . . the media . . . the analysts . . . the rating agencies? And where were investors? Of course, they were all in the same place as the bankers—fantasyland.

And now, guess what? They're still in fantasyland . . . imagining that these trillion-dollar boondoggles will erase the mistakes caused by their earlier fantasy.

Oh, Mr. Gono, wherefore art thou?

Welcome to Zombieland
October 5, 2009—London, England

Welcome to Zombieland . . . where the most amazing things happen. . . .

Starring Ben Bernanke, Tim Geithner, and a cast of millions . . .

The new movie—Zombieland—about a group of survivors in a world of zombies, was the biggest grossing film in America and Canada over the weekend. It must reflect the zeitgeist of the North American public . . . a deep feeling that we are living in a decaying world.

Maybe it comes from the growing awareness that the old bubble economy of the 2002–2007 period is dead. Now, survivors must defend themselves from the zombies.

Survivors are being attacked in the streets, in their homes, and at their workplaces. Zombie banks—kept alive by artificial stimulants provided by the feds—take their money and their houses. Living-dead companies block new competitors. And the zombies at the Fed and the Treasury Department try to gnaw on their savings, encouraging inflation to eat away the purchasing power of the dollar.

As to this last point, the feds have gotten nowhere. They wear down their teeth for nothing. Prices are going down, not up. Houses are 30 percent cheaper than they were in 2006. Hotel rooms are 20 percent cheaper than last year. You want a luxury room? Just ask for an upgrade. Chances are good that no one is renting the luxury suites. Just make them an offer. Discounts are available almost everywhere. The Sony Playstation, for example, is now available—25 percent off.

Stocks are cheaper too. They've been going up for the last seven months, but they're still about a third less than they were in 2007.

Stocks fell again on Friday. Investors began to fret that maybe . . . just maybe . . . the authorities don't have this zombie problem under control.

"Jobs news gets worse," the *New York Times* tells us.

Since the stock market began going back up in March, the United States has lost 2.5 million jobs. It has lost jobs every month since December 2007. Now, unemployment—officially at one in 10 workers—is the worst it has been in 26 years.

What kind of recovery is this? We don't know, but if it continues much longer we'll all be unemployed.

But not to worry, dear reader. Secretary of the Treasury Tim Geithner says the signs of recovery are "stronger" than expected.

We wonder what signs he's looking at. Of course, this is the same doctor who was on the scene at the New York Fed when strange things began happening. The financial industry started acting funny in the bubble years . . . spending money like there was no tomorrow. And then, wouldn't you know it, there wasn't any tomorrow. They dropped dead in the crash of 2007–2008. But with huge injections from the Fed, they've turned into zombies.

Of course, Tim Geithner missed the whole thing. So maybe he's not the best source of recovery sightings.

A survey by the Business Roundtable tells us that the ranks of the unemployed are likely to swell. Only 13 percent of employers have plans to hire more workers. The rest are either sitting tight . . . or turning workers loose.

Naturally, of all those people cut off from paychecks, more than a few are looking a little peaked. Their eyes sink back in their heads. Their skin turns gray. Soon, they're starving for raw meat.

"Personal bankruptcies soar," says the *Wall Street Journal*.

And not surprisingly, when they become desperate, they tend to default on their mortgages. We know already that auto sales drove off a cliff when the summertime Cash for Clunkers program came to an end. Now, summer's over. Housing sales should decline, too—forcing more homeowners into default and foreclosure.

The zombies are having a depressing effect everywhere. The stock market went down again on Friday . . . the Dow fell 21 points. The oil market didn't do much better, with the price of the black gold still below $70.

As for gold, the yellow metal continues to hold above $1,000. It fell below $1,000 for just a couple days. On Friday, it was back to $1,004.

The $1,000 level used to be a ceiling for the gold price. Now it seems like a floor. Are the Chinese buying below $1,000? Maybe. Do we have a Beijing put option available to us? That is, has the risk been taken out of the gold market by China's desire to stock its vault with something other than dollars? It is an intriguing thought. We don't know the answer.

We are holding on to our gold. It's insurance—protection against the feds. If they do something really stupid, the price of gold will soar. If they don't do anything really stupid, well, we'll be surprised. After all, they've already turned America into Zombieland.

On our last visit to the French countryside, in Normandy, we noticed a big pile of hay beside the road, with a sign on it: "Free Milk."

Another pile of hay had another message: "Farmers On Strike."

The story behind these signs has a Depression-era, black-and-white look to it. Newsreels from the Great Depression show U.S. farmers dumping milk rather than sell it at deflated prices. Now, French farmers do the same. Prices have fallen so low that many refuse to sell it at all.

But they can't stop milking the cows. So what do they do with the milk? They give it away. Or, in a few instances, they throw it at the government's farm agency offices.

Meanwhile, a story in the *New York Times* explains one of the reasons why milk has become so cheap. New technology makes it easier and cheaper to produce good milk cows.

Technology and globalization are inherently deflationary. The former increases productivity, thus lowering the cost of output. The latter lowers prices by directing business to the world's lowest-cost producers.

Deflation is the natural order of things. Inflation is always an artifice caused by government. Central banks target a certain level of inflation because they think—or say they think—that a bit of inflation helps create full employment. And it does, sometimes. But it does it by treachery. Inflation hoodwinks the working class. It reduces their real wages, making them cheaper to employ. Then, the proles wise up. They realize that prices are rising. They demand more wage increases. That is when inflation begins to get out of control and presidents get out the Whip Inflation Now buttons.

Every time government offers to solve a problem, it inevitably makes the problem worse—except, occasionally, in rare episodes when a government-organized national defense pays off.

Two interesting news items in the British press, one inspiring . . . one pathetic.

The first concerns how to fight terrorism . . . and win! Terrorists use the local population in Northwest Pakistan like the New Jersey militia used the local population of Pennsylvania when it was putting down the Whiskey Rebellion. That is, they barge into houses and demand food and lodging.

One brave man said "No."

The terrorists were giving him a good thrashing when his daughter took the initiative. She hit one with an axe, took his AK-47, and shot him dead. The other two fled.

Once again, we see how private initiative—at negligible cost—can succeed where trillion-dollar government boondoggles fail. Why make a federal case out of it? Got a problem with a terrorist? Whack him!

The other story was front-page fodder for the *Telegraph* last week. It illustrated the real problem with suicidal people—they think only of themselves.

A young woman was depressed because she couldn't have children. She decided to kill herself. She drank poison . . . and then called the ambulance. At the hospital, she was still conscious and told doctors that under UK legislation she had a "right to die." The doctors were forbidden from treating her. She died.

Naturally, her parents were upset. Hadn't the doctors taken an oath? Weren't they morally bound to intervene, no matter what the law said? She made them all complicit in a homicide. A more considerate person would have stayed home.

When Zombies Attack

July 3, 2009—London, England

Big news yesterday:
"Jobs report dashes hopes on recovery," says the *International Herald Tribune* this morning.

Oh?

Yes, dear reader . . . once again, we're right and they're wrong!

You'll recall from yesterday, the feds said that their monster stimulus program would hold unemployment below 8 percent in 2009. The year's not half over and the rate is already 9.5 percent.

Then, they said the numbers were getting better each month—inevitably leading to a recovery by the end of the year. They predicted a loss of 365,000 jobs in June—considerably fewer than in May. Instead, the figures—even after they had beaten them up—said 467,000 jobs had gone, which was considerably more than May's figure. The important thing is that the trend that economists thought they were watching—which was leading to a recovery—has been broken. Instead of fewer job losses, we have more.

Ha ha . . . we laugh at them. We mock them. We turn up our noses to show our contempt. We turn our backs and point to our . . . oh, never mind . . .

But wait a minute. What are we saying? Hold the self-satisfied congratulations, please.

Yes, we were right: There ain't no green shoots. But we're not vain and stupid enough to think we know what is actually going on. Only morons think they know what is going on. And the more sure they are—the bigger dopes they are.

Where, exactly, is this economy headed? How is it going to get there? When?

Damned if we know. (And damned if we don't!)

Okay, now . . . shush . . . now that we've thrown the jealous gods off our case . . . we whisper to you: Well, we actually *do* have an idea of where this economy is going . . . which we will reveal to you, dear reader, in hushed tones, little by little. For starters, you have to realize: This is a depression. It is not a recession. In a recession, an economy gets a cold and has to take a little bed-rest. In a depression, an economy drops dead. Businesses go broke. The whole structure of the economy changes as the corpses are dragged away and new enterprises take their places.

Economists were 100,000 off on their jobless predictions because they still don't really understand what is going on. We knew the predictions of a recovery were dumb. This is a depression—meaning, it is a major change of direction . . . not merely a pause in an otherwise healthy economy. After more than half a century of debt expansion, debt is contracting. Businesses, households, investors, and the government need to adjust. And that takes time—a lot more than the 20 months of recession we've had so far.

It would happen a lot faster of course, if the feds weren't fighting it every step of the way.

"Rise of the Zombies," is a headline in today's *Financial Times*. It tells a familiar and predictable story: The feds have propped up businesses coast to coast. Instead of being allowed to fail, they are kept alive by the government . . . and continue to take resources that could be redirected to more promising competitors.

But don't bother telling the feds that. They don't care. The old, worn-out zombie businesses still make campaign contributions and employ voters. The businesses of tomorrow don't. The present votes. The future does not.

Investors are wondering if the forecasters know what they are talking about.

"Stock markets disoriented by the uncertainties of the recovery . . ." says an awkward headline in today's French financial news.

The Dow itself lost 212 points yesterday. Oil fell to $66. Even gold dropped $10 as people fled back to the only asset they know they can count on—the U.S. dollar. Or more precisely, U.S. debt denominated in U.S. dollars.

Come hell or high water, the Treasury will come through. When it's time to pay the coupons, they'll have the cash. You can count on it.

But what you can't count on is how much that cash will really be worth. And there lies the great trap for the lumpen investoriat. The lumpen, as you know, get their investment ideas from TV and the newspapers. The poor rubes are the last to buy in a boom and the last to sell in a bust. A day late and a dollar short, they always get the worst deals. When the papers tell them there's a recovery—they believe it. When the Fed chief tells them to use adjustable rate mortgages . . . the silly clumps do it. When a governor of a Federal Reserve bank urges them to "go out and buy an SUV," they head for the dealers.

But thank God for these patsies. Without them, where would we get candy? And where would the U.S. government get its trillions?

The lumpen—along with the sophisticated fund managers who pretend to know what they are doing—are financing the biggest government-borrowing spree in the history of mankind. You don't have to dig too deeply to figure out why that won't work. Financing a little spree of borrowing may turn out well; financing a big one is asking for trouble. Each dollar you lend weakens the borrower's balance sheet. By the time he has gotten to the 12 trillionth dollar . . . you might as well be throwing the money down a well.

And thank God for Arnold Schwarzenegger. What an entertainer! He had it all. Money. A good wife from a bad family. A nice hairdo. And what did he do? He gave up a promising career in the motion picture business to launch himself into the slimy world of politics.

And now the poor man is groveling. Begging. Imploring the banks to take his state's IOUs. He says they are "rock solid." California is the world's sixth-largest economy. But it was a world-beater when it came to debt-based bubble illusions. And now its economy is falling apart. Economists can lie about the inflation rate. They can fudge the GDP. They can torture the unemployment numbers. But when the revenues come in, all they can do is count them up. And revenues are falling. Especially tax revenues.

The feds and the states are losing income. When businesses lose revenue they cut back expenses. But governments—at least those that are modern popular democracies—find that they need to increase spending. They have more people asking for help. And they have programs that become automatically more expensive—such as unemployment benefits—when the economy softens.

Let's see. Expenses down, income up = happiness.

Expenses up, income down = misery.

See how simple it is?

Central Planning and the Parasites It Creates

February 24, 2010—Baltimore, Maryland

Not all economists are charlatans. At Harvard is Robert J. Barro, who just computed the net costs of the government's 2009 stimulus program. It was originally expected to cost $787 billion and is now estimated to come in with a final price tag of $862 billion.

What do you get for that kind of money? Well, Mr. Barro calculates that each dollar of public stimulus spending costs the economy $1.50 in foregone private spending. A "bad deal," he says.

His work involves a purely macroeconomic look at the subject. He believes government spending is subject to a multiplier that reduces or enlarges its effects. In the first couple of years, he assumes, the net effect is positive . . . since the government is spending money without raising taxes to pay for it. But then, tax receipts inevitably have to go up to pay the costs of the stimulus. And taxes are subject to their own multiplier. Take out a dollar in taxes and the economy shrinks by more than a dollar! Which makes the whole transaction not only a waste of time and money . . . it makes the whole society poorer.

"There's no such thing as a free lunch," even in fiscal stimulus, says Mr. Barro. The bill for the stimulus spending must be paid. Taxes must be increased. And when you've done the math all the way to the end of the transaction, you find that you've lost money.

But Mr. Barro has a much more generous spirit than we do. He offers no judgment on the character of the government spending as opposed to the private spending it replaced. Like all modern economists, he assumes that a dollar is a dollar . . . and a dollar spent by government is more or less as good as a dollar spent by the private sector.

But a dollar spent by the government is nothing like a dollar spent by the private sector. A fellow might spend his own dollar unwisely. But at least he gets what he deserves. When the government spends a dollar it does worse than waste the money . . . it perverts the entire economy and creates zombies and parasites.

Here's an interesting item from the *Wall Street Journal* . . . India produces barely half as much rice per hectare as China . . . 3.4 tons per hectare as compared to 6.5 tons in China. Even dirt-poor Bangladesh gets a better yield on its rice land—with 3.9 tons per acre of output.

What's the matter with India's farmers?

We return to a *Daily Reckoning* dictum to explain it. Anyone can make a mess of things, but to really cause a catastrophe you need taxpayer support.

Yes, Dear Reader, India's agricultural sector gives us yet another example of central planning at work. In the 1970s, when India was even more of a socialist country than it is now, the government decided to boost production by giving farmers subsidized fertilizers. This led, as might have been predicted, to the overuse of fertilizers . . . one of which—urea—severely damaged the soil. Subsidies, bailouts, quantitative easing, fiscal stimulus— all produce perverse effects. In this case, the effects are so perverse that India can no longer feed itself. It's forced to import a large part of its food. Naturally, food prices are rising—up 19 percent last year.

But the cost of food itself is only part of the story. There's also the cost of the subsidies. In 1976, the fertilizer subsidy program cost $640 million. Now the price tag is up to $20 billion.

Both the soil and the budget are getting worn out. As crop yields decline, desperate farmers put on more and more cheap fertilizer. And then, as the food output goes down, the government thinks it has to do something to fix the situation. What can it do? Provide more subsidized fertilizers!

Way to go, feds.

Government Growth Does Not Equal Economic Growth

February 24, 2010—Baltimore, Maryland

A couple of years ago, we used to get such a kick out of making fun of the financial industry. Its pretensions were absurd and shocking. Its delusions were breathtaking. Its leaders were lunkheads and grifters.

But the financial industry blew itself up in 2007–2009. Now, what do we have?

The government! Doing all the same things . . . making the same mistakes (only worse) . . . and working hard to blow itself up.

"Basically, it's over . . ." says Charlie Munger. Warren Buffett's partner figures the glory days of the U.S. economic empire are behind it. He spelled this out in what he calls "a parable," in *Slate* magazine.

This puts Munger in direct opposition to all those economists, bankers, politicians, pundits, and meddlers who think they can do better than the financial industry. Martin Wolf, in the *Financial Times,* says the challenge is to "walk the tightrope" between too much additional stimulus and cutting off stimulus too soon.

Richard Koo and Paul Krugman think the feds need to give the economy a lot more stimulus in order to offset the forces of contraction.

Most people think the economy will muddle through somehow . . . thanks to all those geniuses working at the Department of the Treasury and the Fed.

Dream on! The economy might muddle through or it might not. (The *Wall Street Journal* says growth rates have already retuned to normal.) But if the economy does pull out of this depression . . . it will be in spite of all those ham-handed central planners who are telling it what to do, not because of them.

Yesterday, the Dow fell 100 points. Gold dropped $9.

As far as we can tell, we're still in a depression—that is, a deflationary contraction. You'll see a lot of contradictory statistics and BS analyses for the next 5 to 10 years. What you won't see is real growth . . . not until debt is substantially written off, costs are reduced, and a new economic model is discovered. The growth we're seeing now is largely an illusion, a mirage, and an attractive nuisance. We'll have to pay for it later!

To put it another way, you won't see real growth until there's something solid to build on—a new foundation of lower costs and fewer leeches.

Yes, dear reader, the problem is not a liquidity problem. It's not a banking problem. It's not even just a debt problem. The bigger problem is that the U.S. economy—but nearly the same could be said of Japan . . . the United Kingdom . . . Italy . . . and other places—is too expensive, too rigid. and too full of zombies.

Munger is right. At least, he's right about what has gone on so far. The financial industry turned the country into a casino . . . and too many people lost their money.

We don't know what happened in the second part of Munger's parable. We couldn't get the second page of the *Slate* article on our laptop screen. But he's a smart guy. We doubt he missed the government's role. First, the private sector loaded itself up with debt. Now, it's the feds' turn.

Was it Ronald Reagan who said of the Soviet Union, that it was on the "wrong side of history"? The derelict Bolsheviks were definitely on the wrong side of history in 1989. We knew it. They knew it. It was such a glaring problem: They had no choice. Their economy was imploding— thanks to rigid central planning. They gave up and switched sides.

But now it's the United States that is on the wrong side of history. Like the Soviet Union, it tries to impose its will, by force, on Afghanistan. Like the Soviet Union, it has too many expenses and not enough income. And like the Soviet Union, it tries to impose its will on the domestic economy, too—by central planning. Not exactly in the heavy-handed fashion of the old apparatchiks. . . . This is post–Berlin Wall central planning. Collectivism with a clown face.

The United States nationalizes key industry and borrows heavily . . . shifting the weight of economic growth from the private sector to the government. Everything from home finance, banking, insurance, automobiles, employment, and food is now owned, provided, or subsidized by the U.S. government.

After the Soviet Union fell . . . the rest of the world went over to look down the collectivist hole . . . and then slid in, too. In October 2009, the IMF counted 153 separate stimulus or bailout programs. If you bought a house or a car in 2009, you may very well have had the government to help you. And now, if you hire a new employee, you will have the government by your side again. If you get sick, you will have the comfort of knowing that the feds are in practically every examining room, every operating room, every drug laboratory, and every pharmacy. And if Obama has his way—there will be even more of them. Is there any economic act, howsoever trivial, that no longer involves government support, approval, or funding?

Munger may have pointed out. Or maybe he didn't. In either case, we will: The U.S. economy was at its strongest before it was burdened by so many people depending on it . . . and so many smart people helping it along.

It won't make much progress again until it gets rid of those people. And that won't happen until it has crashed . . . and become desperate. Living at the expense of others is a hard habit to break.

The Zombie Economy

March 1, 2010—New York, New York

The zombies are taking over!

Stocks went up 4 points on the Dow on Friday . . . Gold went up $10.

Noise. Distraction. Headlines. Opinions.

The important trend is the big one—the shift of resources from the private sector to the public sector.

During the bubble years, the private sector made a big, big mistake—taking on far too much debt.

Now, it is correcting its mistake . . . reluctantly, painfully, and with plenty of foot-dragging and interference from the government. Instead of letting the dead die in peace . . . the feds are pumping financial adrenaline into their veins . . . turning them into zombies.

It's expensive work . . . so government is now making the same mistake the private sector made a few years ago. It's pretending that debt-fueled spending is the same as growth. Ain't no such thing.

The feds' growth is even more pernicious and counterfeit than the bubble era growth in the private sector. At least people actually wanted houses . . . they just couldn't afford to pay for them.

The feds, on the other hand, produce things that people wouldn't buy even if they had the money—zombie products. Who would buy a billion-dollar software program to spy on other people? Who would pay other people to do nothing? Who would take on the debts of a failing financial institution?

Consider this, from Bloomberg: "Fannie Mae will seek $15.3 billion in U.S. aid, bringing the total owed under a government lifeline to $76.2 billion, after its 10th consecutive quarterly loss.

"The mortgage-finance company posted a fourth-quarter net loss of $16.3 billion, or $2.87 a share, Washington-based Fannie Mae said in a filing yesterday with the Securities and Exchange Commission.

"Fannie Mae, which owns or guarantees about 28 percent of the $11.8 trillion U.S. home loan market, has been hobbled by a three-year housing slump that wiped 28 percent from home values nationwide and led to record foreclosures. The company, which posted $120.5 billion in losses over the previous nine quarters, and rival Freddie Mac were seized by regulators in September 2008."

Did you read that carefully? Fannie Mae guarantees almost a third of the $12 trillion home mortgage market—or about $4 trillion. And guess who guarantees Fannie Mae? You do!

Fannie made bad loans. It ought to be put down, like a horse with a broken leg. But Fannie's bondholders don't take a loss. The losses have been moved to the public sector and Fannie itself has been turned into a zombie company.

Assets, liabilities, spending—it's all shuffling over to the government . . . and sucking the life out of the private sector. In the area of durable goods, only about 4.4 percent of them, on average, were purchased by the Pentagon over the last 17 years. But since the beginning of the financial crisis, durable spending by private industry decreased . . . while Pentagon spending went up. The most recent figures show that 8 percent of durable orders are now bought by the military.

Recovery? Don't bet on it. This government spending only makes it look like a recovery. The numbers may show an increase in durable goods sold, but tanks and armored personnel carriers don't lead to genuine growth. They lead to Soviet-style zombie growth . . . by the government, of the government, and for the government. The rest of the economy shrinks.

Zombieland

March 5, 2010—Baltimore, Maryland

"The world's largest shopping mall is almost entirely empty," says a headline now making its way around the Internet. The mall is not one of America's consumer emporia. It is not in the United States at all. Instead, it is in the Middle Kingdom . . . and twice as large as the Mall of the Americas.

Stimulus spending is a net negative in the United States; what about in China? The China story is largely a stimulus story, too. China's stimulus, compared to GDP, is the world's largest ever—four times the size of America's stimulus program.

When bank loan volume is determined by central planners, you are asking for trouble. But last year, faced with a downturn in demand from their main customer, the Chinese authorities put out the word to banks—increase loans. Loan volume approximately doubled—to $1.4 trillion—the greatest increase, in GDP terms, ever—equal to a quarter of the entire national output.

Investment spending has long been an oversize part of the Chinese economy. As Americans spent too much, the Chinese invested too much in factories in order to make them things they could buy—just as the Japanese had done before them. Investment spending in China increased 200 percent since 2001, making it the world's biggest buyer of raw materials—by a huge margin. Chinese output is less than 10 percent of the world's total but China consumes 30 percent of the world's aluminum, 40 percent of its copper and 47 percent of its steel. Where does all this stuff go? Thanks to China's visionary central planners, it goes just where it is not needed most—into more infrastructure and output capacity. Last year, 90 percent of China's growth came from this fixed investment spending.

There are about five times as many rivers in the United States and five times as many cars . . . but China now has nearly as many bridges . . . three quarters as much road surface. But with easy credit, the connivance of local officials, and the blessing of the central government, it builds more.

Last year, approximately one out of every four square feet of commercial office space in Beijing was empty—about 100 million square feet of zombie space. All over town are dark buildings . . . the Minsheng Financial Center . . . concrete and glass towers on Financial Street . . . the China Life Plaza . . . the Bank of Communications.

This year, the vacancy rate will go up to 30 percent . . . possibly 50 percent, depending on whose estimates you believe. In Eastern Beijing, officials are doubling the size of the Central Business District, even though the vacancy rate there is above 35 percent already. Overall, the city will add another 13 million square feet of commercial space.

Outside Beijing, the zombies are multiplying, too. Whole cities are empty. And in the suburbs of Huairou, a mock alpine village . . . with a 200-foot clock tower . . . rises improbably in the industrial suburbs. Called the Spring Legend, its publicists must be the same people who write fortune cookie forecasts: "The air is so fresh it penetrates your heart," says the sales pitch. You would normally dismiss such descriptions as puffery. But in China's industrial suburbs, the air is often so acidic that it might penetrate the skull, too.

National politicians determine the availability of capital. Local ones have a hand in investing it. Typically, development projects involve bankers, developers, and local politicians—much like Japan's huge public works projects of the past 20 years. Local governments are deep in debt—with total local government debt equal to about a third of GDP. But they keep spending. In Huaxi, for example, they're still planning to build the world's second tallest building, a few feet shorter than Dubai's pyrrhic monument. Huaxi is also the home of the New Sky Village . . . another project that is lost in the toxic clouds.

Property prices are still spiking up. People are still speculating. Ships with dirt and rocks still head for Chinese ports. The capital spending boom goes on.

It looks like growth. But it is zombie growth. People build bridges to nowhere rather than working for profit-making enterprises. Concrete is used to put up cities where no one lives. Savings that might have been used to start a new bank is instead used to prop up an old one.

Japan has been doing it for years. Encouraged by government miscues in the 1980s, private industry created Japan's zombies. Then, after the bubble burst, the government kept them alive. They've been sucking blood from the living ever since.

Economic Zombies Shuffle Toward Bankruptcy

March 23, 2010—Paris, France

Zombies Take Over U.S. Health Care!

"Obama assures his place in history," says the editorial in today's *Financial Times*.

Poor fellow. He'll be remembered as the guy who let the zombies loose on the U.S. health care industry. It wasn't a very good industry even before passage of the reform bill. Not because of the doctors and nurses; they're as competent as other professionals. But they're forced to work under appalling conditions—with lawyers, lobbyists, and regulators on their backs!

This new reform measure just increases the weight. Now, there'll be more parasites than ever. Health care is about to turn into a zombie industry . . . run by brain-dead bureaucrats and kept alive by infusions of blood from the taxpayer.

"Obama should veto the bill," says an American friend. "He should go on TV and tell people that he wants real reform of the health care business . . . not a 1,000 page document full of bribes and boondoggles. That would really assure him a place in history."

But that's not going to happen. Instead, the president will sign the bill, smile in triumph, and the health care sector will come under U.S. government control. One by one, step by step, deficit by deficit . . . the feds take over the economy.

Banks . . . mortgage finance . . . insurance . . . automobiles . . . passenger trains . . . and now health care.

Stock market investors seem to like zombies. The Dow rose 43 points. Gold fell to under $1,100.

What's wrong with investors? What do they think? Maybe each investor looks around and judges his fellow investors fools. He figures the fools will think health care reform is a good thing. So he figures they'll buy stocks. Anticipating a rise, he buys, too.

Or, maybe he figures that the health care act will be such a disaster it will turn voters against the Democrats. . . . And maybe the Republicans will come back into office . . . Who knows what he is thinking . . . or if he is thinking at all. . . .

"U.S. starts to fall in line with other nations," is a headline in today's *Financial Times*.

That is certainly true. The zombies are taking over everywhere. The United States held out against them longer than most nations. But now it, too, is letting government employees run the health care business.

George Wallace once compared the Democrats to the Republicans: "There's not a dime's worth of difference between them," he said. Now, there's not a dime's worth of difference between the world's feds. Whether they speak French or Polish or English they're all taking more and more control of their respective economies. And almost all are going broke.

The latest figures from the IMF tell us that debt in the G7 nations will exceed 100 percent of GDP by 2014. Yes, they're all shuffling along together . . . toward bankruptcy.

Taking over vital industries helps move them down the road. It turns the industries from sources of tax revenue into expense items. The United States has spent $177 billion since it decided to take over Fannie Mae's mortgage finance business, for example.

And how many billions has the United States spent since it took over the nation's passenger rail system in 1971? We couldn't find a figure . . . but it must be around $50 billion.

Amtrak was sold to the public in 1971 as an investment opportunity. With a monopoly on rail traffic between America's most populous cities . . . throughout the biggest economic boom in history . . . you'd think Amtrak couldn't help but make money. It was supposed to turn a profit in 1974. It didn't. Nor did it make a profit in 1975 . . . or 1976 . . . or 1977 . . . 1978 . . . 1979 . . . 1980 . . . all the way up to today. It never made a profit. It just lowered service levels and kept chugging along. And now the feds are still pumping more than $2 billion per year into the zombie railroad.

All aboard!

Tony Hayward Before Congress: No Sympathy for the Oil Man

June 21, 2010—Baltimore, Maryland

Poor Tony Hayward.

The man was devoured by zombies last week.

Now that we've figured out how history works, we're beginning to see the forces of history at work all around us—an eternal fight between the zombies and the producers. We're surrounded by zombies. They are all around us. Tort lawyers. Bureaucrats. Politicians. Welfare slaves. Chiselers. Layabouts. Whiners.

On the way to work, on the Washington beltway, there are so many lobbyists, we have to put up the windows and lock the doors.

Stimulus measures are winding down . . . joblessness is creeping up again. Houses seems to be getting ready for another tumble. David Rosenberg:

> There is no denying the renewed decline in the U.S. residential market, and this transcends the end of the tax credits—the sector is fundamentally weak. Moreover, demand has not reacted to the latest downdraft in mortgage rates and home-buying intentions are, in a word, moribund. The National Association of Home Builders (NAHB) housing market index sagged from 22 in May to 17 in June—a three-month low. Buyer traffic receded from 14 to 16 but the real story was the four-point collapse in the "future sales outlook," to 23 from 27—it hasn't been this low since the depths of the recession back in March 2009.
>
> We ran some regressions and found that the "future" component does indeed have the best "fit" with both housing

starts and new home sales—the latter is set for a renewed 10 percent in coming months, to a 600K annual unit rate, and the latter by 30 percent to the 350K level, which would [be] very close to the all-time low of 338K hit in February 2010. Ouch!

Hey, don't say we didn't warn you. It's a Great Correction, not a recovery.

Stocks began last week with a swagger . . . but by the end of the week, they were barely crawling forward. Gold ran up day after day, adding another $9 on Friday. It looks as though it is aiming for the $1,300 mark.

Meanwhile, the zombies are gaining ground.

Last Thursday must have seemed like the longest day to Tony Hayward.

"Congress mauls BP chief," is the way the *Financial Times* put it.

Mr. Hayward was confronted by a panel of zombies in Congress. They chained him to a rock so the members of the energy committee could take turns feeding on his internal organs.

For seven hours, the BP CEO was asked the same questions, over and over again. No matter how many times he was asked, the answers were always the same. No, he wasn't an expert on the bonding properties of sub-sea cement. No, he wasn't there when the rig exploded. No, he didn't know exactly what went wrong; he was waiting for the results of the experts' inquiry, along with everyone else.

But the zombies didn't really care about getting to the bottom of things. They were going for the jugular. And the right arm. And the liver.

From the reports we've read, Mr. Hayward held up pretty well. He played his part. He did not wander from the script. He remained calm as he was dismembered. His voice did not quake or complain as his liver was removed.

The politicians on the committee, meanwhile, were disappointing. Even for zombies. Hayward was the straight man. The zombies had the TV audience on their side. They should have made us laugh and cry. But for all their theatrical skills they seemed unable to do more than summon up a worn-out look of mock indignation. Like a man who wants to get rid of his wife and then catches her in flagrante delicto; their outrage seemed more stagy than authentic.

Neither Hayward, nor the leading zombies, Henry Waxman and Bart Stupak, will win Oscars. Still, they mostly performed as you'd expect. Hayward said what he had to say. His tormentors feigned profound concern for the fishes and fowl, the flora and fauna of the Gulf area, not to mention the oilmen idled by Barack Obama.

What disturbed us was the crowd reaction. There was a time when Americans had a sense of fair play. At least, we'd like to think so. In a fight between a group of zombies and a real producer, their sympathies should be with the oil man. After all, when they drive into the filling station, it's not the Congressional Record that they pump into their fuel tanks. And when they heat their homes, it's not tort lawyers whom they look to for fuel. Gasoline is valuable. They know it. And they know that someone has to get it. In fact, so keen is their demand for octane, and so high is the price, that the producers are lured farther and farther away from dry land. No one would drill a mile below the water for oil unless a lot of people wanted it badly. Sooner or later, one of the rigs was bound to spring a big leak.

You'd think the public would have more sympathy for the people who risk their lives and their money bringing oil to market.

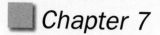 *Chapter 7*

Back It with Bullion

The Dow in Gold Terms . . . Where to from Here . . .

August 6, 1999

'm not making this up. "Pshiiit!" was a popular soft drink in France during the 1960s. But it's hard to find now. Probably out of business. And probably driven out of business by more powerful brands—like Coke.

The advantage of being the leading brand is even more significant with money. This is where Metcalf's law applies. The more people who use one brand of currency, for example, the more valuable it becomes to the users. It is simply more widely and more readily usable. The dollar is the Coke of the currency markets.

Today, you can take a dollar and buy 1/258th of an ounce of gold. Or you can buy 1/10,793rd of the Dow index. As I explained to my assistant, Addison, there was a time within the memory of living Americans at which the ratios were about the same. A dollar would get you either 1/500— more or less—of an ounce of gold, or 1/500th of the Dow. Measured in gold, both the dollar and the Dow have been investment success stories. The dollar has doubled. And the Dow—get this—has gone up 42 times. *DR* readers, however, are cautioned that this trend and this relationship are subject to change without notice.

A lot of things came together to create this trend. The collapse of communism; the restraint of Volcker . . . followed by the more generous habits of his successors and counterparts in America and Japan; the application of Metcalf's law to the dollar. All of these things helped lower commodity prices—of which the gold price is one.

I have not done a statistical analysis on this. But I will bet that gold now (usually) acts like any other commodity. Plotting the monthly price changes will produce a bell curve. (I throw this out to statisticians as a challenge.)

But I will also bet that it is a bell curve similar to the Dow curve. It will have lumpy extremes.

Today's *Wall Street Journal* has an article that takes up one of our themes—Canada would be better off going with a major brand currency . . . the dollar. It notes that there is precious little . . . or little precious . . . backing up the Loonie. ". . . the gold supply, which just 18 years ago made up 80 percent of foreign reserves, now comprises only 5 percent." Like governments almost everywhere, Canada has sold gold and bought paper. And now that the Dow has risen 42 times against gold . . . they are considering buying—the Dow. The talk is not of buying gold while it is cheap . . . but buying the Dow while it is expensive.

The Dow has reached an extreme in dollar terms. In gold terms, it is as much as twice as extreme. At extremes . . . the markets are no longer random. They have a propensity to regress. It is impossible, of course, to say when the regression begins. Or what price levels will result. But, the smart money is probably betting that gold and the Dow will converge.

Under the Big Top, Part Deux

July 19, 2000—Baltimore, Maryland

As I signed off yesterday, our favorite component of the periodic table had been beaten down for the last 20 years. Gold, and those investors foolish enough to buy it, had become a laughingstock—tripping over every piece of news that came over the wire . . . and getting up only to fall down once again, comically.

Even yesterday—which brought news that the dollar would be cut in half in 10 years at the present rate of inflation—gave gold another cue to tumble. Investors would rather own something that loses value at 7 percent per year—the dollar—than something that was supposed to be nature's most perfect store of value—gold.

Goldbugs, people who harbor the quaint and romantic idea that there exist things in this world of real and lasting value, are mute. They have been silenced by 20 years of ridicule. Their only hope—one that I share—is that having indulged ourselves in the greatest investment error that the last two decades had to offer, and suffered accordingly, we might now have some measure of immunity from gross foolishness. We have been there. Done that.

The gross foolishness I have in mind, to disclose the destination of today's perambulation before we have gone far, is not excessive faith in gold, but excessive faith in the alternative to gold—the dollar.

The argument against gold, as I quoted yesterday,★ is not merely that gold is in a slump, but that it is terminal. The voice of progress, you will

---

★The article I am referring to reads, "Andy Smith, a commodities analyst in London is quoted in the *New Yorker* article: 'We're going on a fifty-five or sixty-year aboveground supply. Gold has been marginalized because the world has changed. We have the most robust financial system we've ever had. The thing undermining the many-thousand-year myth of gold is progress!' 'Sure,' the voice of progress continued, 'gold is on the periodic table. Why not choose boron? It's over. Of course, it's over.'" (James Collins in the July 17 edition of the *New Yorker* magazine) recall, told us that the thousand-year-old myth of gold has come to an end. "It's over," he said, referring to the use of gold as a store of value. It's over because the discipline gold provided has been replaced by the discipline of the markets, including the f****** bond traders so much admired by our President.

Gary North explained this in his note to me of a couple of days ago: Bond traders, not gold, are what keep the Fed from flooding the world with dollars.

At the first hint of inflation, the argument goes, bond traders sell bonds . . . the dollar collapses . . . and stocks plummet. And yet, yesterday provided more than a hint of inflation. Bond traders were notified by the Bureau of Labor Statistics, in writing, that inflation is destroying the dollar's purchasing power. Neither the dollar nor bonds fell. They rose.

Instead, gold fell.

Over the long run gold varies inversely with the foreign exchange value of the dollar. When the dollar is strong, gold is weak.

"It is reported," writes Dr. Kurt Richebacher in the July issue of his newsletter, "that measured bullish sentiment on the dollar is at an absolute peak . . . Considering the present unattractiveness of the U.S. financial markets on the one hand, and the excessive and dangerous dependence of the dollar on uninterrupted, huge capital inflows to finance the yawning current-account deficit on the other, the U.S. currency's resilience is certainly most astonishing, if not enigmatic."

The enigma is that so many people seem to have such faith in the dollar for so little reason. Price increases in the United States are greater than those in Japan or Europe—by at least two to one. And American equity prices are at dangerously high prices.

But the measure of faith in the dollar can be taken not only by the drop in the price of gold . . . but also by the incredible increase in the U.S. current account deficit. The current account deficit tells us how many dollars foreign interests are willing to take with no compensating goods or services received in exchange. In 1980, when gold began its epic decline, the number was zero. In fact, in 1981, the United States ran a small current account surplus.

Since then, dollars have swamped the world—with a current account deficit in excess of $1 billion per day.

Meanwhile, Americans have concluded that not only do they not need gold as a store of value—they don't need anything. From 1960 to 1995,

U.S. households ran a financial surplus—roughly equivalent to savings—of about 2 percent.

But, writes Dr. Richebacher, "during the bubble years since 1995 this pattern has dramatically changed . . . the private sector's former financial surplus has turned into a substantial deficit." From an average of 2 percent positive, the figure sank to more than 5 percent negative—a bubble swing of about 7 percent, or about the same as the drop in personal financial surpluses in Japan prior to the collapse in 1989.

There were bond traders in Japan 10 years ago too . . . just as there were on Wall Street before the bear market of 1973–1974 and the double-digit inflation of the late 1970s. Is it possible that the guardians of discipline are as capable of acting like clowns as the rest of us?

"[M]ajor currencies frequently trade like pink sheet stocks," reports James Grant in his *Interest Rate Observer,* "as the dollar did against the yen in early October 1998, dropping by 10 percent in just two days. In the first quarter, according to the Bank of International Settlements, the intra-day trading range of the dollar-euro exchange was greater than 2 percent on more than 21 percent of trading days. . . ."

The implication of this may not be obvious—so I will draw it out: The dollar is as vulnerable as a dot.com. And, the clowns of the future may be the bozos who believe—as the goldbugs did 20 years ago—that today's most dramatic and enigmatic trends are permanent.

The Revenge of Gold

April 19, 2002—London, England

In due course the Japanese people will own over 70 percent of the world's gold! Wrap your mind around the implications of that!

—Harry Schultz

The price of gold hit $305 yesterday. "Buy Golds!!" says the headline of a James Dines ad in *Barron's*.

Dines, whose headline—it seems like it was only a few months ago—was "Buy Internets," now believes that it is gold stocks that are in *"Raging Uptrends!"*

"If you honestly want to make money, it is obvious that you should be interested in uptrending stocks," says Dines. Internets, as all the world has noticed, are no longer in uptrends. Even *downtrend* seems too gentle to describe the white-knuckled descent of the companies Dines used to recommend. Perhaps *death spiral* would be more appropriate. Many of them went down so far, so fast, they will never get up again. But the trends have changed.

One of James Dines's 61 Dinesisms, explains the ad, is that "a trend in motion will continue in motion until it actually ends." We will not dispute this. In fact, the crystal elegance of this dictum makes us wonder about the 60 other Dinesisms. In fact, we have a suggestion for a 62nd one: "The price of gold will go up . . . unless it goes down. Or nowhere."

Dines thinks he knows what direction gold is going in. "It's an actual fact that golds and silvers are in uptrends," continues the author of three-score and one Dinesisms, "and have been outperforming the rest of the stock market. Serious money is made by getting into bull markets early, before the crowd gets it, and precious metals have been sneaking quietly higher, unnoticed by the crowd. . . ."

We've been urging you to buy some gold, too, dear reader. Not because we know something . . . but because we don't.

There are so many things we don't know, we hardly know where to begin to describe them. We do not know how long the world will continue to accept dollars in exchange for goods and services, for example. Nor do we know how long American consumers can continue to spend money that they don't have. Nor do we know when real estate markets might turn downward, ending the illusion of additional wealth caused by rising house prices. But in a world with so many unanswered questions, gold seems the perfect thing to own.

There was a time when we thought we could predict what would happen in the markets. But today, even the dim recollection of those days brings a sigh of regret. How could we have been so naïve, back in the 1970s, we ask ourselves? How could we have been so foolish and so cocksure back in the 1980s, we wonder? Ah . . . but then, we had the confidence of youth . . . the knowledge of the innocent . . . and, most importantly, we had hair.

But by the 1990s, we were losing our mane and gaining our doubts. Age and modesty were beginning to catch up to us. Nature, in her majesty, had already found many ways to separate us from our dignity and our money; we had to conserve what little we had left.

When forecasters told us—back in the 1970s—that gold would rise to $5,000 an ounce, we believed them. For what would stop it? Government was inflating the currency. Government always inflated currency—if it could. There was no example from history of a currency that had not been inflated away to a bare trace of its original value. Why would the dollar be any different?

The logic of that argument was persuasive then, and still is. But the timing proved difficult to forecast.

In a better world, predicting the course of future events would be much easier. If man were merely the homo economicus that economists think he is, he could be expected to do the rational thing at the rational time.

Back in 1971, for example, the rational thing would have been to sell dollars and buy gold. Gold had an established track record dating back thousands of years. It got excited when compared to paper currencies— jumping up and down with the fashions of the time. But, in terms of what it would buy, gold seemed extraordinarily calm.

Through many generations of trial, and mostly error, humans had discovered that paper currencies eventually drifted away to nothing—unless they were anchored to gold or some other solid rock of value. Thus did the Western money system of the nineteenth century function so well—the major nations, Britain, France, and America, had currencies tightly moored to gold. At the end of the century, the franc, the pound, and the dollar were nearly in the same place as they had been at its beginning.

But the twentieth century brought changes. "The classical gold standard died like a soldier in World War I," writes James Grant.

Governments yield to emergency like a dieter to devil's food. In war, for example, restraining influences—gold, habeas corpus, and common decency—give way to mass hysteria. We have already described how the emergency of World War I effectively bankrupted all the major belligerents—save one, the United States.

Britain, France, Germany, Russia—all were on the brink of destitution in 1919. They had lost millions of young men, and billions of dollars, but they had not completely lost their senses. A movement to re-establish the gold standard began almost as soon as the fighting stopped. But it wasn't until early 1924 that Germany ended its hyper-inflation by tying the mark to gold. Then, on the 28th of April 1925, Winston Churchill—then chancellor of the exchequer—announced that the pound would be once-again convertible into gold, as it had been before the war—and at the same rate!

"Why did he do something so stupid?" John Maynard Keynes asked. Answering his own question, Keynes said he believed Churchill was led to his biggest mistake (perhaps even worse than his Dardanelles campaign in World War I) by his own advisors—notably, Norman Montagu, England's chief central banker at the time.

The rate was too high. During the war years, Britain had expanded its money supply and run up billions in debt—most of it to the United States. The general price level in Britain had doubled between 1914 and 1918. Unemployment increased in the post-war years. And exports, even by 1924, were still down 25 percent from their levels of 1913.

A reasonable man might have concluded that the pound—loosed from gold—would likely float lower. It did. But then, a bull market in the pound in the early 1920s produced a sensational run-up in sterling. By 1924, the pound was once again trading at pre-war levels.

Taking the bait, Churchill fixed it by law. The result was disastrous. "The revenge of gold," declared the French newspaper, Le Temps.

Churchill realized his error almost immediately. "Something terrible is beginning to happen to the economy," he said, adding, "If that happens I hope Norman Montagu will be hung."

"It was the biggest mistake of my life," Churchill later said to his doctor.

General Foch, returning from a visit to London in June 1925, described the situation:

"England's government coffers are full. But the economic situation is poor . . . and its industry is operating at half-speed. From every side, you hear complaints that British producers can't possibly compete with foreign suppliers. . . ."

Churchill's mistake had far-reaching consequences. As England grew weaker, Germany grew stronger. Another French commentator: "We thought Germany had been sidelined for a long time, if not forever. But barely seven years after the war, she has become an even more dangerous rival."

Churchill's mistake did nothing to enhance the glory of gold. Many believed it was the gold standard itself that was at fault . . . a few even blamed it for the 1929 crash . . . or for the inability of the government to correct the Great Depression that followed.

Alas, the gold standard had entered a bear market. . . .

A Goldbug's Life

December 2004

M r. James Surowiecki wrote a wise and moronic piece on gold in the *New Yorker*. His wisdom is centered on the insight that neither gold nor paper money are true wealth, but only relative measures, subject to adjustment.

"Gold or not, we're always just running on air," he wrote. "You can't be rich unless everyone agrees you're rich."

In other words, there is no law that guarantees gold at $450 an ounce. It might just as well be priced at $266 an ounce, as it was when George W. Bush took office for the first time. That was just four years ago. Since then, a man who counted his wealth in Kruggerands has become 70 percent richer.

But gold wasn't born yesterday . . . or four years ago. Mr. Surowiecki noticed that the metal has a past, just as it has a present. He turned his head around and looked back a quarter of a century. The yellow metal was not a great way to preserve wealth during that period, he notes. As a result, he sees no difference between a paper dollar and a gold doubloon, or between a bull market in gold and a bubble in technology shares.

"In the end, our trust in gold is no different from our trust in a piece of paper with 'one dollar' written on it," he believes. And when you buy gold, "you're buying into a collective hallucination—exactly what those dot.com investors did in the late nineties."

Pity he did not bother to look back a little further. This is, of course, the moronic part. While Mr. Surowiecki has looked at a bit of gold's past, he has not seen enough of it. Both gold and paper dollars have history, but gold has far more of it. Both gold and dollars have a future too. But, and this is the important part, gold is likely to have more of that too.

The expression, "as rich as Croesus," is of ancient origin. The king of historic Lydia is remembered, even today, for his great wealth. Croesus was not rich because he had stacks of dollar bills. Instead, he measured his richness in gold. No one says "as poor as Croesus," do they? We have also heard the expression, "not worth a Continental," referring to America's Revolutionary-era paper money. We have never heard the expression, "not worth a Kruggerand."

Likewise, when Jesus said, "Render unto Caesar that which is Caesar's," he referred to a denarius, a coin of gold or silver, not a paper currency. The coin had Caesar's image on it, just as today's American money has pictures of Lincoln, Washington or Jackson on it. Dead presidents were golden back then. Even today, a gold denarius is still at least about as valuable as it was then. America's dead presidents, whose images are printed in green ink on special paper, lose 2 percent to 5 percent of their purchasing power every year. What do you think they will be worth 2,000 years from now?

A few years before Jesus, Crassus, who had made his fortune on real estate speculation in Rome, decided to put together an army to hustle the east. Alas, such projects almost always meet with disaster; Crassus's was no exception. He was captured by the Parthians and was put to death in an unusually cruel and costly way. But he did not end his days with paper money stuffed down his throat . . . and certainly not dollar bills. No, they poured molten gold down his gullet—or so the story has it.

Gold has a long history. And during its history, many was the time that humans were tempted to replace it with other forms of money—which they believed would be more convenient, more modern, and most importantly, more accommodating. After all, gold is hard to find and hard to bring up out of the earth. As a result, its quantity is always limited—by nature herself. Paper money, by contrast, offered irresistible possibilities. The list of bright paper rivals is long and colorful. You will find hundreds of examples, from assignats to zlotys. But the story of paper money is short and always sad. Since the invention of the printing press, a new paper dollar or franc can be brought out at negligible cost. Nor does it cost much to increase the money supply by a factor of 10 or 100—simply add zeros. It may seem obvious, but adding zeros does not add value.

Still, the attraction of being able to get something for nothing has been too great to resist. That is what makes goldbugs so irritating: They are always pointing it out. Even worse, they seem to enjoy saying that "there ain't no such thing as a free lunch," which comes as a big disappointment to most people.

Once people were able to create money at virtually no expense, no one ever resisted doing it to excess. No paper currency has ever held its value for very long. Most are ruined within a few years. Some take longer. Even the world's two most successful paper currencies—the American dollar and the British pound—have each lost more than 95 percent of their value in the last century, which is especially remarkable since both were linked by law and custom to gold for most of those years. For the dollar, the final link to real money was not cut until August 15, 1971. That was when the world found out what the greenback was really worth—nothing much.

Whatever promises the Feds made with regard to the dollar, they could unmake whenever they wanted.

Some paper currencies are destroyed almost absent-mindedly. Others are ruined intentionally.

But all go away eventually. By contrast, every gold coin (and silver, for that matter) that was ever struck is still valuable today—and the coins almost always have more value than when they first came out of the mint.

Faith in Faith

June 16, 2006—London, England

Gold investors who had been holding their breath for weeks had it knocked out of them this week. On Tuesday, the price fell $44, enough to put speculators in a tailspin. Even your editor—usually a rock of unproven opinions and a fountain of imperturbable prejudices— began to wonder.

What if we're wrong? What if sophisticated, modern financial instruments have reduced gold's role in modern finance? Wouldn't gold act exactly as it has—that is, as a commodity? It went up with lead . . . and came down with it, too. But what kind of commodity has no industrial use? We wondered then why it had bothered to go up in the first place. After a while, we had wandered so deep into the forest of conflicting and ambiguous thoughts we needed helicopter rescue.

Daily Reckoning readers might be wondering . . . and getting lost, too. Today's reflection is meant to provide them with some breadcrumbs.

We begin with two questions:

1. If we have a faith-based monetary system, what do we have faith in?
2. When this, too, passes, what will take its place?

That second question is the mischievous one. So, we will answer it first: We don't know. But it is the question itself that is most revealing. Were monetary systems permanent and immutable, there would be no need for them. The present financial system could sit there as unchanging as a harbor light—a sturdy guide to the prudent and a warning to the reckless. Instead, monetary regimes come and go, like the lanterns of Cornish pirates, luring ships onto the rocks to be looted.

The financial history of Argentina is instructive as well as entertaining. There, hardly a single generation got through life without washing up— either on the rocks of inflation, the shoals of devaluation, or the soft mud of a financial crisis. One system brought inflation rates of 2,000 percent per year. When that sank, in came a peso as strong as the dollar. And then, when the new peso crashed, a new, new peso, with a new monetary regime behind it.

Just when people had learned how to get around the rocks, the rocks were moved. Along came another regime with another set of standards. Out on the pampas, people finally got used to financial change. They learned not merely from the record of the dead, but from their own living experience: Don't put your faith in any financial system; it won't last.

But Americans can't have learned much from their mistakes; they haven't made enough of them. American paper currencies went bad in the Revolutionary War ("not worth a Continental," was the expression that recorded the mistake), and again in the War between the States (when Lincoln spent more than he could honestly steal from the taxpayers). The Great Depression, with its devaluation of the dollar against gold, might have taught them a thing or two as well. But there is hardly a single person still alive who learned from it directly. No, in matters of financial calamity, Americans might have been born yesterday. Soft and dewy, they are ready to believe anything—even that their financial system might last forever.

That brings us back to our other question: exactly what faith is it that undergirds our faith-based system? It is faith, surely, in the dollar, is it not? The dollar is the unit in which Americans measure their wealth. If the dollar were seriously called into question, so would the system itself be called into question. Everyone knows that the dollar is manmade, of course. Like all man's creations, they accept that it is not without its flaws and is subject to improvement.

Man's automobiles get better every year. And although a man may be happily married, still, walking around a dreary college campus or on a sunny beach . . . he can still imagine how things might be better with a newer model. In the case of the greenback, it has lost 95 percent of its value since the Fed was established. It lost 80 percent of its value while the present financial system has been in effect. That is, since 1971, when the Bretton Woods system, with its limited connection to gold, was abolished by White House decree. But while everyone knows the dollar gives ground, few believe it is unreliable. It is not the ruination of it that disturbs people; it is ruination at an unforeseen rate. Like the Argentines, Americans have learned to live with a greasy dollar. What they're not ready for is one that slips away from them too fast. Or even less—one that doesn't budge.

Their faith is broad. How deep it is, we won't know until it is tested. For the present, "You gotta believe" is the national anthem. Americans believe that their financial leaders have triumphed over sin and science, too. An Argentine recognizes that government will destroy its own currency in order to win votes and power. An American readily agrees that the Bank of Argentina would do such a thing, but of the Bank of Ben Bernanke, he can't believe it. His faith stops at the metal detectors.

Yes, theoretically, government and its central bank may be tempted to try to create more liquidity than necessary, but no, they won't give in to it. Why not? Because the markets won't let them, comes the unwavering reply. Ah yes, their faith stretches to cover free market speculators as well as government bureaucrats. Should the feds create too much money, it is believed, investors will dump Treasury bonds and force up interest rates, thereby reducing liquidity naturally. But for the last 10 years, a huge tide of cash, credit, and credit derivatives has flooded the world without a word of complaint from the speculators.

Instead, they got rich and built gaudy houses in Greenwich, Connecticut. They figured out how to snooker the system . . . shuffling and reshuffling money, slipping an ace up their sleeves when no one was looking. Liquidity—money in all its forms—was lapping around them, but who was going to complain? House prices rose. Stocks rose. Bonds rose. What's not to like? And finally, the head of the most successful money shuffler of all time—Goldman Sachs—has just been invited to Washington to take charge of national finances. Could anything be clearer? The speculators are not watching over the feds; they're watching out for them . . . and for themselves.

Meanwhile, in the popular imagination at least, great strides in the science of central banking have been made since the days of John Law. Asked what exactly those strides are, the modern economist shifts uneasily in his chair and mumbles something about improvements in data available to policy makers.

And this is where we begin to make faces. Our eyes roll toward the heavens.

We think of the improved data itself—of job numbers perverted by seasonal adjustments and changing definitions of employment that flatter the policy makers . . . of inflation figures shrunk by taking out inconvenient prices for food and energy and then hedonically acting as a prestidigitator, so that they practically disappear from the stage of GDP calculations that have undergone so much cosmetic surgery that they no longer resemble anything familiar or even human. And we wonder what kind of jack-ass would take it seriously, let alone rely on such conniving rubbish to formulate public financial policy.

In the past, the detailed information wouldn't have been of much use to bankers, even if they had had it. Their job was simpler. All they had to do was to make sure they could pay their debts—in gold. When they couldn't, they went broke. If they were central banks, the whole nation went broke. As simple as the job was, many still couldn't do it. Shady countries in sunny places routinely went belly up. Even in America, during the Great Depression, 10,000 banks went bust.

The Bank of the United States of America, run by the former chairman of the Princeton economics department, needs data because its mission has crept far beyond policing the value of the dollar. Expectations have inflated, too. Now, the Fed is expected to control the rate of decline of the dollar—a decline of about 2 percent per year is considered optimal. And as if that weren't hard enough, the Fed is also asked to control the economy itself—regulating the availability of credit so as to avoid serious downturns. That is why the Fed lowered interest rates to 1 percent following the defla-tion scare of 2001. It had nothing to do with protecting the value of the dollar and everything to do with avoiding a deep recession.

Not only do central-bank scientists have more data at their fingertips, they have more theories, too. Liberalism. Keynesianism. Monetarism. There's one for every purpose under heaven. It doesn't matter that they are contradic-tory. The banker is merely expected to choose the one that suits the situation and use it like a socket wrench. Crank. Crank. Problem solved.

And so, drawing on twisted data and convenient theories, the banker adjusts rates by quarter points. The prevailing theory in all the Western nations is that centralized planning is ineffective, troublesome, unethical, and stupid. There's hardly a serious economist over the age of 18 who will not point to the former Soviet Union and sneer.

"The market," they will tell you with a superior tone, "does a better job of regulating supply, demand, and price than bureaucrats." And yet, the operating theory of every central bank is that a group of civil servants, working with government data, can fix the price of the key set of components in the entire economic system: credit.

The economists may have their theories, their insights, their models, we allow, but how do they know that what the world needs is a Fed Funds rate of 3.75 percent rather than one of 4.0 percent? And how do they know whether they should be tamping down on inflation . . . or goosing up a business downturn? They may have mountains of data, but they are still lost on the slopes. They cannot tell us what the price of oil will be tomorrow . . . or the price of sugar . . . or the price of gold. They take their guesses along with everyone else.

Because the numbers are corrupted, the theories are a hodge-podge of wishful thinking, myth, and delusion. And the practice is that both officials and speculators collude to take advantage of the corruption and the delusion. Speak the truth to this kind of power? You might as well save your breath . . . and buy gold.

Gold Says, "I Told You So"

January 17, 2008

The battle rages!

    Unstoppable inflation on the one side; immovable deflation on the other. And what's in between?

You are, dear reader . . . keep your head down.

At least you know where you are. Most people have no idea. Most middle-class Americans are caught in this no man's land. Inflation is shooting holes in their family budgets, while deflation blows up their assets.

The headline inflation number for 2007, in the United States, was announced yesterday—at 4.1. Still manageable . . . but it was the biggest annual increase in 17 years.

But yesterday, deflation was on the offensive. The Dow edged down . . . and when we look at the charts of almost any market—France, England, Japan, tech stocks, shipping stocks (keep reading), retail stocks—we see bear markets.

And yesterday, we thought we saw the first signs of a bear market in commodities, too. Oil dripped below $90 . . . and materials and energy stocks suffered, as investors bet that a slowdown would mean less demand for primary products.

France's *Le Monde* chose this for its leading story today: "The Menace of Recession in the U.S. Grows Clearer."

And now, even the candidates for the White House are taking a page from Bill Clinton's playbook, entitled: "It's the Economy, Stupid." As Ed Hadas puts it: Now the candidates are saying stupid things about the economy.

Mitt Romney won in Michigan, largely by telling an outrageously stupid lie. According to *Le Monde,* which is our source for American political insight, Romney pledged $20 billion of taxpayers' money to revive

America's auto industry. We take this readily from *Le Monde,* because the French know how these tricks work; they have more experience with them. You take the money from the people who earn it, pass it out to the unions, insiders, and party supporters; the auto industry goes wherever it is going anyway . . . but the insiders travel in style.

The voters are ready to believe anything . . . especially if it sounds as though someone else's money is headed their way. Besides, everyone feels entitled to a bailout . . . from the lowest assembly line worker to the richest Wall Street bank.

"The source of the problem is debt," Lord Rees-Mogg explained at Wednesday's lunch. "There's too much of it. There's so much that the financial authorities and Britain and America have no choice. They have to try to bail people out. They have to inflate the debt away."

Too much debt is precisely what you'd expect to find at the end of any credit boom. When you give money away, you have to expect that people will take it. At least, as long as they believe they will be able to pay it back.

Presently, the yield on 10-year Treasury notes is lower than the consumer price inflation figure. Which means, they're giving money away. A shrewd investor would probably sell Treasuries and buy something with a higher return—say, gold.

Gold does not typically have any return at all. When its price was fixed to the dollar, it had a rate of return of zero. Which was a good reason not to own the stuff; you'd get a better yield from almost anything. But when the dollar was tied to gold, you didn't need to own it.

Every dog has his day. And it looks to us that the mangy cur that sits at the number 79 slot on the periodic table is having his day at last. He is worthless at producing a profit, a dividend, or an interest coupon. Most of the time he just lies around, doing nothing . . . like a rich man's pet. But there are times when he earns his keep . . . when he is worth every pound of meat you give him: He can be one mean junkyard pooch when he has to be.

If we are right, that stocks are in a bear market . . . and that the nation is headed for a slump . . . the wise *Daily Reckoning* reader will stop worrying about making money and begin to fret about keeping it. He will wish he had befriended gold when the price was around $300 . . . or $500. He will think twice about taking it in at $900. He will think even a third time on the day after gold goes down $20 . . . as it did yesterday. (Yes, deflation hit gold, too . . .) Still, our guess is that this gold bull market has a lot further to go.

How many of your friends own gold? Probably not many. How often do you see articles in the mainstream press about buying gold coins . . . or gold stocks? Almost never.

The last time a major credit contraction and bear market came around, circumstances were different. A top in stock prices was reached in 1968. From there, stock prices fell while loose monetary policy goosed up consumer prices. In nominal terms, stocks held up fairly well. But in real terms, the losses were staggering—about 70 percent to 80 percent . . . from the top in 1968 to the bottom 14 years later. Meanwhile, gold soared . . . up to a high of $850. Gold and the Dow actually came within a few cents of each other in 1980—when a single ounce of gold could have bought nearly the entire Dow.

Adjusting the gold peak to today's dollar, it would be about $2,500. Adjusting the Dow to its 1982 low, it too would be about $2,500. Is that where the Dow is headed? Is that where the price of gold is going?

We don't know. We don't know the destination . . . but we suspect that's the right direction.

A Look Forward at the Final Stage of the Gold Bull Market

November 9, 2010—Baltimore, Maryland

"Is gold going vertical?"

The question was put to us by our family office strategist, Rob Marstrand.

"We could be getting to the final stage of this bull market faster than we thought," he added.

Yesterday, the price of gold rose to new record—over $1,400. This was also the day that news reached the world that the head of the World Bank had defected. Mr. Zoellick jumped the fence . . . he's no longer among the dopes.

You know who we're talking about . . . the vain and foolish economists who think central planning will work. "Give the economy more liquidity!" "Raise rates!" "More fiscal stimulus!" "More austerity."

These guys act like they know what they are talking about. But they are quacks. Mountebanks. Phonies.

Not Zoellick. He said it was time to begin talking about a new gold standard.

Gold jumped $5. What can stop it now?

But there's always a surprise, isn't there? We know that the dollar is going the way of all paper—to the dump. Maybe the surprise is how long it takes to get there.

Maybe gold is going vertical. Or maybe it is just toying with us.

A friend came to us over the weekend. He had four Austrian Corona 1-ounce gold coins. He wanted to sell them.

"I just need some cash now. It breaks my heart to sell them, but I've got to pay expenses."

The expenses were a little unusual. He was buying a ticket for a Vietnamese woman and her children to come to the United States to live. But that's another story. . . .

Somehow, your author has gotten a local reputation as a buyer of gold coins. So much the better. We're not trading. We're not investing. We're just adding a coin now and then to our collection. We buy. We put them away. We forget about them.

"But at $1,400 an ounce?" you ask. "Isn't gold in a bubble?"

Well, yes . . . and no. We liked buying the coins much more at $500 than we do today at $1,400. The price makes us a little nervous.

Gold is in a bull market, not yet a bubble. It will probably stay in a bull market for a long time—until they re-establish a gold standard for paper money . . . or until the international monetary system cracks up . . . whichever comes first.

But there's something a little dangerous about $1,400 gold. Too much, too fast. Of course, in the final stage of the bull market, the yellow metal will trade for far more. Ordinary people will buy gold to protect themselves from inflation. They'll get sick of watching prices on bread, diapers, and gasoline go up. They'll be desperate to grab hold of something more stable. They'll buy gold at almost any price.

But we're not there yet. There's very little consumer price inflation now. The inflation we're experiencing so far is the monetary kind—an inflation of the monetary base, not consumer prices. No one particularly cares about this kind of inflation. The other kind of inflation—in the CPI—could still be years ahead.

Right now, the economy is still de-leveraging. Bloomberg has the news:

"U.S. households cut their debt last quarter, borrowing less against homes and closing credit card accounts," according to a survey by the Federal Reserve Bank of New York.

Consumer indebtedness totaled $11.6 trillion at the end of September, down $110 billion, or 0.9 percent from the end of June, according to the New York Fed's quarterly report on household debt and credit. Households have slashed about $1 trillion from outstanding consumer debts since the peak in the third quarter of 2008, the New York Fed said.

U.S. households, facing a jobless rate that's persisted near a 26-year high, have slashed debt and increased savings following the worst financial crisis since the Great Depression. That's pared consumer spending and slowed the economic recovery, helping to prompt the Fed's decision last week to start another round of unconventional monetary stimulus.★

People still lack jobs . . . which means they still lack money. And while they lack money, they need to cut back on their spending—which helps keep prices down.

The common man is not fretting about inflation. He's not worrying about his savings or the cash in his pocket. He's not desperate to get out of the dollar. Au contraire, he'd like to get into some cash . . . so he can pay his bills.

Which brings us back to this weekend's transaction. If the gold market had entered its third and final stage, our friend wouldn't have come over to offer us gold coins. Instead, he'd be holding on to his gold and would be desperate to get more of it.

"But what if he needed to buy something—like airline tickets?" you ask. "You can't buy things with gold."

True enough. But when we get to the last stage of the gold market . . . when gold really does go vertical . . . gold will be the *last* thing people will sell. Gold may have gone up $5 yesterday. But in the final stage it will go up a hundred dollars per day . . . or more.

Yes, dear reader, the excitement is still ahead. More hurrahs for the gold market. More profits for gold investors.

Trouble is, it could be far ahead.

★Caroline Salas, "U.S. Household Debt Shrank 0.9 Percent in Third Quarter, Fed Says," *Bloomberg* (November 8, 2010).

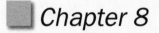 *Chapter 8*

The Gaucho's Guide to Investing in Argentina

Earth's Bright Side

September 27, 2002

"Did you see the news? Argentine workers are taking over the factories. . . ."

"Yeah . . . the factory owners are probably glad to get rid of them. . . ."

Your editor was having dinner with his friend from Argentina, mentioned above.

"My brother still lives there," the friend continued. "He said people are being forced to sell their furniture . . . even their wedding rings. Of course, it's great if you're a buyer."

As you know, dear reader, here at the *Daily Reckoning,* we always try to look on the bright side of things. So, today, we turn away from the darkening days north of the equator and look south—where the sun shines a little brighter each and every day.

It has been a dismal season below the Rio Plata. The Argentine Bolsa has dropped 85 percent in the last five years. If that weren't enough, the country has been in recession for the last four years—one that has been longer and deeper than the Great Depression of the 1930s . . . and worse than any downturn in the last 100 years. This year alone the national GDP is expected to decline another 16 percent.

Since January, the Argentine peso has fallen 60 percent against the dollar. So great has been the currency decline and the recession that typical monthly wages have dropped from near $1,000 at the beginning of the year to only $250 today. This places annual earnings of the average Argentine below nearly every country in Latin America. Even in Nicaragua, average annual earnings per capita beat those of Argentines.

Buy cheap, sell dear. Financial assets in North America and Europe are still dear, but getting cheaper. Financial assets in Argentina, meanwhile, are cheap. Mightn't they get dearer someday?

The latest figures from the Homeland tell us that 1.3 million more Americans slipped below the poverty line last year, bringing the total to 32.9 million. But out on the pampas, nearly everyone has been reduced to living like hogs.

At the beginning of the twentieth century, Argentina was about as rich as Europe, per capita. Penniless English aristocrats would send their daughters either to New York or Buenos Aires in the hopes of making a lucky alliance. Failing that, they could at least support themselves by becoming governesses and private tutors to the upstart families with plenty of money but little else. . . .

And gone are the days when the poor of Italy or Spain would load the decks of cargo ships . . . hoping for a chance to make their fortune in the New World. Now the traffic is in the other direction, with Argentines immigrating to the lands of their grandfathers!

Once a land of boundless opportunity, it is rare to see Argentina described in the press today without a modifier such as *hopeless* or *basket case* attached. This does little for the self-esteem of the proud race of the pampas, but investment value and self-esteem vary inversely, or so we think we've noticed.

For wasn't it the Japanese that had the most magnificent brand of capitalism the world had ever seen—just before they entered the long, slow-motion downturn which shackles them even now, 13 years later?

And wasn't it agreed everywhere that the U.S. model of dynamic, entrepreneurial capitalism represented the crown of all creation . . . at the very moment when U.S. asset prices reached their most absurd excess?

And, last year, wasn't Zimbabwe among the most corrupt, woebegone nations on earth? Yet, the Zimbabwean stock market has risen 120 percent so far this year—the world's top-performing market.

Which leads us to wonder: What market might investors loathe most today?

We have no ready answer. But we do not recall any comments about the wonders of Argentine capitalism lately. Searching the bookstore shelves, we see no books exalting the Argentine system nor any praising the genius of Argentine central bankers. Nor can we think of a single Argentine business tycoon, nor even a single product that makes its way beyond the country's borders.

Come to think of it, we've never heard a single comment about Argentina business or finance that was not a joke.

It is either feast or famine on the bolsa. The Merval index began the last decade below 200. The 1980s had been a lost decade with high inflation rates, incompetent generals, and a disastrous war with Britain. But then, the Brady Plan brought the country's external debt under control and the Central Bank was liberated from direct government control. These measures helped make the Argentine stock market the world's number one performer for 1991. Near 900 at the beginning of 1992, the Argentine stock market index collapsed below 300 in May of 1995. Then, it entered a new bull market that took it up 240 percent over the next 24 months. Since then, it has dropped back below 200 — wiping out a decade of profits.

If this is not the bottom for Argentina, it can't be far away; there is just not that much room left on the downside.

"The unprecedented level of the downfall that the Argentine economy experienced in the last four year presents a unique opportunity for equity investors," writes Marcelo Mindlin in the latest issue of Mark Faber's *Gloom, Boom & Doom Report.* "Argentina is very close to its record bottom and could rebound strongly over the coming months."

Faber makes a recommendation: "IRSA is the largest and most diversified real estate company in Argentina, with interests in office buildings, shopping centers, hotels, apartment buildings, and other residential developments."

The company manages 60 percent of Buenos Aires's shopping center space, for example, and 12 office buildings with 941,510 square meters of gross leasable area.

"Down from a market cap of $800 million," Faber continues, "IRSA is now trading at a market cap of $80 million, with only $120 million in debt. . . . If you can pick up real estate in an emerging economy at less than 10 percent of the value of its London or New York equivalent, I feel reasonably confident that its value will increase significantly in the future."

You can buy low in Argentina. We will wait to find out if or when you might be able to sell dear.

The Gaucho's Union
April 26, 2006

Yo no soy de estos pagos, soy de Arbolito. Lugar de mis amores, pueblo chiquito.

(I'm not from 'round here, I'm from Arbolito. It's a small place, but when I'm away I never forget it.)

— Traditional Argentine gaucho song

We are not from these parts, either, dear reader, nor did we forget you. But, we were not able to write to you yesterday, because we could get neither an Internet signal nor a dial tone—not even a hot bath. Life can be a little hard, out on the high plains. Over the past week and a half, it has been more than a little hard to stay in touch.

When we wrote last, we were explaining why we bother you with the details about our trip to Argentina. After all, the *Daily Reckoning* is—most of the time—about money, but there is more to money than just making it. For many people, indeed, making money is the easy part. Unmaking it is much more interesting and dangerous. A man can go through his life working away at his business with a fair amount of dignity, but only give him a little money, and he is almost sure to make a fool of himself. Usually, he spends so long making it that by the time he finally has some, he has no idea of what to do next. He lacks the taste, the experience, and the judgment to part with it gracefully or with dignity.

Instead, he is likely to squander his money on gaudy houses and expansive cars . . . reckless investments . . . bimbos . . . or even a ranch in South America.

But in your editor's mind, a big spread in Argentina was designed not to expose him to humiliation, but to protect him from it. Way out in the foothills of the Andes, he reasoned, how much trouble could he get into?

Besides, imagine the many sad consequences that could arise from holding on to stocks or bonds: In a few weeks, your investments might be cut in half—or worse. Is the dollar not doomed? Are America's businesses not losing ground to foreign competitors? What will happen to U.S. bonds when Asian lenders figure out that they will never be repaid? What would be the point of holding them? What pleasure could you ever get out of them?

When it comes to raw, mountain desert land—without electricity or central heating—what could possibly happen that would make the place less valuable?

And so, out here, we have gotten ourselves into the cattle business, and we give you the economics of it, lest you be forced to learn it for yourself:

The cattle are all grass fed. Hay is stacked up for the wintertime, but the hay comes from the bottomland on the ranch, too. Almost nothing is purchased, except some supplements and obligatory vaccinations, which only cost a few dollars per head.

On the other hand, you need some gauchos to mend the fences and go find the cattle, give them the required medicines, cut their ears, burn their hides with a brand, round them up, and load them on trucks to be sold. From what we could get out of Francisco, a herd of 1,000 cows spread out over thousands of acres of bad land takes a crew of at least three. Each gaucho costs the farm about 1,200 pesos a month, or about $400. So, setting aside taxes and other miscellaneous costs, you've got to spend about 60,000 pesos a year in labor (not counting the farm manager).

From a herd of 1,000 cows, you get about 500 calves a year, which you can sell for about 150 pesos each, which brings you revenue of about 75,000 pesos. But then you have to pay the farm manager and buy him a pickup truck. So, as near as we can tell you'll lose money forever . . . unless the Chinese start eating Argentine beef for breakfast, which is what every cattleman all over the planet is counting on more than he counts on the eternal life of the soul or Social Security.

But according to Francisco, if we do it right—that is, if we invest more money in larger reservoirs to catch the summer rains and in more and better cows—we'll be able to break even. At least we won't lose money, which is all we ask from any investment.

Thus have we come to Salta Province, and thus were we taking a tour of the property we had bought—on horseback . . . the only way to see it. And thus, also did we end up bedding down for the night under the skies.

At high elevation, even the skies seem more open. The stars seem brighter and there seem to be many more of them. It was a delight for us just to lie in our sleeping bags and stare up at them as they came out. First, they were just a few fuzzy flickers. Then, there were hundreds of them, more distinct. Finally, there were so many that they all ran together like a kind of bright, shining dust. There was the Milky Way, of course. Below it to the south was another batch of stardust we had never seen before, and then another we did not recognize . . . and another.

We could barely close our eyes. Partly because of the celestial lighting, partly because we were uncomfortable in our new sleeping bag, and partly because of the day's events, which like a rich meal, needed to be digested before we could settle into sleep.

The next morning, Francisco and Jorge had saddled up the horses even before daylight, each one of them sporting a montura padded with a sheepskin. You are comfortable in them for the first couple of hours. After that, however, you begin to squirm in the saddle, to twist and turn and try new ways of riding. You even stand up in the stirrups to avoid the bounce, which is how your author ended up spending two days in bed, unable to walk or move, with no telephone or radio, at least an hour's drive from the nearest doctor.

Do you see, dear reader, how one decision leads to another, each of which, individually, is perfectly reasonable, but all of which, taken together, lead ineluctably to an unexpected and disagreeable result?

Jorge, on the other hand, is a man who seems settled equally in his thoughts and his saddle. He barely moves in either. When we speak to him, in Spanish, of course, he looks as though he is working hard to figure out what it is we are saying, but is respectfully reluctant to believe we might be saying anything as idiotic as it sounds.

Translating our own phrases, we realize what our conversation must have sounded like:

"Buen dia," says Jorge.
"I wait that you had a good day both," we reply.
"Are you ready to ride out, señor?"
"We are ready to share. Let's go with God."

"Are you feeling okay today, patron?"

"True. I smell perfectly."

Jorge knits his eyebrows slightly. His smile fades a bit. He must have been wondering what it would be like to work for such a madman. But, he keeps his thoughts to himself and urges his black horse down the hill and out onto the open range. The rest of us follow behind: Elizabeth sitting up straight like a real horsewoman; Edward on his mule, wearing a white hat and a tan poncho made by the same people who made one for Pope John Paul II; the rest of the family and Francisco bringing up the rear.

Spreading his pancho out so that it covers almost his whole body, Edward seems completely happy. The mornings can be chilly, even in the summertime, but warmed by the heat rising from the mule on which he trots along next to Francisco, Edward seems in his element. In London, it sometimes seems we are living with an animal that has never been fully tamed. His instincts are out of place; his energy has no way to express itself that isn't annoying. But out here, he can run around, jump on a horse, ride for hours, and shout at the top of his lungs. In his own way, he is as much at home on the range as Francisco.

Francisco, of course, is a real gaucho, with a certificate to prove it. He even attended a gaucho school, and is currently the president of the local gaucho union.

"Gauchos have a union?" Henry turns the statement into a question by raising the pitch of the last word.

"*Si*. But it is not a union like other unions. We do not go on strike or ask for higher wages. We just teach people the gaucho skills. That's why we have a school for gauchos . . . so the skills are not lost. We also try to preserve the history and culture of the gauchos. You know, in each part of Argentina, the gauchos are different. Here in the northwest, we are not like the gauchos of the pampas—not at all. We wear different clothes, and we do things differently, too. Down there, they barely have to ride a half an hour to find their cattle. Here, we go out for days. And here, it can be much colder. I once rode around this entire valley for 15 days, riding 14 hours a day."

Hot Water

April 21, 2007—Gualfin, Argentina

Our architect, Nick, came up to the ranch a few days ago. He called the solar engineer to try to figure out what was going wrong with our solar hot water system. We are at almost 8,000 feet—nearly on the tropic of Capricorn—with clear skies and the strongest sunlight we have ever seen. We have a whole bank of sleek, modern hot water heaters behind the house; but as near as we can figure, they are producing less hot water than a garden hose in the Maryland summer.

Well, Nick got on the phone to the solar power engineer, and then went behind the house to turn a few valves. Ever since, we've had plenty of hot water. "Go ahead," we told Elizabeth generously. "Take a hot bath . . . use as much hot water as you want."

The water comes down from the Andes. There is no meter to the house. If we don't use it, it flows down into the pasture. The sun shines on the hot water collector . . . if we don't use the hot water it just sits there. Whether we use it or not, the price is the same.

And then, there's the electrical system, which has worked flawlessly since we've been here. The sun hits the solar panels, which charge up a bank of large batteries, which give up plenty of juice. The only trouble is you can't run large appliances—except for one refrigerator/freezer. And those LED lights are cold and unattractive.

The whole system cost $75,000. All you have to do is to clean the dust off the panels from time to time and replace the batteries every three years or so. What's the payoff? No power bills. What's the rate of return on that? We don't know, but if the utilities would cost $500 per month, the implied rate of return is 8 percent. Of course, up here the sun is so bright that conditions are ideal for solar power. And since there is no power grid . . . or any source of fossil fuels within range . . . we had no choice anyway.

But the nice thing about it is that the system works whether we have any money or not. It's . . . well . . . like having savings. If you have to pay $500 a month, it means you have to get $500 a month from somewhere. It is as if you had to pay a mortgage. Unless you have a stock of money somewhere . . . you have to work and you have to earn . . . just to pay your utility bills. In fact, at a marginal tax rate of 34 percent you have to earn about $750 in pre-tax income in order to have enough money.

So the real rate of return, figured on a post-tax basis, is around 12 percent. Not bad. And it's . . . well . . . almost guaranteed. Where else can you get a deal like that?

The only thing that would reduce your rate of return would be a big *decrease* in the cost of utilities. Not very likely, in our opinion. On the other hand, a big *increase* in the cost of utilities would be an implied greater rate of return on your investment.

Besides, if we are ever ruined financially, we can hitchhike out to the ranch and still take a hot bath.

As for raising cattle, yesterday, Francisco announced that the price had gone up.

"Don Bill," (we love it when he says that), "I just heard from some friends that cattle were bringing 2.6 pesos per kilo. Last year, we sold them for 2.2 pesos. This year, we're going to make some money."

Herewith, a brief introduction to the cattle business:

We went over the accounts with Francisco. Just as being an NFL quarterback looks easy to a plumber, raising cattle looks easy to an economist. Each cow produces about 0.6 of a calf. Down on good land, the ratio is more like 0.9. But here, the pumas, the condors, the cold, or the drought tend to carry them off before they can be shipped off to market. The whole farm is littered with the bones of dead cows. Big. Small. And in between. The drought of 2002 killed hundreds of cows, Francisco told us.

"It's a hard place to raise cattle," Francisco explained. "It's too high . . . too dry . . . and too wild. But it's all you can do here. I tell people that the condors kill the calves and they don't believe me. But they do. They attack them just after they are born, before they can run away. One of two of them kill the baby calf . . . then the rest come down to feed on it."

While the output is thin, so are the costs. The cattle are not fed. They are not kept in pens. Nor do they get any medication . . . other than government-required vaccinations. They're on their own. The only costs are the expense of employing the gauchos who look after them, which isn't much. And each calf weighs in at about 120 kilos when it is sold. So you can do the math.

Plus, up in the hills, the local people who live on the ranch have a deal where they pay us a percentage of the animals that they raise, in lieu of rent. As we understand it, we get 16 percent of the goats, sheep, and llamas. It doesn't amount to much, since there is little market for these animals, but they are tasty when cooked over an open fire.

Sowing the Wind,
We Reap the Whirlwind

April 11, 2008—Buenos Aires, Argentina

N ever did God give man such a sunny day that the authorities couldn't make it rain.

As near as we can tell, nature favored Argentina as she did few other places. She caused the Andes to rise up, and then over millions of years, let their hillsides wash downriver to be deposited in a vast, flat, well-watered, plain, with topsoil so thick farmers can abuse it for generations.

On the edge of this fertile farmland, and in the middle of one of the biggest booms in farm prices in history, the politicians in Buenos Aires have achieved what might have seemed nearly impossible; they have created a crisis in the agricultural sector.

"Day 20. The Strike Continues: Farmers Reject Government's Nine New Initiatives," says the headline on *La Nacion.*

But farm problems are not limited to the pampas. Thanks to globalization, they're sprouting everywhere. "Fears Grow over Rice Crisis," is the front-page story at the *Financial Times.* "Silent Famine Sweeps the Globe," reports *WorldNet Daily.* "Thirty-Three Nations Face 'Unrest' Because of Food Shortages," says the IMF.

All over the world, food fights are breaking out. Not because there is too much food or too little, but because it has gone way up in price. Of course, you could put that another way: The paper money in which food is priced is going down faster than usual. There's no less food than there was five years ago. But there is a lot more paper money. Modern central banking was invented so that we could have paper money—and have it in abundance. Now, we have so much that it is causing food prices to soar. But food is hardly in a class by itself. When one bubble pops, the authorities immediately begin pumping up another one. After the dot.com bubble deflated in 2000–2001, for example, up came even bigger bubbles in residential housing and the financial industry. Now, both housing and finance are losing air. But the central banks are still pumping hard. Where's the air going? Apparently into commodities. In other words, worldwide inflation of food prices is a monetary phenomenon, as Milton Friedman might put it, not an agricultural phenomenon.

To show you the scope of the phenomenon, we pull out a copy of the *New York Times* from October 19th, 1896. There, it is recorded in black and white that the average wheat price was about $1 a bushel—in gold— during the previous 20 years. An ounce of gold would buy you 20 bushels of wheat. Today, you can buy a bushel of wheat for about $12, which means, an ounce of gold will buy about 75 bushels of wheat. In terms of real money—gold—the price of wheat has gone down for more than 100 years. However fast farmers have added to the world's wheat output, in other words, central banks have outdone them, planting far more acreage in paper money.

And now that governments have caused a crisis, they are hard at work making it worse. In Argentina, the farmers are few; city dwellers are many. Argentina's peronistas can do the math. They make out the farmers— historically patrician landowners with large holdings—to be greedy and insensitive. The politicians imposed a 49 percent windfall tax on foreign sales. The measure should lower prices for Argentine consumers and raise money for the government, they reasoned. It seemed like a no-brainer. That is, until the gauchos blocked the roads into Buenos Aires and threatened to starve the city.

In America, the math is different . . . but the result is equally imbecilic. There aren't many farmers out on the prairie, but in Washington, there are more farm-state U.S. senators than pigs. They push and shove up to the taxpayers' trough to get huge subsidies for their hometown campaign donors—lately, in the form of bio-fuels. Corn-fed ethanol may make no sense in environmental terms or energy terms, but it lubricates the big wheels of national politics. In the event, it takes a third of the U.S. corn crop out of the food chain and puts it to use in the drive train—further driving up grain prices.

With bread prices on the rise, politicians feel compelled to intervene. And every intervention falls upon the crops like a cloud of locusts.

Last Friday's 10 percent spike in rice prices came as governments moved to corner the market. Three billion people, many of them with very marginal incomes, eat rice every day. The price of rice rose 50 percent in the last two weeks, causing Thai farmers to sleep in their fields to protect their harvests . . . while the Philippines posts armed guards at its granaries. Vietnam, India, Kazakhstan, and China have all restricted foreign sales. The exporters are coming under pressure to export less—in order to lower prices at home. The importers, meanwhile, have no choice but to try to get as much of it as possible, as soon as possible, in order to head off shortages. Result: a run on rice.

India's trade minister warned hoarders: "We will not hesitate to take strong measures. . . ."

Of course, hoarding is exactly what a smart family should do. Most likely, there will be runs on other commodities too . . . and then a run on gold itself. People will want something real . . . something sure . . . something with which they can buy rice, without having to worry about it doubling in price two weeks later. That something, traditionally, is gold.

Hoard it now, while you still can. Maybe we just had our last chance ever to buy gold for less than $900 an ounce. And maybe what we have now is our last chance to buy it for less than $1,000. The price today is $931. We are bullistic on gold because we are realistic about human nature. Give someone an opportunity to print money and you can be sure that sooner or later, come what may, he'll take it.

The feds no longer tell us how much money they're printing, but experts say M3, the broadest measure of new money creation, is higher than 15 percent per year. Let's see, money increases at 15 percent per year . . . and how fast is the supply of goods and services increasing?

Uh-oh . . . the IMF says the United States is headed for recession. Some economists think the country is already in recession. What that means is that the supply of goods and services is barely increasing at all. Which means, the extra money has to bid for the *existing* goods and services.

No need to beat around the bush about it. What this means is that monetary inflation is driving up prices.

The price of oil is $112. Wheat, corn, soybeans, rice—all the grains are near record highs, too. Many countries are banning exports. Many are controlling prices. Mexico, for example, has price controls on tortillas.

Of course, the real cause of rising food prices is a falling value of paper money. But only the European Central Bank seems to take its mission to protect the euro seriously—it's holding rates steady. While the ECB tries to hold the line against inflation, the rest of the world's central bankers are giving inflation all the slack they can. The Bank of England, following the U.S. lead, cut its key rate yesterday by a quarter-percentage point.

Let's go back to our war analogy. It's a battle between the forces of inflation and the forces of deflation, we keep saying—one side unstoppable . . . the other immovable.

But what kind of war is this? Glad you asked because we were thinking about that very question as we sat in front of the fire up in the mountains yesterday.

The Franco–Prussian war of 1870 was a great war. The French declared war on the Germans, for some reason that no one seems to recall. The Huns attacked, rolled up the French army . . . and laid siege to Paris. In the city, residents soon had to eat rats and cats to stay alive. Parisians exchanged recipes and made the most of it.

The whole thing was over fairly quickly. The Frogs capitulated, agreed to pay reparations, and the Germans withdrew (keeping the Teuton-speaking area of Alsace.)

It was a nice war because it had a clear winner . . . and because it was over like a good street brawl, before the cops came. And the Germans were very civilized about it. They didn't set up bases in France. They didn't stretch out the war for years . . . or make the French learn to speak German. They won it fair and square, and then went back to their strudel and frauleins. Which made Europeans think that war was not such a bad thing.

Then, came World War I. Ooh là là . . . this was a war of a different sort. It went on for four years. At enormous cost to everyone . . . millions of dead . . . trillions in financial losses . . .

. . . and who won? Nobody.

We bring it up because this financial battle looks to us like that kind of war. A war of liquidation . . . in which people lose money they thought they had—either to inflation or to deflation. Yesterday, Lehman Brothers liquidated three of its funds. And, as mentioned earlier, a big part of the stock market has been liquidated. And housing gains are being liquidated at about 10 percent per year. . . . Remember, inflation liquidates almost everything . . . including the value of American labor. As consumer prices go up and the dollar goes down, the relative price of American labor falls. The working man is liquidated.

But if this is a World War I kind of war . . . everyone gets liquidated—investors, lenders, borrowers, consumers, businessmen, householders, working people . . . everyone. People who worry about money will have less to worry about, in other words.

We thought about not coming back to civilized people—people who worry about money, that is.

Hard against the Andes, wine makers such as our next-door neighbor, Donald Hess, are making some of the best wine in the world. Next door is a long way away—about a 40-minute drive. But it's worth it. Not only can you stock up on wine, Hess operates a great restaurant, too.

Later, after we returned home, we sat in front of the fire and dozed off.

Maybe it was the lack of oxygen, (it takes a few days to get used to the altitude), or maybe it was Donald Hess's Malbec wine. . . . Whatever the cause, we drifted into such a state of relaxation that Juanita, who tends the kitchen, thought she should sound the alarm.

"Señor Bonner?" she asked.

Then, seeing that we awoke readily, she was reassured, and offered us a cup of tea—maté, of course. We drank it, put a few more sticks on the fire . . . and drifted off again.

In the morning, we had mounted up and ridden out to a little valley about two hours' ride to the east.

"That's where I was born," said Jorge, pointing to what appeared to be a pile of washed out adobe bricks. Jorge, now 54, had such a broad smile we wondered what kind of a childhood he must have had.

"I lived there until I was 17. Then, we moved down into the valley."

We had been riding for about an hour. The place where Jorge grew up was an hour's horseback ride from the ranch house, itself a 40-minute drive away from the closest neighbor, which is more than four hours from the nearest major city. Jorge must have had no other means of transportation except horseback. He must have had no access to school . . . or not much. He must have had little or no access to TV or medical attention.

Even now, as foreman of the ranch, Jorge gets a house to live in—basic, but not bad. He has no television, but he does manage to get a weak signal on his radio. His electricity comes from the same source as ours—a power plant we installed on the property last year. His hot water comes from a solar heater on his roof.

(Solar power was supposed to be cheap. But it hasn't turned out that way. Something is always going wrong. And each time something goes on the fritz an engineer has to make the four-hour drive from Salta to fix it.)

We know Jorge's finances too—since we pay his salary. He earns less than a trash collector in America . . . less than a hamburger flipper . . . all of $500 per month. But our bet is that his net worth is higher than most Americans. Jorge can't spend money—and can't borrow it, either. There is nowhere to spend it. And no bank would lend to him. And yet, there he is—a picture of health and happiness, a smile always on his lips, ready with a kind word for everyone.

Which makes us think the whole thing is a fraud. Worrying about money, we mean.

"You really should give Jorge a raise," said our business manager down here. "He hasn't had a raise in three years, and inflation has been running between 10 percent and 20 percent per year. Nobody knows for sure because the government lies about the numbers. But anyway you figure it, Jorge should get more money."

"Of course . . . of course," we replied. "But Jorge is already richer than any of us. We have never met such a good-natured, happy fellow. Obviously, money has nothing to do with it."

(We gave him a raise anyway.)

The Happiest Day in a Man's Life

April 23, 2010—Gualfin, Argentina

D ust swirled up so thick you could barely see what was going on in the corral. Edward had lassoed a calf. He was holding on to the rope and digging in his heels. But he wasn't heavy enough to hold the young animal. He skidded on the dirt and looked like he was water skiing.

The other *changitas*—the boys who helped with the round-up—threw their lassoes over the calf, too. One got another rope on his neck. The other caught a foot. The three of them slowed him down and then grabbed him, trying to turn him over. The idea was to reach over his back and grab him under his chest or belly . . . and pull him over onto the ground.

The boys struggled and tugged but they couldn't bring the calf down. Instead, the four of them looked like a rugby scrum, with the calf in the middle. Then, Javier came over. Javier was wearing chaps. He's Jorge's nephew and his right-hand-man . . . second in command of the gauchos and first in command of the cows. About 5 feet 10 inches, dark and muscular. He has a wide face, stretched even wider by an ever-present wad of cocoa leaves in his jaw, topped by a broad, blue Andean-style hat. A handsome man, in a rough, gaucho style.

Javier walked through the cloud of dust to where the boys were rasslin' the calf. With a single, swift movement, he reached over the animal, lifted it off the ground and put it down, bringing his knee down on its neck to hold it in place. He then drew a knife from behind his back, while the boys held the animal. A few seconds later, the calf had been castrated, tagged with a piece of yellow plastic on its ear, and released.

Javier put his knife back and walked over to another calf being held in place by another group of changitas.

The *hierra*—the roundup—had started early in the morning. Jorge and Javier put on their chaps and checked their syringes as the other cowboys began driving the animals from a holding pen into the long, narrow stone-walled entrance to the wooden chute where they would be held in place and vaccinated. We were a little short-handed, because some of the cowboys were still out in the field, collecting cows over about 10,000 acres of open range. Boys—the changitas—did the work of driving the cattle around the pens. Included among them was one little blond boy, Alejo, only five years old.

Alejo is the son of our farm manager, an Anglo-Argentine, originally from Buenos Aires. He ran along the top of the eight-foot-high stone wall, whooping and hollering along with the other boys . . . and occasionally jumping from side to side of the chute. The boys tried to frighten the cattle so they would move into the wooden stocks where Jorge and Javier could work on them. The boys didn't know whether they were working or playing; it was all the same to them. They practiced lassoing the cattle in the pens . . . and yelled with such gusto that the animals occasionally stampeded on top of each other.

Cattle will try to avoid you. You can get down in the middle of them. They'll run all around you. They'll keep away from you. Except for the bulls, when they get angry. The danger was that one of the boys would fall into the chute, where the cows were so crammed up together they stomped on one another by accident. Your editor operated one of the gates and tried to keep an eye on the boys. But there was no point to it. The changitas would have been trampled in seconds.

The roundup, tagging, castrations, and vaccinations continued all day. By the time the light began to fade, we were covered with dust and had barely enough energy left to walk back up the hill to the ranch house.

But this was not the beginning of our visit. It was the middle. We had arrived the day before.

After we landed in Salta, we went straight to the bootmaker. His shop was on a broad avenue, where we were able to park at an angle to the curb. Inside, there were large piles of boots and shoes, mens' and womens' . . . right on the floor. There were so many shoes. We didn't think the city had that many feet.

In the back of the room was an old cobbler sitting on a stool, with a blue apron and a workbench in front of him. He was hammering at a boot. There was no sign of modern technology. Or even any kind of technology.

A young apprentice sat near him, in front of one of the enormous piles of footwear . . . applying shoe polish to a woman's slipper.

The shoes were all in jumbled heaps. How did they know whose were whose? Maybe it didn't matter. Maybe customers left off one pair and came back the next week for another pair. As long as they fit, nobody complained.

At the front desk was a cheerful man with a round face, talking to an even more cheerful customer with an even rounder body. On the wall was a newspaper clipping with a photo. The man in the yellowed photo was a younger version of the man behind the counter. Smiling, then as now. With a little mischief in his smile, like a cobbler who enjoyed making pairs of shoes with two left feet.

The woman was making jokes. Or maybe just laughing at nothing. She was talking so fast, we couldn't understand what she was saying. And then, she stopped and turned to us.

"He's the best bootmaker in the North of Argentina."

For a second, we wondered who was his rival in the South. And then we got down to business.

"I'd like a pair of boots made to fit my feet."

"Well, of course . . . we wouldn't make them to fit your head. Nobody wears boots on his head."

"Good point."

After a little negotiation over time and money, we each took off our shoe and placed our right foot on a piece of white paper. He traced the foot and took measurements of the circumference of our calf and the height of the arch.

"That's all I need," he said.

"But what if the left foot is not the same as the right foot?"

"Then I don't want to make you a pair of boots. They're supposed to match. If they're different, they're not a pair . . . they're two separate boots for two separate feet."

"Oh . . . "

After the bootmaker's shop, we went over the Caterpillar dealer, on the outskirts of town. We had come in search of a backhoe. We needed it at the ranch to dig new reservoirs and canals. The rainfall in the area has been going down for many years. Two years ago, we got 120 milliliters of rain. Last year, we got only 100 milliliters. The rainy season is already over for this year and we got only 80 milliliters. If this trend keeps up, the whole place will dry up and blow away.

We've already sold off half the herd; the farm is huge. But size is a liability here. It can only support about 600 cows now. And, in the winter months, we need to irrigate some fields or there will be nothing for them to eat. So, we need to build bigger, deeper, better reservoirs to catch the little water that comes our way.

Your editor's cousin, Calvert, came along. He is in the construction business in Maryland. An economist can eat and drink as well as any man, but he is no good at buying backhoes.

Calvert inspected two used machines. He worked the levers and tried out the controls.

"This is just too beat up . . . it's only got 5,000 hours. But they were hard hours. The bucket wobbles a bit. And one of the hydraulic cylinders looks like it's been hit by a rock."

"And this other one is just a mess . . ." It was a local brand. On the surface, it looked like a Caterpillar, but it was made in Argentina.

"Easy to get parts," said the salesman.

"Yeah . . . and you're likely to need them," said Calvert.

Then, we looked at a third one. It was just two years old. Only about 2,700 hours on the chronometer.

"This one looks like someone took care of it," said Calvert. He got up in the cab and started it up. The motor made a low rumble . . . even . . . and smooth. The front bucket worked like it should. Calvert then swiveled around to test the back bucket. Everything seemed in order.

Then, we checked it over for signs of leaks in the hydraulic system and other indications of wear and tear. After a few minutes, Calvert came to the point:

"Ask them how much they want."

"He says it's $70,000," we reported.

"Well, a new one of this model, down here, is about $20,000 more. And you'll have to wait for it. This one is here . . . and ready to go. And I doubt that there's $20,000 worth of difference between this and a new one. So, if I were you, I'd go for it."

We went for it.

"Good Lord, Bill," said cousin Calvert. "This must be the happiest day of your life. You bought a pair of handmade boots and a backhoe in a single day."

The machine arrived at the ranch the day after the hierra. Javier was appointed the designated operator. That is because Javier is the only one of our farmhands who knows how to drive. Javier has an old Chevy pickup. The rest of the crew ride horses . . . or walk.

So Javier climbed up into the driver's seat. Calvert showed him how to operate the big rig.

"What you want to do," Calvert explained, "is not to think about it too much. You want it to be instinctive . . . you just try to operate these controls so that the machine works as smooth as silk."

We translated as best we could: "*Hagalo suave. Naturalement. Instinctivamente.*"

Javier's expression rarely changes. He shook his head and went to work, digging a hole in the rocky, dry ground.

We were going to build the reservoir near the house. This was decided after Jorge took us on a four-hour horseback ride to examine another place—the site of an abandoned reservoir. It didn't take us long to figure out why it had been abandoned.

Our horses struggled to get down one side of the mountain, across a stream and up the other side. The incline was steep, with huge boulders blocking the way.

"There's no way we could get the backhoe in here," said Calvert. "And if we tried, it would turn over or something . . . we'd never get it out. I wouldn't come anywhere near this place with a backhoe."

The horses barely made it up the far side of the mountain. We were so preoccupied by their progress . . . picking their way between the rocks . . . that we didn't notice the rocks themselves. There were rows of stones piled at right angles to the hillsides, forming low walls. We were making our way across one of these walls when Calvert remarked, "Ask Jorge what these walls were for . . ."

"We're in an old Indian settlement," Jorge explained. "These are the walls that held the terraces. Over there is a *pucara*—a fortress."

Jorge pointed to a hill in the middle of the valley.

"How many of these Indian settlements are there?"

"They're all over the place. The archeologists know about some of them. But they don't know about all of them. And maybe they don't care . . . there are so many."

"You mean to tell me that you're considering building a road through an impossible stretch of hillside . . . right through the middle of Indian ruins . . . and then digging them up to make a reservoir?

"It's amazing that you could even think of it. In America, you'd need an act of Congress to do something like this . . . and then you'd never get it."

Javier learned fast. Within an hour or so, the backhoe's movements were fluid. The hoe dug into the hard earth, curled toward the tractor, and came up full of dirt and rocks.

The new reservoir was under way. . . .

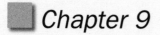 *Chapter 9*

The Expatriate's Experiment Abroad

The Accidental Investor

February 19, 2001—Ouzilly, France

"You got a very good deal," said Maitre Boulzaguet. "You bought at the very moment when prices hit bottom. Good move."

Maitre Boulzaguet is the *notaire* who organized the deal when we bought our farm in France. I saw him on Saturday night at a dinner party organized by Blanquita, a woman from Venezuela who is married to a local Frenchman.

"But you can't worry about prices," said the notaire. "You never know if they're going up or down. You just have to buy something you like. If you worry about money . . . well . . . you are doomed to be miserable."

By way of further introduction to new readers, my family and I moved to France a few years ago. Our intention was to come for the summers, while I was trying to develop business in Europe. But without ever really intending it, we found ourselves making a much bigger investment—in both time and money—in our French property. The house is a huge chateau-style agglomeration from various epochs and various owners— which was in desperate need of attention when we arrived. We have been working on it, and spending on it, for the last four years.

Maitre Boulzaguet is the kind of man you want to know when you enter a new area. He knows everyone . . . and everyone's business. If there is a local deal to be made, chances are he is in on it.

"Cuba is great," he said suddenly, changing the subject. He and his wife had just returned from a vacation. "But people are so poor. I gave the woman who did our laundry a 50 cent tip. But she gave it back. She said it was too much money."

Maitre and Madame Boulzaguet travel frequently. Their children are grown. They take advantage of their free time and excess money by touring the world.

"One of the best trips we ever took," he said, his eyes lit up with the pleasure of recalling it, "was when we went to the United States. We rented a car in Phoenix and then drove all over the Southwest. We went to Santa Fe and Taos. Taos Pueblo . . . *c'est fantastique.*

"But you know," he confided, his gray head bending in my direction, "you never know. Sometimes the trips you think are going to be the best turn out to be not so good . . . and often, those that you take without much expectation turn out to be your favorites."

So much of life is ruled by chance, dear reader, I feel it my duty to call it to your attention. Thus, I pass along this little memoire for no other purpose than showing you how some people cope with uncertainty.

When you marry a woman of 25 you can scarcely predict what she will look like at 50. When you get off the plane for a vacation, you cannot be sure whether your time will be well spent or not. And when you make an investment, you cannot know at the time of purchase whether the asset price will rise or fall.

Yet, you have to make choices. You have to decide to do one thing and not another . . . to buy one investment and not another. . . . And, important decisions are almost impossible to hedge. When you marry, for example, if you try to keep your options open after you tie the knot you are almost certain to wiggle the knot loose.

"You know what my wife and I do, though . . ." Maitre Boulzaquet continued, "we decide in advance, before we leave the house, that we're going to have a good time, no matter what. And guess what, it works. We've been to some rotten hotels. Even in America, we stayed in . . . what are they called . . . the Motel 5. . . ."

"Motel 6," I corrected him, "where they leave the light on for you."

"Well, I wished sometimes that they had turned the light off. Some were pretty good, but some were not. But it didn't matter because once we decided that it was something we wanted to do and that, good or bad, we were going to enjoy it. Well . . . we did."

The Boulzaguets had decided to make the best of their trips—in sickness and in health . . . whether at the Four Seasons or Motel 5 . . . they were going to have a good time.

Could there be an equivalent in the investment world?

Also at the party was an older gentleman, with a youthful face, but hair the color of snow and a pronounced forward stoop. I did not catch his name, but he helped me understand a little more of the French rural mentality.

"I think it is so nice what you have done with Ouzilly," he said. "So often, when a grand old property passes out of a family's hands, it goes downhill. It may have been in the family for centuries, but the new owners don't really have any attachment to it. Usually, it is on the market again in a couple years—after they see how much work and expense it is to keep it up. Then, it is flipped around, broken up . . . and is never quite as nice as it used to be."

"But you seem to have stepped right into the previous owners' shoes," he continued.

"Yes," literally, I thought, as someone left a pair of slippers up in the attic, which I have used from time to time, "they were broken by the weight of it. And now I am being broken down by it, too."

"Ooh là là," added Maitre Boulzaguet, "I bet you wouldn't want to add up all you've spent on the place."

"But it's a good thing you did," replied the white-haired gentleman, "because it was on the edge of ruin."

"Yes," I couldn't help myself, "and now it is I who am on the edge of ruin."

But we are all going to be ruined in one way or another. At least here I can enjoy my poverty in genteel circumstances, like the previous owners.

"But at least the land has gone up in value," Boulzaguet reminded us.

At the time we bought the farm, property was at the bottom of a cyclical low. At about $700 per acre, it was the cheapest farmland in Europe . . . and about a tenth the price of land in Maryland.

It was also about a tenth the price of farmland in England or Holland, which attracted a number of foreign farmers willing to master the complex farm subsidy system.

Whether it was the marginal buying by farmers, or an upturn in the French economy, I don't know. But between 1995 and 2001, prices of French farmland have doubled.

Of course, it doesn't matter. We've decided to enjoy the place. For better or for worse.

Planting Trees

August 27, 2001

"How is the garden doing?" I asked Mr. Deshais yesterday.

Our gardener has been a disappointment to me lately. He's stopped talking to himself. I used to enjoy his comments—spurting out of his mouth like water out of a hole in a garden hose.

But now I have to work to have a conversation with him, as if I were laboring on a rusty old pump handle.

"Oh, it is too dry. We need rain."

"Wasn't there a lot of rain this summer?"

"Yes, but that was earlier in the summer. . . . It has been dry for the last three weeks."

"I thought it rained hard a couple of nights ago."

"Ah, but that was the wrong kind of rain. Too hard. We need a soft rain . . . so the water gets down to the roots."

"You're getting very picky . . . "

"Well, water is the key ingredient. . . . There are only three things that really matter," he continued. "Earth, sun, and water. . . .

"If I had a lot of money, I know what I would do with it—I'd buy land. You can't own the sun. And water . . . some of the best companies in France are water companies. But I don't trust people who run big companies. I would buy land."

"But agricultural commodities are near all-time lows." I protest. "It's very hard to get a decent return on farmland."

"No, I wouldn't bother farming. Farming is finished in Europe. All the farmers have such big, expensive equipment. . . ."

He pointed toward Pierre's huge new tractor. "Sooner or later they're going to eliminate the subsidies and the farmers are going to be out of business. No, I would buy land and plant trees on it. Hardwoods, like oak and walnut. Every year, the trees grow. I'd rather leave my children land with timber on it than money.

"Children would just waste the money. Or money might waste them! But land and trees is a good patrimony. The land doesn't go away and the trees just keep growing. Every year they're more valuable.

"And you know what else, . . . " he continued, thinking big. "When you clean up around the good trees . . . you cut out the bad trees and thin out the plantation . . . you can use that wood to heat your house. So, they're another line of profit."

"In real terms," wrote Porter Stansberry recently, "according to Julian Simon, one of the most well-respected economists of the 20th century, the typical American worker produced about $2 to $3 worth of output every hour in 1900. Today that figure is between $20 and $25—a 10-fold increase."

Porter and many others believe there is a direct relationship between higher productivity, higher profits, and higher stock prices. That was, after all, the promise of the New Era. Information technology was supposed to increase productivity—justifying much higher stock prices than Americans were accustomed to.

Like a man who might have enjoyed a ham and cheese sandwich, but for the fact that he had neither bread, ham, nor cheese, American investors might have enjoyed the benefits of a productivity-driven profit boom . . . except that there was no extra productivity, and even if there had been, it would not have led to greater profits.

The rate of productivity growth today is still 50 percent less than it was in 1917–1929. And Jeremy Grantham of Grantham, Mayo, Van Otterloo explains (in *Barron's*) why productivity doesn't lead to profits and higher stock prices:

"People say productivity justified higher P/Es through higher profits. But I'll give you a simple thought experiment. . . . Say you come out with a seed corn that is twice as productive—that is, for every dollar of seed it will grow twice as much corn in an acre. Give it to everybody at the same price as the old seed. Productivity will double. But what will happen to the price of corn and what will happen to the profits of the farmers in the following year? I think it is fairly obvious to everybody that they will be drowning in red ink and there will be corn coming out of every silo . . . The whole productivity argument was interesting but it has no relevance to how much money the system makes and how high a P/E you should pay for it."

A report from the U.S. Department of Agriculture tells us what happened in the real farm economy. "Productivity growth is a more important source of output growth in agriculture than it is for other industries," it says. Working the earth, in other words, has benefited more from productivity gains than working computer terminals. Thanks to machinery, even a Democrat, out on the plains, can produce more wheat than thousands of farmers before the Industrial Revolution. (Think what he might have done if he had had access to the Internet!)

Yet, a quick glance at Forbes's list of the richest Americans reveals not a single person who has made his fortune tilling the soil. On the contrary, farmers have become so productive that they have shrunk as an occupational group from 70 percent of the population in 1840 to less than 5 percent today . . . and those few who are still planting and hoeing are now almost all sustained—in America as in Europe—by taxpayer handouts.

If rising farm productivity has not produced investment profits . . . what has?

According to Jeremy Grantham, "Timber is the only low-risk, high-return asset class in existence. People are not familiar with it. What they are not familiar with they avoid. But timber is the only commodity that has had a steadily rising price for 200 years, 100 years, 50 years, 10 years. And a unit of wood, just the price of a piece of wood—in real terms—beat the S&P over most of the twentieth century, from 1910 to 2000."

Thus does Mother Nature in her wisdom reward patient investors while punishing the day traders . . . and give the highest profits to a business that has benefited little from productivity enhancements. Even in this Information Age, dear reader, it can take 50 years for a hardwood tree to mature. But the annual return from planting trees has been 40 percent higher than the S&P.

"The price of a piece of wood actually outgrew the price of a share of the S&P, which is an unfair context, because there is some growth embedded in the share of the S&P and there is no growth embedded in a single cubic foot of wood. The yield from timber averaged about 6.5 percent. The yield from the S&P averaged 4.5 percent. The current yield on the S&P is 1.25 percent and the current yield on timber is 6.5 percent."

Not only have trees proved to be good for good times, they've also proven good investments for bad times. "In each of the three great past bear markets . . . 1929 to 1945 and 1965 to 1982, and a third one that's off everyone's radar screen, which is post–World War I, 1917 to 1925—the price of timber went up. It is the only reliably negatively correlated asset class when you really need it to be.

"One reason for that is that you can withhold the forest. If you find the price of lumber is no good, you don't cut. Not only is there no cost of storage, the tree continues to grow and it gets more valuable."

But no investment is risk-free.

"What about what happened two years ago," I remind Mr. Deshais, "when that storm flattened forests all over France? Nobody expected it. And the trees weren't insured. Growers must have lost a fortune."

"Well, at least they had plenty of firewood to heat their houses."

The Episcopalian's Guide to Airport Security

June 3, 2002—Paris, France

E arly yesterday morning . . . after his flight was cancelled . . . your editor had the illusion that comes so readily to him—of profundity.

"Coat . . ." the security guard had said to him a few minutes earlier.

"Pardon me? . . ."

"Take off your coat," came the explanation from the factotum.

"What's the magic word?"

Common civility has given way to security needs, it seems, along with common sense and common convenience.

You have no particular reason to be interested in my travel adventures, dear reader, but in today's letter I will try to think of one. And if not, well . . . the *Daily Reckoning* is, after all, free.

It was 6 A.M. For the second time in less than 12 hours, the passengers on Air France flight 028 had answered the same dopey questions:

"What do you mean, has my bag been in my custody . . . it's been in your custody. . . . I didn't even have a toothbrush. . . ." answered a grumpy passenger with bulging forearms, after a night in the airport.

Now we were getting another round of unsolicited close inspections. Many travelers were not happy. But few complained. After all, at least they were still alive. Their flight, scheduled for the night before, had been canceled after the pilot dropped dead of a heart attack.

"Take your shoes off. . . ." the guard continued.

"I guess you have a lot of trouble with people trying to hijack 747s with penny loafers," I commented.

But the guard was as insensitive to sarcasm as he was to courtesy.

A search of the computer databases at NSA or CIA or FBI would turn up few Episcopalian businessmen on the lists of suspected terrorists. Nor has anyone who voted for Jimmy Carter ever been accused of terrorism. Still, in the interests of security you can't be too careful.

"Smile," I tell Jules, "and the world smiles back at you. Common courtesy, like common law, common sense, common decency . . . and traditional architecture and value investments . . . have a kind of magic to them. Pay attention to them and good things happen. Ignore them . . . and you end up with monstrosities."

People gripe about what morons these security guards are. But at least they get paid for their part in the national charade. The rest of us are the real idiots—unpaid extras, standing in line under the pretense that every girl scout who boards a plane menaces the republic.

Your editor was witness to an amazing scene on a previous flight. In addition to the scrutiny given to everyone, airport security now includes deeper checks—in which a few passengers are selected at random. If you are chosen, the guards put on rubber gloves and riffle through your underwear and papers.

In the Saint Louis airport, the fickle finger of fate pointed at—you guessed it, a group of girl scouts. The odds that the girls—on their way to a jamboree—would pull out plastic knives and force their way into the pilot's cabin were, shall we say, remote. The plane would be struck by a meteor first! Still, the security guards worked their way through the girls' panties and mosquito repellant with the seriousness of an orangutan defusing a bomb. Even more astounding—other passengers neither laughed nor scoffed.

Often, we noted later, in our reflective mood . . . common sense finds few buyers . . . while absurdity is over-subscribed. For there on the table in front of me in the waiting lounge was a copy of Sunday's *Washington Post*. A headline tells us that the Bush Administration has just reversed more than 200 years of military policy . . . and thousands of years' worth of accumulated experience.

"U.S. Will Strike First at Enemies," said the headline, describing the president's new line. ". . . the United States can no longer deter attacks from other nations by threatening massive retaliation, but instead must strike looming enemies first," explains the *Post*'s report.

How will the United States know who is an enemy and who is not? That was not explained. Generally, a man waits until he is attacked. Then, he knows he has an enemy and has to defend himself. Striking first is considered bad manners. Plus, it seems to lead where good people would rather not go. A man who throws the first punch is sure to get himself into trouble—sooner or later—swinging at enemies real and imagined, until he finally meets his match.

"It is a dangerous situation," commented a friend in Washington. "I mean, the United States is the world's only super-power. Not having any competition makes people arrogant and lazy. . . ."

Success is self-correcting, we noted earlier. The greater the success . . . the bigger the correction that follows it.

Napoleon, you may recall, decided to attack Russia because it posed a security risk to his continental empire. Along the Seine, the vapors of arrogance and complacency had gone to the little Corsican's head. But his campaign against Russia slapped him in the face; it was a total disaster.

Later in the nineteenth century, Napoleon's nephew declared war on Prussia for much the same reason: national security. There was no time to wait, he argued. He feared the growing power of a unified Germany and decided to strike first, before the Germans could organize themselves and do real damage. The French army was not exactly prepared for action . . . but even after Waterloo, the Seine still reeked with the lingering odors of a bull market in French power. Like American investors today, the French believed "we will always manage somehow." A few months later, Parisians still managed . . . just barely; they were eating rats . . . as the city was besieged by von Moltke's army.

"With hindsight," writes Paul B. Hatley, "historians realize that Napoleon III's decision to go to war with Prussia ranks among the great military blunders in history."

The French learned from this experience. They've attacked nobody since. The god of war, they noticed, turns his back on those who strike first.

But the intoxicating stench of mindless pride drifted across the Rhine, where it took up a long residence. Kaiser Wilhelm II decided to take the initiative in 1914—sending his armies into action against Belgium and France. By 1919, there no longer was a Kaiser.

Then, in the late 1930s Adolf Hitler went on the attack, his nostrils flared with maniacal self-assurance. He struck first to the west . . . and then to the east. In both directions, he enjoyed great initial success—followed by terrible catastrophes. By 1945, Hitler was no more.

Of course, we do not presume to know whether the Bush Administration's attacks will be more successful. But there is so much we don't know. We don't know if the people we meet are good people or bad . . . so we smile and say please and thank you, anyway. We don't know if stocks are going up or down—so we buy only those that represent real value for our money. We don't know if striking at presumed enemies will make the world a better place or a worse one. But in Dulles Airport Sunday morning . . . we thought we smelled a strange and unsettling aroma wafting in from the Potomac. . . .

Reformation

May 13, 2002—Paris, France

Bonner—give up your passport and your citizenship. . . .

—A *Daily Reckoning* sufferer

"This is a quiet Sunday," explained a gray-haired woman speaking from the pulpit, "between the ascension of Christ last week and the coming of the spirit at Pentecost next week."

It was as quiet as a tomb this past Sunday in the church at Bourg Archambault. Almost no one was there—not even a priest. Your editor and two of his children could choose almost any pew they wanted—even arriving at the last minute. Entering, we stepped upon a granite threshold worn into a bowl shaped by centuries of feet, marking the rhythms of the church calendar. At our back, the balcony—which must have been built to house the overflow of the faithful—was completely empty.

So low has the stock of the Catholic church fallen that churchgoers in France no longer have to get there early. Except on certain ceremonial occasions, there are always plenty of empty seats. Spiders can spin their webs in almost any corner of almost any church in the Old World and rest at ease; they will not be disturbed.

The old priests are dying off—along with the parishioners . . . leaving little groups gathered on Sunday mornings to worship without clerical guidance. There is a shortage of new priests. But what does the church have to offer the young? Celibacy? Poverty? Dreary lives spent in dreary places listening to dreary passages from ancient texts? And no stock options . . .

While the star of traditional Catholicism has fallen, new bulbs have been plugged in to take its place—reason, politics, and the state! While the world once basked in the light of faith, religion, and the church . . . now an unnatural neon light shines into nearly every heart . . . and flickers into every nook and crevice of the modern world.

Today's world is lit up by politics as the medieval world was once illuminated by religion. But when a light is everywhere, all the time, who notices it? "That's just the way things are," people say to themselves—until the light goes out.

People in the Middle Ages did not even notice religion. It was everywhere. Their lives were organized around it—with religious events punctuating every important phase of life . . . and providing meaning and explanation for all that happened.

"Well, we can bring the lemon trees out now," said our gardener on Sunday. "The 'ice saints' are past." The "ice saints," are the two Saint's Days in early May that, in our area, traditionally mark the end of the risk of frost.

Religion was so important, people could not imagine life without it. The saints told them when to plant. The priests told them what to think . . . and what to do.

In today's world, it is politics that is everywhere and in nearly everything. The newspapers are full of it. There is scarcely any little hideaway in the entire economy where a man can nap away from the glare of politics. Yet, Americans hardly notice. Even the libertarians think that politics is the way to freedom; they can't imagine anything else. Got a problem? Think about it. Argue it in public. Put it to a vote. Pass a law.

Today, people think they can invent their own ethics and their own rules—binding themselves and others to whatever claptrap they come up with. Would it surprise you, dear reader, to discover that the rules they invent happen to be the most convenient for the fads and fashions of the time?

Nowhere on earth has this new faith reached such a zenith as in America. Hardly anywhere else on the planet are politicians, the stock market, and the state held in such esteem.

The French are proud to be French, not because of their government— but in spite of it. In the time since the founding of the American republic, France has endured five republics, two monarchies, and two empires, not including Vichy France, which we're not sure how to classify. They are no strangers to defeat . . . nor to treason . . . nor to complete confusion and national bankruptcy. They've seen governments, and currencies, come and go many times.

A friend gave me a book describing how nearly all of Napoleon's top generals betrayed him—even Lafayette, whose help was critical in winning the American war of independence from Britain. Some of the generals betrayed him more than once . . . first when he was exiled to the Isle of Elba and again before the battle of Waterloo. Some were actively negotiating with enemy forces, passing on critical information at vital points in the campaign.

This kind of back-stabbing doesn't contribute to battlefield victories, but it is a great boon to national cynicism. America's weakness is that it has been too successful. People do not reflect carefully when things go well; they save their serious thinking for when things go badly. The Frenchman is a skeptic; he knows that things are not necessarily what they seem and that even this government and this year's franc will one day be gone. The American, by contrast, is a true believer. In the long journey from feeble colonies to the edge of empire, Americans seem to have chucked their cynicism by the roadside.

The U.S. government and its money are considered permanent—like the Catholic Church in 1400. And in America, "freedom and democracy" are no longer subjects for examination, but objects of worship . . . popular myths, like the Virgin birth and the transubstantiation of the flesh . . . and similarly, beyond question. Doubters risk excommunication. (See note from a *Daily Reckoning* reader, earlier.)

We realize, dear reader, that our criticism of American democracy puts us in a very small minority—so small, we might be all alone!

And why do we bother? We're not sure. But we have a sneaking suspicion that politics, the Fed, the dollar, the stock market, and America itself are all overbought.

Until recently, foreigners admired the United States even more than Americans. What greater act of flattery is there then to send $1.5 billion per day to a foreign country—in exchange for pieces of paper?

But foreign investors are more skeptical than Americans. And they are beginning to ask questions. What will happen to our U.S. investments if the dollar goes down, they want to know. How can a nation maintain the value of its currency when it produces so much of it? Might not the Americans be biting off more than they can chew . . . with their worldwide War Against Terror? What would happen if we foreigners stop financing the United States?

We have no way of knowing, of course. The present trend could last another century. Then again, there could be a reformation at any time.

All Saints' Day

October 31, 2003—France

Pumpkins, witches, and cobwebs. With all the decor around Paris at the moment, you'd never know Halloween was once an unknown holiday. This essay was originally aired on November 1, 1999.

"Pumpkins. I'm going to plant pumpkins next year." Pierre has been raising beef—big, beautiful Limousin beef—and sheep for many years.

But the European Union is forcing down the subsidies for beef. And sheep are disappearing from the region altogether . . . there are no longer any subsidies available for sheep farmers. French farmers cannot compete with those in New Zealand and Australia. And wool prices are so low it no longer pays to shear the sheep.

Cereals, on the other hand, are heavily subsidized. The difference, Pierre explained, came about because the cereal growers could leave their farms in slack seasons and go to demonstrate in Brussels. Large groups of farmers always strike fear in what passes for the hearts of politicians, so the cereal farmers typically get half to two-thirds of their income from the subsidies . . . not from selling food.

Farmers who raise livestock, on the other hand, cannot get away. They're forced to stay on the farm day after day to take care of the animals. They pose less of a threat to the taxpayer's purse.

Even with the subsidies still in place, raising cattle is not a way to get rich. Pierre has suggested that we put our farms together. Apparently, you need bigger and bigger holdings to make money. And he needs to build a big new barn to make the operation more efficient. The return on investment? About 2 percent.

Hmmm . . .

Maybe pumpkins are the answer. The big orange vegetables are new to France. So is Halloween. All Saints' Day has been recognized and celebrated for many centuries. But Halloween is a new import from America, along with the whole shebang of decorations, customs, and commercial opportunities that accompany it. Department store workers wore costumes in Paris last week—stimulating interest and sales, no doubt. Even out here in the middle of nowhere, Halloween is catching on.

Our children held the first Halloween party in this region three years ago. The invitees had barely heard the word at the time. The kids took a candlelight tour of our attic, with staged shows of various spook-house exhibits. In one room, however, we decided to surprise them. We lay on a bed . . . in a room with wallpaper peeling off the walls and creaking floorboards . . . and put a sheet over ourselves as though we were corpses waiting for an undertaker.

As the kids came in, we began making a low growling noise . . . and then sat up. The kids were so alarmed and shrieked so loud we were afraid someone would call the police. Then they flew down the circular steps so fast that their little bodies were still spinning like tops as they swirled out the front door and into the yard.

That was three years ago. Now, Halloween decorations are in many stores.

Along with new things to buy and a new opportunity for secular celebration.

There is a world of difference between All Saints' and Halloween. The spirits that one honors on All Saints' were not, after all, all saints. They were real. They were spirits that might be honored . . . or feared. (Of course, if you don't believe in the spirit world . . . you have no business celebrating All Saints' anyway.)

But regardless of your views on the afterlife, All Saints' requires at least some reflection . . . on the lives of our forebears, on the challenges they faced and perhaps the lessons that could be learned from them. At the very least, you might stand before the grave of someone you knew . . . offer flowers . . . and spend a moment recalling the person.

This is not a ritual that lends itself to the Internet age. (But who knows . . . maybe you'll be able to order flowers via the Internet . . . and maybe the screen will prompt you to think about certain aspects of the deceased. And maybe AllSaints.com will be a big hit as an IPO, giving people a way to celebrate the ancient holiday without ever leaving their day-trading terminals.)

Halloween, on the other hand, is an example of what Philippe Muray calls *Festivus*. Muray has noticed the way in which the genuine, dark, primeval, wild, and dangerous currents and undercurrents in society have been tamed . . . and transformed into harmless celebrations. This applies not merely to the shift from All Saints' to Halloween, but also the political process, where genuinely revolutionary parties have been replaced by a token opposition and emasculated rebels.

We have often noted how you cannot even say what you want about taxes anymore . . . without fear of criminal prosecution. Yet, is there any real opposition—of a sort that might be described as dangerous to the government? No, we celebrate the First Amendment now; we do not practice it.

Likewise, America celebrates liberty. It is like Halloween . . . an empty expression . . . a hollow festival . . . something to feel good about. No reflection required. No risk, either. But what would the ghosts of Jefferson and Adams think of us?

Who cares? As the GDP increases . . . stocks rise . . . and the spirits of Liberty remain in the grave . . . pumpkins are the business to be in.

The Money Pit

January 14, 2005—Paris, France

The financial media is full of bores and quacks—just like Congress. But all the hacks share a common and vulgar hustle: They all promise you more money. There is something unbalanced about it. Only half a man's life is passed in trying to make money, and not necessarily the better half. The other half is spent trying to get rid of it. The following little letter is designed to help.

Last week, we drove out to a small town in Normandy. There, we spent two hours in a grim office signing papers. From that day forward, we would be responsible for the town's most remarkable building—the former seat of the local marquis . . . an eighteenth-century chateau. The place had been on the market for more than a year. Since no buyers who knew anything about it could be found, nor any who hailed from anyplace within 4,000 miles of it, your editor became its *chatelain*.

It was a moving occasion. The seller had owned the place for many, many years. There were so many family memories attached to it, she said. The poor woman had a small tear in her eye at the end; we barely noticed her winking at the notary when the deal was done.

There is something timeless and dignified about owning a magnificent pile of stones. It makes you think of the next generation . . . of eternity—that is, of blowing your brains out.

A man buys a house to live in. He keeps an apartment as a convenience. He has a beach house for fun. But he buys a chateau to inflict pain—either on himself or his family.

We bought our first one 10 years ago. It was an ideal investment, we discovered. Unlike stocks, or real estate, or gold—a chateau in France is a sure thing. Your stocks might go up, or down. Real estate, too. And gold . . . who knows what the gold price will be a year from now? But a chateau—a huge, old stone house—is much more reliable. It is practically guaranteed; there is almost no way you can win. You see, dear reader, the correct translation of the word *chateau* is actually *money pit*. There are more enjoyable ways to part with a fortune. There are quicker ways, too. But none is surer.

But even the vast expense does not fully describe the suffering that a chateau causes. Writing checks is one thing. But you cannot simply write a check. You must write it to someone. And therein lies a punishment—suitable for a serial killer. Each check requires a payee as well as a payer. And the payee of your chateau checks will be the local artisans, roofers, electricians, merchants, plumbers, cabinet makers, tax officers, half-wits, and miscreants. None will present himself readily. None will present his bill clearly. Not a single one will complete the transaction without innumerable meetings, compromises, delays, mishaps, threats, and misunderstandings. The process will not stretch out over years . . . for that suggests movement and flexibility. No, it is more like a long stay in a federal penitentiary, punctuated only by tedious visits from an incompetent lawyer—who bills by the hour.

Our first chateau fix-up project stretched out over nearly 10 years. It is still not complete. Not that there hasn't been any progress. When we arrived, the chateau was broken down, but at least we were in pretty good shape to tackle it. Now the chateau is in good condition, but we are broken down. And is it any wonder? We spent nearly every weekend and holiday for the last 10 years in a cold, dirty, drafty, smoky, uncomfortable place—our own chateau. We scraped the lead paint off the walls; we laid up stone walls in the icy rain; we choked in front of open fireplaces . . . trying desperately to get warm, we stood so close to the flames that our buttons melted, while our backs were still cold. We climbed up to the top of chimneys, 50 feet above the ground—this is a chateau, remember—to clear out the crows' nests. We slept amid the mold and mildew and contracted strange and wondrous diseases that haven't been seen since the nineteenth century, and excited the curiosity of medical school students. And we felt lucky; we survived.

But what is the purpose? Why make such sacrifices? Because, once you get the place fixed up, you can throw a big party, invite your friends and enemies, and show off. Just don't forget to do it in the summer. In the winter, the place will still be drafty, cold, and dangerously unhealthy. Even if you had a nuclear reactor next door, you would never be able to get the place warm. All the energy in the world is not enough to warm up these places in January. Which is why your nose will always run . . . you will have a lingering cough from October to May . . . and your friends—if they ever do come to your celebration—will look on you with pity and ask if they can call an ambulance.

All of that, though, is the good part. The bad part is that after buying this pile of rocks . . . and spending a fortune fixing the place up so that you will have something to leave to your children . . . the children themselves will want nothing to do with it. By then, they've spent hundreds of weekends shivering in front of an open fire, too . . . being asked by Dad to help with this or that. Whatever scales Dad still has over his eyes dropped from theirs years ago. They can barely wait to get rid of the place so they can return to a tidy apartment in Paris with a bistro next door. When you tell them that you intend to leave it them in your will, they will scarcely be able to wait; they are likely to club you with a fireplace poker right on the spot, and have the place up for sale before the sun sets.

To make matters worse, even after enduring the torture of buying and renovating a chateau (every one of them is apparently in urgent need of repair), the owner hardly gets the respect he thinks he deserves. The French look at him in awe; how could anyone be that stupid, they ask themselves. They've spent years trying to offload their own piles so they could buy a trouble-free place on the Cote d'Azur. Americans, meanwhile, look at him in shock; why would he want to do such a thing, they wonder. Even his fellow chateau owners give the man no more admiration than he would get from a Paris waiter. In fact, they regard him as pathetically *petit*. For no matter how much you spend, your place will always be small in comparison with others in the area. Here we enter into the strange realm of middle-aged male psychology . . . and the real reason we get involved with chateaux in the first place. For no matter how big yours is—viewed from whatever angle—it is never big enough. There is always someone fifteen minutes away with a bigger one. And when he gets drunk and flirts with your wife at cocktail parties, your sense of jealousy and inadequacy gets the better of you.

Which is why, of course, you buy your second chateau. It is a bigger money pit than the first. It requires even more meetings, more checks, more decisions, more drafty weekends, and more resentment from the family. But at the end of it you end up with a bigger place—and then you get drunk and flirt with his wife!

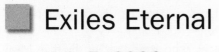

Exiles Eternal

July 7, 2006

"Is the weather nice? How's Aunt Gertie? And how's Tempest, the dog? He must be getting up there in dog years. Are the tomatoes ripe yet? Did you have corn on the cob for the Fourth? Did the relatives come up from . . . Virginia, right? And is that old honey locust tree in bloom? How I remember that smell. It used to intoxicate me. On a warm spring day, I remember I used to lie in the hammock and suck so hard at the air I almost fainted. Couldn't get enough of it, you know. People ask me what I miss over here, and that's all I can think of is things that smell. Yes, I miss the odor of the beech leaves in late autumn. You know, under the big tree in the driveway, and the grass after the first time we mowed in May. And even the odor of the crisp northern wind before the snow flies."

Exiled from our homeland . . . far from kith and kin . . . thus we write to our countrymen.

A man doesn't choose what he is. His culture sinks in to him without his knowing, like the scent of the trees and the swamps. He can ignore it. He can disguise it. But he can never get the smell out of his nostrils, like Proust with his madeleines. Traveling in a strange country, even many decades after leaving home, he catches a faint aroma that seems to waft into some part of the brain that is normally closed off, like a room in an old house where the dearest memories are stored. And then it comes back to him. Not distinct images. Not words. Not even actions. But a feeling that picks him up and transports him thousands of miles to a place he once knew and had forgotten all about. And that is what he really is. He knows it. He is not necessarily happy or sad about it. But he cannot get away from it.

American tourists wandering the streets of Paris or London squeeze their passports tighter than their wallets. They can't imagine anything worse than being cut off from the smell of home. When they go overseas it is as if they were visiting the underworld and in danger of getting trapped in hell forever.

They are not alone. There are many who would rather die than leave home. Socrates, for example. Told to shut up or face the consequences, he refused to stop philosophizing. His fellow citizens decided to put him to death. When his friend Crito asked why he did not simply leave Athens, he replied:

> Or is your wisdom such that you do not see that
> more than mother and father and all other ancestors
> the country is honorable and revered and holy
> and in greater esteem both among the gods
> and among humans who have intelligence,
> also she must be revered and more yielded to and humored
>
> and suffer whatever she directs be suffered,
> keeping quiet, and if beaten or imprisoned
> or brought to war to be wounded or killed,
> these are to be done,
> and justice is like this,
> and not yielding nor retreating nor leaving the post,
> not only in war and in court but everywhere
> one must do what the state and the country may order

Socrates might have gotten away from everything. He could have run off to Rome, for example, as was the custom. In fact, 300 years later, there were so many Greeks in Rome that Juvenal complained that they were ruining the city. "I cannot abide . . . a Rome of Greeks . . . there is no room for any Roman here." Nothing about the Greeks appealed to him.

Ovid, by contrast, didn't have to worry about any Greeks crowding into Rome since he was exiled to the Black Sea for writing what was either naughty or critical; historians are not sure which. He couldn't bear being away from Rome—even if it was filling up with low-life Greeks.

From his exile, he kvetched about the weather (too cold), the people (barbarians), the language (incomprehensible)—everything.

And to the poetry he continued sending back to Rome, he added plaintively, "I wish to be with you in any way I can." He even concocted a few lies about the climate—complaining about the snow lying on the ground all year round and wine freezing in the bottle—to get Augustus to let him go back.

We began to have doubts about Socrates when we learned that the neo-conservative bunglers behind the Bush Administration were inspired by the classics. It was a little like saying our broken-down pony was inspired by Man of War; the only thing similar about them may be that they have four legs. Still, it aroused our suspicions.

Of course, not all the ancients were homebodies like Socrates and Ovid. When the Cynic Diogenes, for instance, was asked where he came from, he replied: "I am a citizen of the world." He meant he was not ruled by local concerns and customs but by a more universal code, what the Stoics elaborated as a *kosmou polites*—or worldwide citizenry.

Marcus Aurelius extolled the virtues of the kosmous polites. "One must first learn many things before one can judge another's action with understanding," he said. But here at the *Daily Reckoning,* we have noticed that the more we learn, the less we know. Hardly have we got one idea down then another comes along to challenge it. We develop a taste for French wines, and then we discover Italian ones. We like living in London and then we fly off to Buenos Aires where we find we can afford twice the lifestyle at half the price. We were content in the paleo-anarcho-Christian wing of American conservatism—a voting bloc of at least two or three people— and then we discover that the French national health system actually works quite well. We finally master fundamental, deep-value stock analysis, and then we find someone who outperforms us using Vedic astrology. If we keep going in this direction, we wonder what will become of us.

In Socrates' view, the masses need shared values to make the city-state work. Today, the lumpen can't live without Social Security, central banks, and Major League Baseball, he might add. Certainly, the world's governments would have trouble selling their bonds if the next generation showed itself unwilling to pay off debts incurred by the generation that preceded them. And maybe it is true; maybe most people need the warm embrace of familiar places, familiar people and familiar holidays, pastimes and rules.

Elizabeth came back from Paris last night. She reported on the madness in the streets:

> It was unbelievable. When the French beat the other team—I think it was Portugal—people went crazy. They leaned out of windows shouting and flying flags. Everyone was blowing his

horn. It was amazing. We were trying to drive across town to the apartment, but there were mobs in the streets. They would come along and rap on the top of the car. It was kind of scary.

A few days before, we were in a cab in London. The cab driver said, "I guess you were watching the game earlier."

"What game?" we replied.

We cosmopolitans don't know or care. We are cut off. Exiles from everywhere, and nearly everything. We work in the office on the Fourth of July, and miss the Super Bowl, too. We have no voice in local politics. We get involved in no local action committees. And we only read the local newspapers for entertainment. "What will those dumb Frogs do next?" we ask ourselves. Meanwhile, the dumb things Yanks do irritate us so much we can't bear to read the headlines at all.

Are we lonely? Not so we've noticed. Do we miss the Rose Bowl? We never watched it, anyway. Are we starved for information? On the contrary, at a distance, we see more clearly what goes down in the homeland than do people living in the middle of it.

But who protects us? Who looks out for us? Whom can we turn to to get our highways and speeding tickets fixed? We exiles are exposed to the harsh elements—always in danger of getting rounded up and shipped off. We are in danger of having our visas revoked, or having our property confiscated. But why would anyone want to get rid of us? We are no trouble. We do not vote. We do not ask for any services or benefits. We do not complain. What would be the point? We spend money and pay taxes. Who could ask for better citizens?

But the more cosmopolitan we become, the more we wonder about home. Out on the Maryland tidewater, the old families spoke their own tongue—derived from a seventeenth-century dialect from Southwest England, we are told—for 300 years. With the language and time came history and eccentricities that made local life rich and interesting. But then came a homogenization that washed out the particularities. In a few decades, the place came to resemble every other suburb of America. Local accents were replaced by the English you hear on television. Tobacco and oysters yielded to government jobs. And local customs were replaced with national rules and regulations. You couldn't smoke in a restaurant. You couldn't build without a permit. You couldn't drive without a seat belt. Toss an empty beer can into the river and it's a federal case.

Ol' Cap'n Earl used to live out on a pier in the West River. He had built himself a rickety cabin over the water to get away from his wife. He would sit outside, drink his beer, and throw the cans into the water. In the summer, after work, when the river smells rose up so strong they were almost overpowering, men would gather out on the pier with him. They would talk. And drink. Sometimes they would pull a crab up out of the water. And the hours would pass.

But then some agency showed up. His cabin was condemned by about 12 different government agencies. Cap'n Earl, an old man by that time, was moved onto dry ground and died soon after. And then, the sailboats came, owned by Washington lawyers. They were soon so thick on the river that you could walk from one bank to the other, hoping from boat to boat.

No, all the baroque odors and smells have been scrubbed away. Now, the Maryland tidewater is no different from any other place in America. Our friends have grown up and become middle class Americans. There are no front porches, no rocking chairs, and no screens in the windows—no shutters. The old folks are almost all dead. No one speaks the local dialect anymore, except a few diehard watermen and unreconstructed tobacco farmers. And even the church seems to have been amalgamated into the general faith of America's great religion—where the greatest sin is being intolerant and the greatest virtue is recycling.

We are happy here on the other side of the globe. And then, when the wind comes off the Atlantic, we sometimes get a whiff of it . . . a ghostly trace of what we once knew. We pause. We stagger. And then, we remember:

There are a lot of exiles in this world. Each one has his own reason; we have ours. Long before we left America, the America we knew left us. We travel not to get away from it, but to find it.

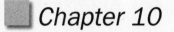 *Chapter 10*

The One Appointment We Must All Keep

Memento Mori

January 26, 2000—Paris, France

We arrived at the cold, stone church on a cold, windy day to put the cold body of my aunt into a cold grave in the nearby cemetery.

As we stood outside, waiting to follow the body into the church, one of the gravediggers tapped on the coffin as if to make sure a mistake had not been made. I listened intently, too . . . though I was sure there would be no sound from the other side.

He then began a conversation with Michel, a farm worker who spent his whole life—except for a stint in the Algerian War—on our farm, as his father had done before him.

Michel said he wanted to walk behind the casket, in the procession into church, along with the grieving family. He must have wanted to keep death in front of him—where he could keep an eye on it. He spent a career working with dangerous farm equipment and being shot at by Algerians. But it was his hobby, bicycling, that nearly killed him. A car knocked him from the road, and he hit his head on a rock. A year later, one eye still doesn't work right . . . and he tastes nothing.

His brother, Francois, was there, too. So were far more of our neighbors than I had expected. They could not have known Aunt Jacqueline. She had a stroke and lost the power of intelligent conversation before she arrived in France. But she still smiled at people when they came to visit and seemed glad to see them.

Mr. Goupil was there . . . the communist mason with Royalist tendencies. Madame Brule, whose husband masterminded the renovation of our house as well as the stocking of its wine cellar. Madame Livet played the organ. Mr. Ducellier, his mother, and his sister were all there. His uncle, Pierre, was there too. Pierre remembers growing up in a huge chateau with a staff of retainers to serve him. But that was then, this is now. The family fortune was divided amongst seven children and socialist governments. Pierre's old money is gone . . . he now earns a precarious living on a small farm, and tends to the local business affairs of an American family whose money is so new they haven't even made it yet.

His wife, Chantal—baroness by birth, goose stuffer by profession— was there, too. We followed the coffin toward the altar, preceded by Mr. Hepper, the Anglican priest, whose voice boomed with such authority I first thought a truck had run into the church. Aunt Jacqueline was as serious about religion as an Episcopalian can be. She would have liked Mr. Hepper. He looked the part in his black vestment, red hair, and bright, florid face.

She would have liked the whole thing. Aunt Jacqueline was never in tune with the modern world. She was a romantic who would have been much happier in the nineteenth century than the twentieth. In fact, she lived an Emily Dickensian life, in a house straight out of the last century— without central heating, electricity or plumbing—until the 1960s.

She had seen almost the entire century. Born in 1911—she had lived through the most remarkable events of the most remarkable era in human history. But she wasn't the least bit interested in them.

Elizabeth read a passage from the Bible in English. Maria read another in French. We sang hymns in English—feebly. And I delivered a lame eulogy in French.

Mr. Hebber then gave his talk. He spoke of the way nature works— with death as a necessary feature . . . and a prelude to new life.

I was doing my part. I looked somber. Grieving in a dignified way. But my mind wandered, as it does during church sermons. I could not help but think about the way the fevers of markets mirror the tempers of life itself—cycles of boom and bust . . . episodes of madness . . . greed, fear, the whole gamut of emotions.

A number of readers have written in response to my note a few days ago about the way Internet stocks have become a kind of currency. Companies are using stock to pay the rent . . . and almost all the expenses of doing business. They're exchanging them for advertising. They're paying off professionals—such as lawyers, consultants, and accounting firms with shares. Copywriters have been offered share options, too. And paying employees with shares has become not only possible, it's necessary. Employees insist upon it. Maybe they should print up some shares in small denominations for cab fare and restaurant tips, too.

Of course, other businesses accept the shares as payment for stock—as in the AOL Time Warner deal. But Internet stocks are not the only ones creating new currency. UPS launched the largest IPO ever last October. Their stated purpose was to get a currency that could be used for acquisitions. But this deal illustrates how currencies inevitably go bad over time.

The idea of investing is that the money you put in is used for capital improvements that end up producing something that can be sold at a profit. The UPS money, however, will do no such thing. UPS is owned by employees. They are selling their shares to the public. The money ends up in the pockets of the employees, not in capital improvements. In fact, a UPS spokesman admitted that the men in brown had no particular need for capital. They have plenty of trucks and airplanes already.

If you can create wealth just by saying so—you will say so often. You will do so until your say-so becomes completely worthless. Even UPS—which is a real company with real profits—sold 100,000,000 shares in October. But over the next 18 months, employees will be free to sell more and more of the shares they still hold. If they all decided to sell, the market would have to absorb more than one billion shares! If you have a currency, in other words, it is just a matter of time before it is an inflated currency.

This is why most currencies have a shorter lifespan than a drug dealer in Baltimore.

The Federal Reserve was begun in the year Aunt Jacqueline was born. The currency that had been stable for a century then began a decline that took 95 percent of its value away by the time of her death. The competition had been removed from the currency market. The Federal Reserve could create money—just by saying so. But compared to a lot of other currencies, the dollar has been as upright as a Baptist.

Back in America, I have a few currencies framed on my wall. They are beautiful—but, except as art, totally worthless. I bought them from Doug Casey, more than a quarter century ago . . . at a time when his own business fortunes were at a cyclical low.

Aunt Jacqueline was still a young girl when the Reichsmark became worth less than the paper it was printed on. Even before that, the Tsarist-era Russian bonds, which were plastered all over France, and practically used as currency, had become worthless. She was 18 years old when the U.S. stock market crashed . . . and her father almost went bankrupt.

In the years that followed, hundreds of currencies became extinct. Dozens in South America. Remember the austral? Colons. Pesos. Sucres.

And currency destruction is not limited to Latin countries. Rubles. Dinars. Lire. Baht. Just say the words and smile, because they are what American tourists call *funny money.*

I remember traveling in Poland in the 1970s. Zlotys were practically worthless then. God knows what happened to them. Here in France, the franc had lost about 99 percent of its value since 1913 when DeGaulle knocked two zeros off in 1958.

Among Aunt Jacqueline's effects is a U.S. War Bond from 1942. The issuer is still solvent—and now paying off its debts. But the currency is not the same currency it was in 1942. Were she alive to collect, the $25 bond might be worth only about $1.09 in real terms.

Currencies expire as people do. But no one comes to the funeral. Christians believe that the sadness they feel at a funeral is for themselves . . . not for the dead. When a person dies, he goes on to a better life in a better place. The veil of tears is lifted. We say Hallelujah . . . "even unto the grave." But there is no cause for celebration when a currency goes bad.

After the service in church, the mourners filed by the coffin and sprinkled holy water on it. The casket was then turned around by two spindly men, who looked like they might lose control of it, and placed back in the hearse. We followed, on foot, in procession to the graveyard, where the coffin was lowered into the ground and Mr. Hepper tossed the dirt upon it. "Ashes to ashes," he said, "Dust to dust."

Thom Hickling, R.I.P.

*December 28, 2005—Rancho San Jose
de los Perros, Nicaragua*

Mornings are always the same in paradise. The sky lightens. Clouds always seem to hang over the mountains to the east. They turn crimson on the edges and then, gradually pink, until the sun shows itself beneath them. It is a new day, just like the last one . . . and like none that has ever happened before.

Far out on the horizon, the sea is completely flat. Then, closer to us, we see a chaos of small waves. But as we look to the shore, the waves form great rolling swells that crash into the rocks and pound down on the soft beach like an avalanche on a small mountain village. Except, it happens about once every 12 seconds and goes on night and day for all eternity. It is amazing that there are any rocks or beach left.

Today, we shuffle to our computers and sit with our shoulders stooped and our heads low. We reckon today, as we do every day, but we reckon with a heavy heart. For we have lost one of our *Daily Reckoning* founding fathers . . . a dear reader . . . and a dear friend.

Thom Hickling was visiting his daughter, Holly, in Zambia, Africa, where she manages a refugee center. He had gone to spend Christmas with her. He sent us a photo just a couple days ago, showing the two of them, guitars in hand, entertaining a local crowd with Christmas carols, blues, rock and roll, and gospel songs. But the family got a call yesterday. Thom died in an auto accident. We are still not sure what has become of Holly.

We have always had a fondness for minstrels, misfits, and lost causes. At one time or another, Thom was probably all those things. He also had a wonderful habit of being around when you needed him . . .

We recall the first time we saw Thom—about 35 years ago. He wore a snappy outfit from the 1970s . . . and had a guitar on his back. The last time we saw him was only a week ago, at our Christmas party in Baltimore. He had not changed. He wore a pair of silver-trimmed cowboy boots, a shimmery silk jacket, and one of those Texas string ties you could hang a man with. It was an odd get-up for Baltimore, but Thom could make something like that work. Earlier in the day, Thom had led our annual meeting; he managed to turn a dull corporate event into lively entertainment. Same thing at the party; Thom took over the microphone. Pretty soon, the whole place was rocking. Somehow, Thom could create a party just by walking into a room.

We also recall that when the *Daily Reckoning* was only an idea, Thom came along and got it going. He didn't know much more about the Internet than the rest of us, but he was willing to try almost anything. And he had a network of contacts all his own. He brought in some of his musician friends. They wore their baseball caps backward, but they were forward looking when it came to technology. Somehow, the reckonings started going out in the last summer of the twentieth century.

Another time, Thom was on hand when your editor thought he was dying. You need a good man around when you think your time has come. Thom comforted the family. Thom called the ambulance. Thom recorded our last words. And Thom prayed. Who knows? Maybe it was the prayers that turned the event from a tragedy into a farce. Thom was there when we needed him. He almost saved our life. We only wish we could have saved his.

And so it is a new day . . . and a new world . . . It is not the world we wanted. It is not the one we made.

But it is the old world, too. For the waves keep coming, one after another. Yesterday, they were glorious and beautiful. Today, they are dreary and relentless. Never stopping. Never slowing. The sea never goes quiet. The noise of it this morning was so awful we had to close the windows. But the groan continued, like a monster howling outside the city walls.

The waves keep bashing against the shore . . . wearing it down . . . pulverizing every rock . . . bleaching out every shell and tree . . . pounding, smashing, crushing, rubbing, melting, grinding . . . until every heart is broken . . . and every dream is turned to sand.

Thom, R.I.P.

Requiem for an Economist

September 12, 2007

D
r. Kurt Richebächer died about two weeks ago in his home in Cannes, France. He, and his insights into the world financial markets, will be greatly missed by long-suffering *DR* readers and editors alike.

One of our greatest complaints is the way the modern world pays homage to its dead.

When a good man finally has the mud tossed on his face, he is almost instantly forgotten; so little notice is taken, it hardly seems worth dying. Meanwhile, those who are widely mourned and greatly regretted usually don't deserve it. When Lindsay Lohan dies, for example, America will probably declare three days of national mourning and hang black crepe on the Capitol.

Kurt Richebächer met his end with hardly an *ave* from anyone but friends and family. We pause to remember him here for both sentimental reasons and practical ones. On the sentimental side, we remember him as an old friend and fellow idealist. On the practical side he, and practically he alone, understood the worldwide economic boom for what it really is—a sham.

Frank Laarman, R.I.P.

December 1, 2009

The older you get, the lonelier you become. That is not because you become anti-social. It is because your friends die.

Your editor is only 61. He is not a particularly social fellow. His wife thinks he is a curmudgeon, because he does not tarry at cocktail receptions or join in Super Bowl parties. He rarely stays up after midnight; and has never heard anyone say anything after the midnight bell that was worth staying up for. And to make it worse, he is an economist of the finger-wagging, I-told-you-so school.

A man of this sort does not accumulate many friends. So when he loses one, he feels like a bum whose last quarter rolled down a storm drain.

On Monday, we went to a funeral for a dear friend, Frank. The service was held in an old and beautiful church in the heart of Paris, St. Julien Le Pauvre.

"Isn't that just like Frank," said a fellow mourner. "He couldn't even be buried like everyone else."

Frank was Catholic. "Not to believe would be vulgar," he said after receiving last rites.

He chose St. Julien le Pauvre for his funeral service because it is a Catholic church, but it is also much more than that. It is in the hands of a sect we had never heard of—the Melkite Greek Catholics. The group comes from the Near East, with its headquarters still in Damascus, and now has parishes all over the world, with an important cathedral in Roslindale, Massachusetts. It claims descent directly from the apostles Peter and Paul, but through a long and twisted lineage, threading itself through the history of the Levant. Melkite Christians are the product of an old schism. They were part of the Eastern Empire and subject to the authority of Constantinople for centuries. Then, the Muslims took over . . . adding

Arabic flourishes and poetry to the Melkite rites. Later, the Melkites joined with the Roman Catholics, with whom they remain united.

Frank was an architect. The last time we saw him—when he was already feeling the heavy hand of the Reaper on his shoulder—we talked about building. We told him about our project at the ranch in South America, where we are planning to build, by hand, a vaulted ceiling out of local stone and adobe. It is fairly easy to imagine it, but very difficult to figure out how to build it in practice. How do you frame it up so that it is rounded in the right places . . . and intersects a different curve going in the other direction?

Frank had done a vaulted ceiling himself, in stone, in a house he built with his three sons. If he could do it, we reasoned, we could do it, too. But Frank was an architect; we are only a feral economist.

Frank took us over to the basement door. Leaning on a cane, he invited us to go down and have a look. We saw what he had done, like a wine cellar with a vaulted roof. It was not exactly what we had in mind, so we explained and Frank took out paper and pencil to instruct us. Still it was difficult to grasp the intersection of the two curves, at a 90-degree angle one to the other, from his drawing.

"I need to see this in stone in order to understand it," we said.

"Don't worry, you'll see it soon enough," he said.

"What do you mean?"

"Just keep your eyes open."

Saint Julien is a marvelous old church, built in the thirteenth century. It was built and rebuilt and built again, according to the history books. But in the thirteenth century, the present shape took form.

Then, as recently as the 1920s, Saint Julien became the scene of an important event in the art world. Tristan Tzara, Andre Breton, and Philippe Soupault staged the last major "Dada excursion" there. The Dadaists shouted a stream of idiotic and absurd remarks to passersby. That was the idea: to stir up interest in the absurdity of life itself. It was a form of marketing, designed to raise the public's awareness of Dada and perhaps give the artists more street cred. It failed. The public ignored them. Breton and Soupault then split off from Tzara and formed the surrealist movement.

Frank had little interest in the Dadaists. As far as we know, he had no particular interest in the Melkite schism either. It was the building itself and the richness of the ceremony he admired. The church is built entirely of stone. It is small, intimate, with an ornate wooden panel that embellishes the sacristy in front of worshippers. On the walls hang religious paintings and icons in the Eastern Orthodox style. The priest was dressed in the Eastern style, too. Though not Orthodox, he could be easily mistaken for one of that ilk, with a black cloth stretched over a flat rack on the top of his head, falling gracefully to his shoulders and down his back.

The service began with chants and a sung Greek liturgy. It had the flavor of monasteries, minarets, and strong coffee. . . . At times, the words were clearly French. At other times, we weren't sure. There were the usual bible readings . . . and a homily from the priest.

We were lost in thought . . . mostly remembering Frank and wondering why we had seen so little of each other in the 30 years we had known each other. Frank was a much more reflective man than we are. We write. Frank thought. And when he talked, we listened carefully. Because his thoughts were not the rough brew of columnists and pundits. They were the distilled spirits of the serious thinker. Rich. And strong. Often, when we were considering a subject, we would ask ourselves . . . "What would Frank think of this?"

Now, it is too late to ask him. We'll have to think for ourselves.

As we were thus occupied with our thoughts, our eyes rolled upward. There were columns running down both sides of the church, spaced about the same distance as those we intended for our project at the ranch. We followed them up to where they branched out, expanded . . . and vaulted over the ceiling. And yes, there were the criss-crossing supports . . . the frame on which to rest our ceiling . . . and the angles, formed naturally by the intersection of the two vaulted sections . . . just as we had imagined it.

Our mouths were open. We tilted our heads upward. We studied the ceiling. And we thought we heard a voice whisper: "Just open your eyes."

Adieu, Frank.

Remembrance of Fanny

September 8, 2010

Last week in Paris was a wonderful, awful time. Left on our own, we saw old friends. We dined at sidewalk cafes in neighborhoods we had never seen before. And on the weekend, we did something we hadn't done in years—nothing. We walked the streets and enjoyed the low, warm sun of late summer.

But a pall hung over the week too. We were on death watch. A friend and colleague was dying. She was only in her 30s . . . young and beautiful, with two small children. It didn't seem possible. Not in this age of medical miracles. But one course of treatment had not stopped the cancer. Neither did the second. Or the third. No one wanted to believe it was happening . . . least of all, the patient herself . . . not until the end drew close.

We went to see her in the hospital. She had lost all her hair and much weight. But her face never looked better . . . with skin so clear and fine, it looked as though she was already among the angels.

"What do you think?" she asked. "Did I do something wrong? How come this is happening to me?"

What could we say?

"I don't know. . . . Things happen. We don't know why."

"It would be so much easier to be a believer [in God . . . in the Resurrection . . . in Eternal Life . . .] . . . I'd like to think I was going to Heaven. . . ."

"What do we know? Maybe it's true. Why not believe?"

Where she was headed, we don't know. But she left this world yesterday.

Let it be. Let it be.

R.I.P.

Life Goes On

April 23, 2010—Gualfin, Argentina

"The poor little girl saw her mother in the house, naked, with a man. . . ."

The adobe houses that people live in up in the mountains are not very big. Usually just one or two rooms. There are not many secrets in family life.

"At least they could go outside, behind some bushes or something. . . . You'd think this place is a paradise. . . ."

In many ways, it is paradise. The valleys are green. The sky is blue. The sun is hot. There are no traffic jams. No drug dealers. No TV. No stone-hearted tax collectors. No stonehead politicians. No crackpot economists.

"But these children are not innocent . . . they've seen everything. . . . Well, not the same things that kids in the city have seen . . . but they are not innocent. The problem here is that they don't have families. . . . Not all of them, of course. But a lot of the girls just have babies. First with one man . . . then with another. . . . And sometimes they start as young as 12 years old. They see their mothers . . . and then they do the same thing."

We had invited the entire local school over for an outing. Two teachers—Olivia and Lilliane—along with their 23 students. Lilliane, a slim, attractive woman in her 40s, with black hair pulled back in a bun and bright read lips, was telling us about the problems they face:

"I've been here for 26 years. We used to have twice as many students as we do now. But now the girls don't have as many children. They know how to avoid getting pregnant. But they still carry on. . . .

"And they're bolder and naughtier than they used to be. I woke up one night and found one older boy had snuck into the school and was in bed with one of the girls. We had to make a rule . . . no one gets to stay in the school after they are older than 12. But even that doesn't seem like enough. One night we found a boy of 10 in bed with a girl of 11. They're just too young for that kind of thing.

"Many of the children stay with us because they live too far up in the hills to go home at night. And some of them live so far away that they have to stay with us on the weekends, too. We have nine who stay with us on the weekends now.

"But it's exhausting for us, because we have to keep an eye on them at night. . . . We can't trust the children to behave themselves."

When the children arrived, they filed into the house quietly, timidly. Many of them had never been in a real house before.

"Have a seat . . . sit down," we told them.

They sat down without a word. The house was silent. Our Spanish is not good enough to entertain a group of 23 children. In a flash of inspiration, we picked up the guitar and started singing the first song that occurred to us:

"Your cheatin' heart . . . will tell on you. . . ."

The kids giggled.

By the time we finished the final verse, Elizabeth had brought in the *pan casero* (homemade, unleavened bread) with marmalade on it. They had brought their own cups, into which we poured *mate cocido*—a type of herb tea.

The kids seemed satisfied. When they were finished, they went out into the courtyard.

"Gimme five," said Calvert loudly, to a group of boys. "Up high . . . down low . . . uh oh . . . too slow."

The boys laughed. One by one, they tried to slap Calvert's hand before he jerked it away. Then, Edward got out his soccer ball and the boys all played.

As for the girls, we don't know what they were doing. But our Argentine friend, Maria, had gotten back to the house by then. She had been on a long ride on a short, uncomfortable mule. Maria plays the guitar and sings too, only people don't laugh at her. She must have entertained the girls somehow.

Maria was the last to come back from our outing. We had left the house early in the morning to ride up to see Dona Ileena—an old woman who lives high in the mountains. Her husband, Felix, fell down a few weeks ago and hit his head. He was taken down from their lodge and driven to a hospital a couple of hours away. That left Ileena alone. No one had seen her in several days; we thought we should pay her a visit.

We don't know how Maria ended up on the mule. But she was a good sport about it. On the way back, she switched mounts with someone else, but then went back to the mule.

The horses took up a steady trot for a couple of miles across the plain . . . up the valley . . . until they arrived at the pass. Then, they slowed to a walk to pick their way down the rocky road that led to the smaller valley below. It took two hours to reach the alfalfa fields. We dismounted for a few minutes, drank some water, tightened our saddle girth straps, and headed upstream. The river was dry at first. Then, a trickle of water appeared. We continued up the valley, making our way between thorn bushes, alamos trees, pampas grasses, and the rock cliff wall on the side of the river. On the right, we passed two abandoned adobe houses. On the left, there were Indian ruins . . . the stone walls that once held small terraced fields.

After another hour and a half, Gustavo, who was leading this expedition, pointed up to the right.

"We have to go up there. That's where Ileena lives."

It was not obvious how we were going to get up there.

Gustavo didn't hesitate. He found a path through the thorn bushes . . . that turned into a path through the rocks. The horses strained to get up the hillside. It's amazing where they can go. Soon, they were on a green mesa, their riders still on their backs.

The pasture looked over-grazed, but we saw only one horse, tied up near the house, and two cows lying under a tree. Our horses stepped over a low stone wall, another relic of the Indian days. The place was naturally fortified. Steep cliffs guarded the access on three sides. On the other, the mountain went up rather than down. Over on the edge of the cliff was an enclosure of sticks and logs, where a herd of goats was kept; the enclosure was not meant to keep them from getting out, but to keep the puma from getting in. It must have been moved from in front of the house, where there was about three feet of goat manure, forming a large circle.

The house was made of adobe, with a low, mud roof and a few openings to let out the smoke. Off to the side was another low building, also of adobe, probably used for tools and storage.

No one came out.

"Ileena . . ." Gustavo yelled, urging his horse closer to the house. Still, no sound came from the house.

Then, a moment later, Ileena came out, dressed in a dirty, dusty, torn dress . . . a sweater, and a pair of cloth shoes, torn open at the toes. Her gray hair was pinned behind her head and her face was crossed by hundreds of wrinkles. She might have been 60 . . . or 90 . . . we couldn't tell.

She smiled. We got down off our horses, and greeted her warmly with kisses and hugs. But we couldn't understand what she said. Gustavo had to translate.

Then, when we were satisfied that all was well, we mounted up again for the long ride back.

"The Indians never left here," Maria explained. "This place has probably been inhabited for 1,000 years. Nothing much has changed."

This is not the first time we've met Ileena. She and Felix were often down in the valley when we visited. They always seemed to be in a good humor. Thin and spry, it looked like they would live forever. But now Felix is in a hospital with a head injury and no one is sure he'll ever be completely right again.

Life goes on.

The following day, life went on some more. We rode up to the old reservoir. Uphill and down. Over rocks and streams. Among ancient Indian ruins . . . and saddle sores. The old reservoir is still there. Perhaps it too dates from the time of the Inca or even before the Inca—the Diaguitas—or even some more ancient group. A long time ago, after the hunter-gatherers began settling down to plant corn and potatoes, people figured out that if they were going to live in this valley they had to find a way to store and direct the little water they had. Life needs water.

And there was not enough water falling from the sky to support much of anything.

We examined the old reservoir and then gave up. There is no way to get machinery to it. And it is too big to dig out by hand.

Riding back, we passed one of the adobe houses where *la gente* live. An old woman, short and fat, came running out. She had a handkerchief to her face, as though he had been crying.

"Jorge . . . Jorge . . ."

Jorge turned his horse around. He rode over to the old woman and spoke to her for a few minutes. Then, he rejoined our group . . .

"She told me my father died. . . . She heard it on the radio. He lives in Salta. But they make announcements on the radio for the people in the mountains to inform them of important events.

"He was 85 years old . . . and sick. . . . I'll confirm it when we get back to the house. [We have a satellite phone for emergencies.] If it is true, I'll have to leave to go get the body. . . ."

Life goes on . . .

Santa Maria, Madre de Dios, Ruege Para Nosotros

Sunday morning, the padre gave a mass at the little chapel next to the school. Then, he came over and blessed the new backhoe: "Lord, we ask that this machine may help make the farm more productive and may make it a better place to live and work for all who live here."

"Amen," we said.

Local priests are in short supply. Ours is an intelligent man with thinning hair, who came from Spain to minister to the poor of the Andes. He and another priest take care of 22 different churches, covering a region bigger than the state of Rhode Island. Once he left on Sunday, he could not come back to bury Jorge's father. So, the blessing of the clergy was performed in Salta, before the journey to our ranch began.

Javier caught on quickly. After a few minutes of training, he could operate the backhoe better than your editor. There are some things economists can do well. At least, in theory. In practice, we've never found anything.

Backhoes were not designed for intellectuals. By the time we have calculated the angle of attack, a good operator has already dug two holes. Maybe most things in life are like that—better done by instinct than by calculation.

Javier turned off the motor and came down from the cab. We were giving him instructions in maintenance—*graselo cada dia, sin excepcion*—then we heard the deep, full-throated noise. It was an old Chevy truck coming up the hill.

"That must be Jorge, with his father's body," we said to Javier.

"*Mi abuelo* [my grandfather]," said Javier. The cowboy's face was as hard and immobile as the stone mountains behind him. It was not an unfriendly face. But it was not a face you'd like to see in a bar fight, either, at least not unless he was on your side.

The old truck usually ran on bottled gas. But it could only get gasoline at the station in Molinos . . . so it switched back to gasoline, which caused it to run poorly, occasionally coughing and sputtering.

Still, it made the trip from Molinos in an hour and a half, across the desert to our ranch, with the coffin of Jorge's father in the back. Along with it came four other dusty pickups—each one carrying more of Jorge's family. Brothers and sisters, nieces and nephews . . . all came back to the cradle of the family itself, where Agostin, father of Jorge, Evo, Rosa, Candelaria, Josephina, and Fermina, was born.

The body already lay in the chapel, in front of the altar, when we got there. Candles were lit on all sides. A few people kneeled, praying in their pews. Others milled around outside.

We shook hands with the men standing outside our church. The women inclined their cheeks upward for a kiss. All were shy. Many of them had never met a real economist; probably, they never will. Then, we went inside, took off our hats, stood before the closed casket, and made the sign of the cross on our chest before going back outside to await events.

Soon after, Jorge's wife took charge.

"In the name of the Father, the Son, and the Holy Ghost," she began. "We are gathered here to say goodbye to Agustin. . . . He has taken a road we all must take. Santa Maria, mother of God, pray for us."

"*Santa Maria, Madre de Dios, Ruege Para Nosotros. . . .*

"*Santa Maria, Madre de Dios, Ruege Para Nosotros. . . .*

"*Santa Maria, Madre de Dios, Ruege Para Nosotros. . . .*

Once the litany began, it seemed like it would never stop. Maria called upon the saints, by name . . . and asked for the help of the angels and Heaven itself . . . counting out the beads of her rosary . . . reaching out to the Kingdom of God and imploring its denizens to welcome her father-in-law, to take him up into their celestial hotel and make him feel like he belonged there. As for those left still alive, she asked for help for them, too. Would God give them a little help . . . a raincheck . . . she asked . . . a reservation for the future, for the time when we too must join Agostin . . . and all the saints . . . in our eternal home.

When the litany ended, the choir assembled. Gustavo led it in a death chant . . . a simple tune sung over and over, with old women keening in the background. The effect was unlike any church music we had ever heard. There were no musical instruments in the chapel, but the keening filled the air, like an organ or bagpipes. It was soothing and melodic . . . but deeply sad. . . .

"It's the music the Indians sang when they came down from the mountains," Maria explained. "It's called a *baguala*."

Each person in the church then stood in line to take communion . . . and touched the casket on his way back to his seat, some merely placing their hands on it for a moment, others making the sign of the cross.

When the last of the Eucharist celebrants had sat down, Jorge's wife blew out the candles, while Jorge, his brothers, and nephews moved up to the front of the church. They picked up the coffin, and put it back onto the pick-up truck. The rest of us got in our trucks too, in order to follow the procession out to the graveyard.

Across an arroyo from the chapel is an old adobe house. It was the house where Agostin lived as a child and where Javier lives now. The procession drove to the house; the casket was taken out of the back of the pickup and carried around the house. Then, it went back in the truck for the trip to its final resting place.

About a half mile from the house, out on the range by itself, is the graveyard. It is a giant square, surrounded by stone walls, about six feet high, so remote that life above ground is almost as peaceful as it is below it.

Here, in the high plains of Boot Hill, some 50 or so bodies lie unmolested by the living. Here, the dead are on their own . . . save when someone comes to join them. They enjoy their sleep without interruption—no lawnmowers and no Internet signal.

Some graves are marked by piles of rocks. Others by concrete tombstones. Still others only have a wooden cross to mark the spot. Some of the dead appear to have been forgotten completely. Other gravesites are garnished with a few faded, plastic flowers.

Off to the right, as we enter, is a pile of pick axes and a little farther is a hole, much deeper than we expect. It must have been hard work digging it.

"I guess the next one will be dug with the backhoe," we said to Calvert.

"I don't know. They might rather dig those graves by hand."

Jorge's wife spread a blanket on the bottom of the grave while Jorge and his kin attached ropes to the coffin. They then set the coffin on the top of the hole supported by a couple of metal bars across the opening.

Again, mourners began their lament, while one by one the rest of the group, beginning with the closest family, approached the casket. Each one dipped a sprig of green leaves into holy water and made the sign of the cross on top of the casket.

Now that the body was closer to the grave, the keening grew louder and eyes grew redder. Some cried. Some merely looked blank and sorrowful.

When everyone had paid his last respects, a bent gray felt hat, the kind an old ranch hand might wear, was put on top of the coffin. Jorge and his brother pulled out the metal bars while other relatives held the ropes. Then, the body was lowered into the hole. When it came to rest on the bottom, they pulled up the ropes.

The wailing and keening continued. The relatives each took a hand of dirt and threw it on the coffin. Then, one of Jorge's sisters threw on some of his clothes. Another tossed a pack of cigarettes into the grave.

When the symbolic burial was over, three of the ranch hands, Natalio, Omar, and Juan, picked up shovels and began seriously filling the hole with dirt. A cloud of dust formed around them. Juan smoked a cigarette as he worked.

Soon, the grieving friends and family were beginning to drift away. Bottles of Coca-Cola and orange soda came out. Anna and Juan's son came over and offered us a cup of Coke. Out of the corner of our eyes, we noticed Javier, the toughest hombre in the Calchaqui Valley, wiping away a tear.

Santa Maria, Madre de Dios, Ruege Para Nosostros.

■ *Acknowledgments* ■

While writing *The Daily Reckoning*, I have had both the responsibility to develop my own view of economic events and the opportunity to develop the voice with which to communicate it.

It would be impossible to thank everyone with whom I have dissected and discussed the ideas in these pages, but I would like to thank a few people who made this particular collection possible.

Thanks to Addison Wiggin, who's been with me from the earliest issues of *The Daily Reckoning* and without whose stamp I would never have released such a collection.

Thanks to editor Samantha Buker and the team of Debra Englander and Kelly O'Connor at John Wiley & Sons for pulling these pages together.

And thanks to Greg Kadajski for sifting through the archives for this special project, as well as seeing my words posted on the Web and sent daily to my readers.

Mostly, I would like to thank my wife, Elizabeth, and my children, Will, Sophia, Maria, Jules, Henry, and Edward, for often appearing as characters in the ongoing saga that is *The Daily Reckoning*.

WILLIAM BONNER

■ *About the Author* ■

William Bonner is president and CEO of Agora Inc., one of the world's largest financial newsletter companies (www.agorafinancial.com). He is the creator of the *Daily Reckoning* (www.dailyreckoning.com), a financial newsletter with more than 500,000 readers in the United States, Great Britain, and Australia, which is translated daily into French and German. Mr. Bonner is also the coauthor, with Addison Wiggin, of the international bestsellers *Financial Reckoning Day* and *Empire of Debt*. With political journalist Lila Rajiva, he wrote his third *New York Times* best-selling book, *Mobs, Messiahs, and Markets*. He divides his time among a ranch in Argentina, the Agora home office in Maryland, various joint ventures, and other places around the globe.

Index